Visions of Tragedy in Modern American Drama

RELATED TITLES

Visions of Tragedy in Modern American Drama

From O'Neill to the Twenty-First Century

Edited by
David Palmer

Bloomsbury Methuen Drama
An imprint of Bloomsbury Publishing Plc

B L O O M S B U R Y
LONDON · OXFORD · NEW YORK · NEW DELHI · SYDNEY

Bloomsbury Methuen Drama

An imprint of Bloomsbury Publishing Plc

Imprint previously known as Methuen Drama

50 Bedford Square	1385 Broadway
London	New York
WC1B 3DP	NY 10018
UK	USA

www.bloomsbury.com

**BLOOMSBURY, METHUEN DRAMA and the Diana logo are trademarks of
Bloomsbury Publishing Plc**

First published 2018

British Library Cataloguing-in-Publication Data
A catalogue record for this book is available from the British Library.

ISBN:	HB:	978-1-474-27692-4
	PB:	978-1-474-27693-1
	ePDF:	978-1-474-27696-2
	eBook:	978-1-474-27694-8

Library of Congress Cataloging-in-Publication Data
A catalog record for this book is available from the Library of Congress.

Cover design: Adriana Brioso
Cover image: Curtis McClarin in South Coast Repertory's 2012 production of
Topdog/Underdog by Suzan-Lori Parks. (Photo by Henry DiRocco)

Typeset by Integra Software Services Pvt. Ltd.
Printed and bound in Great Britain

To find out more about our authors and books visit www.bloomsbury.com. Here
you will find extracts, author interviews, details of forthcoming events and the
option to sign up for our newsletters.

*For all those who ever believed
that we create our better selves
by coming to understand
the trials and terrors of other people
and the ways they are like our own,
leading us at last to compassion
—which since the beginning
has been the purpose of tragedy*

CONTENTS

LIST OF
CONTRIBUTORS

Susan C. W. Abbotson is a Professor at Rhode Island College, where she specializes in modern and contemporary drama in the English Department. She has authored several books, including *Critical Companion to Arthur Miller, Masterpieces of Twentieth Century American Drama, Thematic Guide to Modern Drama,* and the forthcoming *Modern American Drama: Playwriting in the 1950s,* part of the *Decades of Modern American Drama* set (Methuen Drama, 2018). She also has published essays on Tennessee Williams, Thornton Wilder, Sam Shepard, Eugene O'Neill, August Wilson, Mae West, and Arthur Miller, and she is the Performance Review Editor for the *Arthur Miller Journal*. She is currently working on a piece about Ivo van Hove's production of Lillian Hellman's *The Little Foxes* and an essay on William Inge.

Natka Bianchini is an Associate Professor of Theatre at Loyola University Maryland in Baltimore, where she teaches theatre history, directing, and dramatic literature. Her monograph *Samuel Beckett's Theatre in America* was published by Palgrave Macmillan Press in 2015. Her articles and reviews have appeared in *Theatre Survey, Theatre Journal,* the *Journal of Dramatic Theory and Criticism,* and the *Journal of American Drama and Theatre,* among other places. She is the founding vice president and conference planner for the Edward Albee Society and the editor of the forthcoming fourth volume in the series *New Perspectives in Edward Albee Studies* published by Brill.

Christopher Bigsby, an award-winning academic, novelist, biographer, journalist, and broadcaster, is a Professor of American Studies at the University of East Anglia, where he founded the Arthur Miller Center for American Studies. A Fellow of the Royal Society of Literature and the Royal Society of Arts, he has published more than fifty books, among them the three-volume

The Cambridge History of American Theatre (edited with Don B. Wilmeth); the three-volume *Critical Introduction to Twentieth-Century American Drama*; *Modern American Drama, 1945–2000*; a major commentary *Arthur Miller: A Critical Study*; his acclaimed two-volume biography of Arthur Miller; and his multivolume series *Writers in Conversation with Christopher Bigsby*. As a broadcaster, he has had regular series on BBC radio and has done television documentaries on John Steinbeck, Mark Twain, and Edith Wharton. Published widely in academic journals and anthologies on many twentieth-century American dramatists, he recently has turned to exploring drama on American television. His most recent book is *Twenty-First Century American Playwrights*, which was published by Cambridge University Press in 2017.

Jackson R. Bryer is a Professor Emeritus of English at the University of Maryland, where he taught undergraduate and graduate courses in American literature and dramatic literature for forty-one years and authored or edited more than thirty books ranging widely over theatre and American literature and culture. He is the president of the Thornton Wilder Society, editor of *Conversations with Thornton Wilder* (1992), and coeditor of *The Selected Letters of Thornton Wilder* (2008) and of *Thornton Wilder: New Perspectives* (2013).

Soyica Diggs Colbert is an Associate Professor of Theater and Performance Studies and has a joint appointment in African American Studies at Georgetown University. She is the author of *The African American Theatrical Body: Reception, Performance and the Stage* (2011) and *Black Movements: Performance and Cultural Politics* (2017). She edited the Black Performance special issue of *African American Review* (2012) and coedited *The Psychic Hold of Slavery: Legacies in American Expressive Culture* with Robert J. Patterson and Aida Levy-Hussen (2016). She is currently working on two book projects, *Lorraine Hansberry: Artist/Activist* and *Performing Seeing: Blackness in Visual Culture and Performance Theory*. She is vice president for research and publications of the Association for Theatre in Higher Education.

Anne Fletcher is a Professor of Theater at Southern Illinois University and a specialist in 1930s American drama. She is the author of *Rediscovering Mordecai Gorelik: Scene Design and the American Theatre* (2009) and *Modern American Drama:*

Playwriting in the 1930s (2018), part of the Bloomsbury decades series on twentieth-century American theatre. She coauthored *The Process of Dramaturgy: A Handbook* (2010) with Scott R. Irelan and Julie Felise Dubiner, and with Irelan she coauthored *Experiencing Theatre* (2015) and coedited *Contextualizing New Plays* (2017). Her articles appear widely in anthologies, including *Blackwell Companion to American Drama* (2005); *Brecht, Broadway, and United States Theatre* (2007); *Interrogating America Through Theatre and Performance* (2009); *Death in American Texts and Performances: Corpses, Ghosts, and the Reanimated Dead* (2010); *Thornton Wilder: New Perspectives* (2013); and *Experiments in Democracy: Interracial and Cross-Cultural Exchange in American Theater, 1912–1945* (with Cheryl Black, 2016).

Sharon Friedman is an Associate Professor in the Gallatin School of New York University. Specializing in modern literature and drama, feminist criticism, and adaptation, she is editor of *Feminist Theatrical Revisions of Classic Works* (2009) and coauthor with Cheryl Black of *Modern American Drama: Playwriting in the 1990s*, part of the *Decades of Modern American Drama* set (Methuen Drama, 2018). Her essays have appeared in *Theatre Journal*, *American Studies*, *New Theatre Quarterly*, *Women and Performance*, *New England Theatre Journal*, *Text & Presentation*, *Codifying the National Self: Spectators*, *Actors and the American Text*, and *Intertextuality in American Drama*. Her current book project is titled *The Gendered Terrain in the Theatre of War*. She is on the executive council of the International Susan Glaspell Society.

Claire Gleitman is a Professor in the English Department at Ithaca College, specializing in modern and contemporary American, Irish, and world drama. She has published numerous articles on modern and contemporary drama in journals such as *Modern Drama*, *Eire/Ireland*, *The Canadian Journal of Irish Studies*, *Comparative Drama*, *New Hibernian Review*, and *The Arthur Miller Journal*. She is the founding director of the *On the Verge* play-reading series at Ithaca College, for which she produces and directs staged readings. She is currently working on a book-length project focused on anxious masculinity in American drama.

Jeffery Kennedy is an Assistant Professor in the Faculty of the New College of Interdisciplinary Arts and Sciences at Arizona State University, teaching courses in Interdisciplinary Arts and

Performance. A leading scholar on the Provincetown Players, he created the website www.provincetownplayhouse.com, an award-winning research source, curated the historical gallery at the Provincetown Playhouse after its refurbishment in 1998, and is finishing a book tracing the artistic legacy of the Provincetown Players. His work on O'Neill is widely published in journals and anthologies such as the *Eugene O'Neill Review*; *Journal of Dramatic Criticism and Theory*; *Text & Presentation*; *The Eugene O'Neill Companion*; *Eugene O'Neill and His Contemporaries: Bohemians, Radicals, Progressives, and Lefties*; *Eugene O'Neill's One Act Plays: New Critical Perspectives*; and *Critical Insights: Eugene O'Neill*. He was president of the Eugene O'Neill Society from 2014 to 2015 and chaired the Society's triennial international conference in 2011 in New York.

Stephen Marino is the founding editor of *The Arthur Miller Journal* and an Adjunct Professor of English at St. Francis College. His work on Arthur Miller has appeared in many journals and essay collections. He is the author of *A Language Study of Arthur Miller's Plays: The Poetic in the Colloquial* and the editor of the Methuen Drama critical student edition of Miller's *A View from the Bridge*. His recent book *Essential Criticism: Arthur Miller's "Death of a Salesman" and "The Crucible"* was published in 2015 by Palgrave/Macmillan. A new collection he edited, *Arthur Miller's Century: Essays Celebrating the 100th Birthday of America's Great Playwright*, came out in summer 2017 from Cambridge Scholars Publishing.

Brenda Murphy is a Distinguished Professor of English Emeritus at the University of Connecticut. She is a past president of the American Theatre and Drama Society and the Eugene O'Neill Society and serves on the board of the Arthur Miller Society. Her twenty books on American drama and theatre include the *Cambridge Companion to American Women Playwrights* (1999), *Understanding David Mamet* (2011), *The Theatre of Tennessee Williams* (2014), and *Remembering Eugene O'Neill* (2016), which she edited with George Monteiro. She contributed the essay "Tragedy in the Modern American Theater" to the *Blackwell Companion to Tragedy* (2005) and has written articles on a wide variety of topics in American drama and theatre, including Mamet's plays and film adaptations.

Deirdre Osborne is a Reader in English Literature and Drama at Goldsmiths, University of London. She co-convenes the Masters in Black British Literature and teaches undergraduate modules on Shakespeare, cultural theory, feminism, modernism, and postmodernism. Her research interests span late-Victorian literature and maternity, Landmark Poetics, mixedness, adoption aesthetics, and black writing. Publications include editing the first *Cambridge Companion to British Black and Asian Literature: 1945–2010* (2016); a critical edition with commentary of Lorraine Hansberry's *A Raisin in the Sun* (Methuen Drama, 2011); a critical edition of plays by Kwame Kwei-Armah, Malika Booker, SuAndi, Lennie James, Courttia Newland, and Lemn Sissay in *Hidden Gems*, vol. 1 (2008) and vol. 2 (2012); and guest editing the special issue "Contemporary Black British Women's Writing" for *Women: A Cultural Review* (2009). She is contributing coeditor of *Modern and Contemporary Black British Drama* (2014) and associate editor of the scholarly journal *Women's Writing*.

David Palmer spent most of his career in book publishing in New York before returning to academia in 2005 to teach philosophy in the Humanities Department at the Massachusetts Maritime Academy. His interest in ethics, philosophy of mind, and theories of the self led him to explore a cognitive studies approach to conceptions of tragedy in plays by Samuel Beckett, Arthur Miller, and Eugene O'Neill, and he has published on all three of these dramatists. He began work on this anthology when he was a Travis Bogard Fellow, funded by the Eugene O'Neill Foundation, at the Eugene O'Neill National Historic Site in Danville, California, in 2015. He is on the board of the Eugene O'Neill Society and is president of the Arthur Miller Society.

Jonathan Shandell is an Associate Professor of Theater Arts and co-chair of the Theater Arts Program at Arcadia University. His book *The American Negro Theatre and the Long Civil Rights Era* (working title) is forthcoming from University of Iowa Press. Other publications include the anthology *Experiments in Democracy: Interracial and Cross-Cultural Exchange in American Theatre, 1912–1945* (coedited with Cheryl Black, 2016), chapters in the anthologies *Cambridge Companion to African American Theatre*, *Authentic Blackness/"Real" Blackness*, and *African American*

National Biography, as well as articles in *African American Review*, *Journal of American Drama and Theatre*, *Theatre Topics*, and other leading journals. He served as president of the Black Theatre Association and an affiliated writer with *American Theatre* magazine.

Sandra G. Shannon is a Professor of African American Literature in the Department of English at Howard University. A leading scholar on August Wilson, she is the author of two books—*The Dramatic Vision of August Wilson* and *August Wilson's "Fences": A Reference Guide*. Shannon also has edited the Modern Language Association's *Approaches to Teaching the Plays of August Wilson* and *August Wilson and Black Aesthetics* and is the volume editor for *Modern American Drama: Playwriting in the 1980s*, part of the *Decades of Modern American Drama* set (Methuen Drama, 2018). She has been editor of *Theatre Topics* and president of the Black Theatre Network. She founded and is the current president of the August Wilson Society, is editor of the *College Language Association Journal*, and is a founding board member of *Continuum: The Journal of African Diaspora Drama, Theatre, and Performance*. She was a featured scholar in the PBS-American Masters documentary *August Wilson: The Ground on Which I Stand* (2015).

Shannon Blake Skelton is an Assistant Professor of Theatre at Kansas State University where he teaches courses in theatre history, dramaturgy, and film. He is the author of *The Late Work of Sam Shepard* (Bloomsbury Methuen Drama, 2016). Currently he is working on a book-length consideration of masculinity in the writings of Tracy Letts, Martin McDonagh, and Neil LaBute, as well as projects on the films of Stuart Gordon, the plays of Woody Allen, and mid-twentieth-century American radio drama.

Werner Sollors, a PhD from the Freie Universität Berlin, has been Professor of English and Afro-American (later: African American) Studies at Harvard University since 1983. Coeditor with Greil Marcus of *A New Literary History of America* (2009), his major book publications include *Beyond Ethnicity* (1986), *Neither Black nor White yet Both* (1997), *Ethnic Modernism* (2008), *The Temptation of Despair: Tales of the 1940s* (2014), and *African American Writing: A Literary Approach* (2016). He is a Fellow of the American Academy of Arts & Sciences, a corresponding member of the Austrian Academy of Sciences and the Academia Europaea, and an honorary member of the Bavarian America Academy.

Harvey Young is Chair and a Professor of Theatre at Northwestern University, where he also holds appointments in African American Studies, Performance Studies, and Radio/Television/Film. He is the author of three books: *Embodying Black Experience* (2010), *Theatre & Race* (2013), and with Queen Maccasia Zabriskie *Black Theatre Is Black Life: An Oral History of Chicago Theatre and Dance, 1970–2010* (2013). His edited books include *The Cambridge Companion to African American Theatre* (2012), *Reimagining "A Raisin in the Sun": Four New Plays* (2012, with Rebecca Ann Rugg), *Suzan-Lori Parks in Person: Interviews and Commentaries* (2013, with Philip C. Kolin), and *Performance in the Borderlands* (2014, with Ramón H. Rivera-Servera, part of Palgrave's Performance Interventions series). Young is president of the Association for Theatre in Higher Education and a past editor of *Theatre Survey*, the journal of the American Society for Theatre Research.

Toby Zinman is a Professor of English at the University of the Arts in Philadelphia. She has been a Fulbright professor at Tel Aviv University, has been a visiting professor at SIAS International University in Henan, China, has won five grants from the National Endowment for the Humanities, and has published six books. She publishes widely in academic journals and lectures internationally on American drama as well as being a broadly published arts journalist and the chief theatre critic for the Philadelphia *Inquirer*, where she reviews New York and London in addition to Philadelphia. She recently was named by *American Theatre* magazine "one of the twelve most influential critics in America."

FOREWORD

Christopher Bigsby
University of East Anglia

When Marion Starkey published her study of the Salem witch trials, *The Devil in Massachusetts*, she declared, "Here is real Greek tragedy" (1949: 12). Arthur Miller, drawn to the same events and an enthusiast for Greek tragedy from his days studying it at the University of Michigan, wrote a note to himself that in the play he was writing, *The Crucible*, the hanging with which it would end "must be tragic," the result of a flaw in the individual as well as the state (Bigsby 2009: 443). For Miller, tragedy invested the individual with significance precisely because, as he was fond of saying, it is a form in which "the birds came home to roost" (Miller [1999] 2015: 486), and as such coincided with his social and moral ethic, which held people responsible for their actions. He reacted against the theatre of the absurd because it depicted people as victims of a cosmic joke. Indeed, for Beckett the prevailing mood is one of tragicomedy; Vladimir and Estragon in *Waiting for Godot* are true heirs to Cervantes' Don Quixote. It is not accidental that the modern form of the absurd was born in a postwar Europe that had witnessed genocide, a conscious mocking of human hopes—hope being the last item out of Pandora's box. Genocide is not tragedy but its denial.

As an atheist, and despite the Greek theatre's embracing of gods as an expression of determining forces, Miller rebelled against the idea of a God who offered not only consolation but also an external sense of justice, a meaning independent of human will. He was closer to Sartre's existential declaration that man is condemned to be free, free to bear the burden and consequences of personal decisions that have a public as well as a private significance. Tragic heroes might be obedient to necessities in which they believe themselves to believe, but rebellion ultimately lies at the heart of the tragic sensibility. In Hemingway's formulation, the tragic hero can be destroyed but not defeated (1952: 50). He rages against the dying of the light, immortality denying the tragic for, as Miguel de Unamuno observed in *Tragic Sense of Life*, consciousness and finality are the same thing.

According to George Steiner in *The Death of Tragedy*, Ibsen, with whom "the history of drama begins anew," seemed a creator of modern tragedies. Steiner looked not to the social dramatist whom Miller embraced when he adapted *An Enemy of the People* but to the Ibsen of *The Wild Duck* (Miller's model for *All My Sons*) in which an obsession with the ideal brings down the sky (Miller [1994] 1996: 544–51).

O'Neill is perhaps closer to Beckett's sense of being lost in life's incoherence than Miller, at least as expressed by Edmund in *Long Day's Journey Into Night*: "For a second there is meaning! Then the hand lets the veil fall and you are alone, lost in the fog again, and you stumble toward nowhere, for no good reason!" ([1956] 2014: 156). O'Neill's characters seem to exist in some anti-room to life, each inhabiting fictions as the characters in *The Iceman Cometh* do pipe dreams. They exist in a series of tensions between love and hate, compassion and its denial, staging their lives as performances the better to avoid the sharp edge of reality. They become tragic only in their awareness of their plight.

O'Neill was conscious that the United States was not a natural home for the tragic spirit, having been wed since its beginnings to a melioristic ideal. There were those who thought Dreiser's *An American Tragedy* was ill-named, its title yoking two words that sat together uneasily in the clean air of the New World. Certainly tragedy's Darwinian sense of the implacable seemed to offer neither redemption—a central faith, religious or secular, in an American culture committed to re-invention—nor transcendence while in fact offering both, except with a cruel sense of prevailing ironies to which the national spirit wishes to see itself exempt. "It's morning again in America," declared a famous campaign slogan for Ronald Reagan. Tennessee Williams's gypsy can have her virginity restored at every full moon. There always is a green light across the bay representing possibility, even though F. Scott Fitzgerald knew otherwise and showed how Gatsby's belief that innocence could be simply declared and restored ends with his corpse face down in a swimming pool still fatally illusioned. Americans' cheery sense of endless opportunity can seem designed as an antidote to the tragic seen as a product of another age and place, abandoned, with much else, on the voyage to a new Eden free of the weight of history and tragedy alike. No wonder writers have felt obliged to resist a Pollyanna account of human affairs, an obligation to hold the culture to account.

A sense of loss pervades key American dramas, a feeling of values abandoned and connections broken. Surely the proper fate of a country ever eager to declare its unique virtues is that those claimed virtues be inspected by writers whose characters sense a disjunction between their own lives and promises made. This may lead to satire, social critique, or withdrawal into privacies. It also may lead to a profound feeling of abandonment—a quest for meaning resolved too late, a sense of failure reaching down into the soul that can lead either to the tragic or the absurd. In play after play a gap opens up between life as proposed and life as lived.

Mourning Becomes Electra was a self-conscious effort to recreate a modern Greek tragedy, but O'Neill's other great plays stage the lives of people who have brought their fates upon themselves in a more modern setting where, beyond a flawed self, fate is the product of social and psychological pressures. His characters, much like Miller's Willy Loman, cling to an interpretation of experience at odds with their inner needs thus obviating the connections with other people that might constitute the meaning they seek. They are abandoned because on some level they have abandoned themselves. Is this tragedy? Perhaps so, for they have denied their own culpability, failing until the very end to understand the source of their misdirections. Beyond that, there is a sense in which their plight is shared by all as they seek to create meaning in a context in which none is offered.

The Iceman Cometh, Long Day's Journey Into Night, The Glass Menagerie, A Streetcar Named Desire, All My Sons, Death of a Salesman, The Crucible, A Delicate Balance, American Buffalo, Glengarry Glen Ross, Buried Child all end with characters stunned, staring into a future which is no future, the mere consequence of events having run their course. There are moments of self-realization of a kind we look for in tragedy. Certainly Joe Keller and John Proctor experience such moments; as different as their deaths are, they are preceded by a belated understanding of what they have brought upon themselves as well as what they have suffered by internalizing suspect values. Willy Loman and Blanche DuBois, however, meet their fates still blinded by illusion, leaving others to recognize the desperation that drove them through events that seem fated but with which they in fact colluded.

American drama does not exist in isolation. Behind Albee lurks T. S. Eliot; behind O'Neill, the Greeks; behind Williams and Albee, Strindberg; and behind Miller, Ibsen and, again unavoidably, the Greeks. There is a line of succession. All have tasted tragedy and savored it. Is there, then, a single definition? Certainly there are critics who have patrolled its boundary seemingly in an attempt to keep out the taint of impure immigrants, to resist its accommodation of the modern. What is common is the attempt by the protagonists of these dramas to invest their lives with meaning in a context in which such meaning is neither gifted nor apparent, indeed in which they feel the pressure of unmeaning. What is common is a sense that the past presses unbearably on the present. What is shared is an awareness that beyond the individual's sense of dislocation is a more profound fragmentation in our social, moral, and metaphysical experience of the world. How, in the end, is it possible to discover a shape to experience in the face of its evident denial? That is surely where art steps forward and in tragedy makes a desperate gamble on the only immortality available.

References

Bigsby, Christopher (2009), *Arthur Miller: 1915–1962*, Cambridge: Harvard University Press.

Hemingway, Ernest (1952), *The Old Man and the Sea*, first published in *Life*, September 1, 34–54. Available online: https://books.google.com/books?id=WVYEAAAAMBAJ&pg=PA35#v=onepage&q&f=false (accessed January 12, 2017).

Miller, Arthur ([1994] 1996), "Ibsen and the Drama of Today," introduction to James MacFarland (ed.), *The Cambridge Companion to Ibsen*, Cambridge: Cambridge University Press. Reprinted in *The Theater Essays of Arthur Miller*, revised and expanded edition, Robert A. Martin and Steven R. Centola (eds.), 544–51, New York: Da Capo Press.

Miller, Arthur ([1999] 2015), "*The Price*—The Power of the Past,"
    reprinted in *The Collected Essays of Arthur Miller*, introduction by
    Matthew C. Roudané, 484–6, London: Bloomsbury Methuen Drama.
O'Neill, Eugene ([1956] 2014), *Long Day's Journey Into Night*, William
    Davies King (ed.), New Haven: Yale University Press.
Starkey, Marion L. (1949), *The Devil in Massachusetts: A Modern
    Enquiry into the Salem Witch Trials*, Garden City, NY: Doubleday.
Steiner, George ([1961] 1996), *The Death of Tragedy*, New Haven: Yale
    University Press.
Unamuno, Miguel de ([1912] 2005), *Tragic Sense of Life*, trans. J. E.
    Crawford Flitch (1921), New York: Cosimo Classics.

ACKNOWLEDGMENTS

I wrote the various drafts of the proposal for this anthology while I was a fellow in the Travis Bogard Artist in Residence Program at Tao House, the Eugene O'Neill National Historic Site in Danville, California, in the spring of 2015. I am grateful to the Eugene O'Neill Foundation for its support, and in particular to Linda Best, Wendy Cooper, Florence McAuley, and Carol Sherrill for organizing the fellowships and for their many kindnesses during my time at Tao House. I also thank Mary Camezon for her help in the O'Neill Foundation Archives and Eileen Herrmann for her gracious encouragement of this project. Paul Scolari, PhD, was the chief of Natural and Cultural Resources for the National Park Service for this region of California when I was at Tao House, and Tom Letterman was the regional superintendent. I am grateful to them and to their staff for the work the National Park Service did in conjunction with the Eugene O'Neill Foundation to make the Bogard Fellowships possible. I also thank the Franciscan Brothers of the San Damiano Retreat for working together with the O'Neill Foundation to provide me with such splendid living accommodations during my time in Danville.

In developing the proposal for this anthology, I benefitted—as I always do—from email exchanges with Susan Abbotson and Brenda Murphy. I am grateful to them and to Stephen Marino for their encouragement and guidance, which have been generous and ongoing.

Guidance from Mark Dudgeon, Publisher for Theatre Studies, was valuable both in shaping the proposal and in refining the project as it developed. I am grateful to Mark for both his guidance and his patience, as I am to Susan Furber, the editorial assistant for Bloomsbury Methuen Drama, who guided the project to completion.

I also have benefitted for more than a decade from enthusiastic encouragement for academic projects from Nelson Ritschel, my colleague at the Massachusetts Maritime Academy, and from financial support for conference travel and a sabbatical provided by the college, which the Vice President for Academic Affairs, Bradley Lima, has been generous in approving.

The following people and experiences were significant in shaping both my interest in and my ideas about themes in this anthology: Kathryn and Leo Palmer; Amy and Leon Kass; Paul Mitchell; Hannah Arendt and Hans Jonas; teaching the Literature Humanities course in the undergraduate core curriculum at Columbia University; Jim and Deb Morgan; Mark Patrick; Calvin and Kathy Bruce; Greg and Nadine Mort; Joe and Jeff Bukhari; Elisabeth Hasslacher and Lindsay, Caitlin, and Julia Schreiber; Richard Palmer and Jo Circle; Sophia Palmer; and Andrew and Jameson Palmer. In particular, two excellent women provided patient understanding and support as I pursued these academic interests: Hilary Palmer and Christine Morgan. Nearly all the good things in my adult life I owe to these two people.

The point of an anthology is to bring together individuals who as a group provide much clearer and broader insights into a varied topic than any one author could develop alone. I believe that has been the case with this book. The contributors to this volume are a mix of well-established, influential scholars and younger academics whose recent work shows great promise for the development of theatre studies. In editing each essay for this volume, I found my old ideas often challenged and new ideas come into focus. I am grateful to all the contributors for finding time amid busy schedules and the demands of many other projects to participate in this exploration— an investigation both of the concept of tragedy and of Americans' sense of identity over the last century.

David Palmer
New York

Introduction

David Palmer

Massachusetts Maritime Academy

In George Orwell's *Nineteen Eighty-Four*, Room 101 is a torture chamber—personalized for each victim. When the novel's protagonist, Winston Smith, asks O'Brien, the agent of Oceania's autocratic regime, what is in Room 101, O'Brien replies, "You know what is in Room 101, Winston. Everyone knows what is in Room 101 ... The thing that is in Room 101 is the worst thing in the world" (Orwell [1949] 1992: 273, 296). For Winston, the way to that worst thing is rats. When O'Brien threatens to place a cage of hungry rats around Winton's head, Winston is overwhelmed by uncontrollable terror. "You can't do that," he cries, "in a high cracked voice ... You know this is not necessary. What is it that you want me to do? ... But what is it, what is it? How can I do it if I don't know what it is?" (297–8). O'Brien brings the cage close to Winston's face and clicks open the first of two releases on the cage. A "blind, helpless, mindless" panic seizes Winston. What is it O'Brien wants? By this point Winston has been brutalized nearly to death, has admitted to lies, has confessed to anything they asked. What more is there? He must think, think, in the few seconds he has left. What more could they need? ... "and then—no it was not relief, only hope, a tiny fragment of hope":

Do it to Julia! Do it to Julia! Not me! Julia! I don't care what you do to her. Tear her face off, strip her to the bones. Not me! Julia! Not me! (300)

Julia is Winston's former lover, who also has been captured by the Thought Police. Throughout his pain and degradation and the contemptible actions he has done to keep alive, the one piece of his self Winston has clung to and protected from them, the one element of his self-respect he was sure they could not take was his loyalty to Julia (240). He would not betray her ... but now he has ... by his own words ... deep in his heart ... completely.

A slogan of the Oceania autocracy is, "Who controls the past controls the future: who controls the present controls the past" (260). The terror of the present moment in Room 101 severed Winston from the past self he thought he knew. Throughout his ordeal, Winston had maintained the idea that despite the humiliations he had been forced to perform he was still, as O'Brien says of him, some kind of "guardian of the human spirit" (283): Winston believed that at his core he still held an indestructible integrity—a way of continuing to be the person he took himself to be. The destruction of that lingering pride and sense of self is the purpose of Room 101: as O'Brien says, "You shall see yourself as you are" (283). Having destroyed in the present any story Winston clung to about who he was in the past, the regime has destroyed Winston's connection to the future. There is no Winston Smith any longer. He does not know who he is. He has no purposes or direction left in his life. Starting points cannot be remembered, no longer seem real; a significant destination cannot be imagined. Both Winston and Julia had thought, "They can't get inside you"'

But they could get inside you. "What happens here is *for ever*," O'Brien had said. That was a true word. There were things, your own acts, from which you could not recover. Something was killed in your breast: burnt out, cauterised out. (303–4)

Since their origins in ancient Greece, tragic dramas have depicted this kind of collapse of the self when it confronts overwhelming force—the abandonment in ruins of some fundamental element in the stories we tell ourselves about who we are. That collapse is "the worst thing in the world," which in his response in Room 101

Winston shows he knew implicitly, just as O'Brien said he would; the rats were merely an implement, a motivator toward seeing "yourself as you are."

Arthur Miller, in his most famous essay on tragedy, "Tragedy and the Common Man" (1949, the same year Orwell published *Nineteen Eighty-Four* and the year in which *Death of a Salesman* opened on Broadway), calls these cherished and essential elements in a person's story a sense of "dignity" and points out that even the most ordinary of us have them, not merely the grand; a sense of dignity is part of being human. Tragedy depicts overwhelming forces assaulting this dignity, leading the characters to "the underlying fear of being displaced, the disaster inherent in being torn away from our chosen image of what and who we are in the world" (Miller [1949] 2016: 7, 9). As O'Brien says to Winston, "What happens here is *for ever*"; there will be no way back. Something you had trusted—some basic necessity for your way of being in the world—is shown to be false and "burnt out."

For the Greeks, the overwhelming force driving tragedy was fate, their sense of the fundamental balance and orderliness of the cosmos, the natural order with everything in its proper place. Early on fate is envisioned as a power in the universe external to individuals, a handmaiden to *diké* (justice), the force of an objective moral order: Aeschylus's depiction of Orestes, the loyal son, caught in the curse on the House of Atreus, murdering his mother, Clytemnestra; Sophocles' Oedipus, the savior of Thebes, learning his true identity and the reality of his actions. Later, in Euripides' plays, fate is more the inescapable, internal psychological facts of human nature: Medea succumbing to rage as she acknowledges that Jason has abandoned her; Pentheus moving from a rationalist's disdain for emotions to his destruction by them. In either case, fate is inescapable and overwhelming: an implement in Room 101 that forces us to see ourselves as we really are when, as Miller says, our "chosen image" has been "torn away."

Collapse alone, however, is not sufficient to establish tragedy; tragedy requires our collusion in events. We must be complicit in our agony and destruction. For Rita Felski, tragedy is "a particular shape of suffering ... an uncanny unraveling of the distinction between agency and fate, internal volition and the pressure of external circumstance" (2008: 10–11). As Winston and Julia learn, "There were things, your own acts, from which you could not recover." Without this complicity, there is not tragedy, only pathos in which we are merely helpless abused victims. Winston is pushed beyond terror, but the words betraying Julia are his own. Lear has greedy and vengeful daughters—who succeed by manipulating his vanity. While the court in Denmark is corrupt, Hamlet remains uncertain and ambivalent. Iago plays on Othello's insecurity and pride.

Perhaps Macbeth, however, of all of Shakespeare's tragic victims understands most explicitly his own role in his destruction. This happens not when Birnam Wood seems to move to Dunsinane, and he realizes his interpretation of the weird sisters' prophecy has been deluded. It happens long before, immediately after Duncan's murder, when Lady Macbeth chides her husband for cowardice, thinking he fears Malcolm's dead body in his unwillingness to return to the king's bedchamber with the bloody daggers. Numbly, as they hear knocking at the castle's gate, Macbeth replies that she deeply misconceives the source of his inaction:

> I'll go no more.
> I am afraid to think what I have done;
> Look on't again I dare not ...
> To know the deed, 'twere best not know myself.
> Wake Duncan with thy knocking! I would thou couldst! (*Macbeth*, 2.2)

Macbeth has been driven by an overwhelming temptation, an ambition he could not resist, by the taunts of his wife who questions his manhood—a fundamental part of his story to himself of who he is—claiming he is a coward if he does not act on that ambition. But Macbeth also knows the act itself was his: he is complicit. The murder is something he has done, not merely an irreversible misfortune that has befallen him. Misfortune arises from sources completely external; it is mere pathos for which the victim cannot be held responsible. Macbeth's situation is tragedy, an action of his own in which he has lost his self.

Further, as O'Brien said to Winston, the destruction is "*for ever.*" Duncan will not wake. There is no way for Macbeth to return to his story of himself as a loyal and noble warrior, his old self. The only way forward is either into numbness and loss—the path Macbeth takes, sinking further into villainy, and that Winston takes, succumbing to a life of meaningless drift—or into a search for forgiveness, which is why stories of struggles for forgiveness "after the fall" often also are elements of tragedies. Oedipus from Thebes wanders toward Colonus (Palmer 2015).

Because of this, tragedy is inherently ironic for it requires both our complicity in our own destruction and our rebellion against that collusion, be the rebellion wistful, terrified, or furious. Tragedy requires both our colluding with the forces that have "torn away ... our chosen image," as Miller said, and also our struggle against those forces. This ironic tension is the fundamental factor distinguishing tragedy from melodrama or pathos: "In tragedy the conflict is within man; in melodrama, it is between men, or between men and things" (Heilman, page 79, quoted in Felski 2008: 7). Tragedy is James Tyrone's wistful remorse as he remembers his early career before "that God-damned play I bought for a song"; Blanche DuBois's journey from Belle Reve through her role in her young husband's suicide to the Hotel Flamingo to New Orleans, where she struggles with memories of her own cruelty and urges her sister to leave Stanley and not "hang back with the brutes"; John Proctor's simultaneous sense that he is morally unworthy to fight the duplicitous injustice of the Puritan court because of his past affair with Abigail Williams and his raging refusal to cooperate; Dodge's killing and burying the child that reveals the lonely despair of his own marriage while continuing to fuel that despair; Troy Maxson's hanging on to angry bitterness as he fulfills his job as a garbage man so that he can pay his rent, put food on his family's table, and not be whiffed by "strike three" in life.

This conscious rebellion is what distinguishes tragedy from the absurd. Characters in absurdist dramas do not rebel against the forces defeating them; they endure, though confusion or ignorance or comfortable denial or an ever-growing numbness to the degradation of their lives. Enduring, though a kind of resistance, lacks the understanding to rise to the level of rebellion. This is Samuel Beckett's "I'll never know, in the silence you don't know, you must go on, I can't go on, I'll go on" from the end of his novel *The Unnamable* (1954). Arthur Miller called Beckett's *Waiting for Godot* "a vaudeville at the edge of the cliff" (Miller [1994] 2016: 167). The characters' full awareness of their situation would tip them into tragedy and rebellion, but they have not yet reached that point; they wait and endure, on the edge.

As a result, the absurd makes a space for tragicomedy in a way that genuine tragedy does not. *Twelfth Night* could be made a tragedy by focusing on Malvolio, making him aware that he is despised and betrayed, and forcing him to confront the destruction of his self-story and the ways in which he has been complicit in its ruin; but as Shakespeare renders him, Malvolio is oblivious and thus absurd, merely comic or in some productions tragicomic. Tom Stoppard's *Rosencrantz and Guildenstern Are Dead* makes the opposite journey from the tragedy of *Hamlet* to comedy by taking away the lead characters' understanding, making them confused and unaware while on the brink of destruction. They endure, but they are too unaware to rebel. Certainly tragedies can have comic scenes or subplots: the porter in Act 2, Scene 3 of *Macbeth*, or Eugene O'Neill's send-up of the pompous titan of industry T. Steadman Harder toward the end of Act 1 in *A Moon for the Misbegotten*. But the tragic plot itself requires characters both to have an awareness of their own role in creating the depth of their destruction and to rebel against it. This leaves no space for comedy.

From Aristotle to Schiller, Hegel, Schelling, Kierkegaard, and Nietzsche, and on to Arthur Miller, Albert Camus, Raymond Williams, George Steiner, and Terry Eagleton, there have been distinguished discussions and debates about tragedy (see Bushnell 2008; Poole 2005; Wallace 2007; Young 2013), but generally these have been debates about the source of tragedy: what causes people to come to the tragic situation, to become complicit in their own destruction. On the nature of the tragic situation itself, however, there is more general agreement: tragedies depict people being overwhelmed by a set of events in which they are complicit that threaten to destroy their sense of self, against which they rebel, and which leave them in agony. Some tragedies depict the moment when the character confronts this agony and collapse; others focus on a time "after the fall," on the character's struggle to engage with the consequences of the collapse. But in both cases, as Miller said, we are presented with characters who have a painful and deep understanding that they have been "torn away from [their] chosen image of what and who [they] are in the world" ([1949] 2016: 9) and thus have lost their way in life.

* * *

This collection of essays is not only about tragedy in general but about American tragedy in particular. Is there something about America that causes its dramatists to write their tragedies from a certain perspective or set of attitudes that make American tragedy distinctive or peculiar in some way? Except for Toby Zinman, who was asked to capture the broad ethos of the entire past quarter century in American theatre in her wide-ranging concluding essay, each contributor here was asked to focus on a single canonical author and to approach this question empirically. Rather than starting with preconceived notions of what tragedy is and then forcing them down upon the works to see if they fit the mold, contributors here were asked to look directly at the plays themselves and to explore what they showed about their author's vision of the nature and sources of human suffering, the ways the self is assaulted, and the ways characters respond. From that, it was hoped, distinctive elements of the author's vision of tragedy would emerge. (For a different approach, see Andreach 2014, where he argues that traditional conceptions of tragedy, far from being outmoded, continue to be found in contemporary American drama.)

The vision of tragedy described in the first part of this introduction, with its focus on overwhelming forces, complicity, and rebellion, despite its many references to the ancient Greeks and Shakespeare, is in large part the vision that resulted from this exploration of American dramatists. This shows the universality of the human experience of tragedy, the basic elements of human nature that enable dramas to move across time and cultures and to continue to have cathartic effect.

In addition, however, there also are specifically American themes here, grounded, as Arthur Miller suggested, in the American Dream, which he calls, "the largely unacknowledged screen in front of which all American writing plays itself out—the screen of the perfectibility of man" (Miller and Roudané [1983] 1987: 361–2). Because European colonists myopically disdained Native American cultures, they saw America as a wide-open frontier, a land where the social and class impediments of the Old World basically did not exist and opportunity was unimpeded. This is the vision expressed by Benjamin Franklin both in his *Autobiography* and in the aphorisms of *Poor Richard's Almanack*. Americans, according to this unfettered optimism, are limited only by their own characters and ability.[1] According to the American Dream, the New World, as Jefferson decreed in the *Declaration of Independence*, is a land where more enlightened and progressive social systems guarantee each individual "life, liberty, and the pursuit of happiness." Capitalism together with these libertarian democratic ideals supported and extended this vision. As the frontier closed, the market place became the new wide-open frontier where individual skill, initiative, and diligence were promised to lead to a flourishing life.

The American Dream is America's version of Romanticism, a glorification of the individual's potential and experience that flowered in both the jingoism of George Babbitt in Sinclair Lewis's 1922 novel and the contrarian bohemianism of Greenwich Village in the 1910s that gave rise to O'Neill, Glaspell, and the Provincetown Players. The Dream is a core commitment to the significance of the individual in Western liberal democracy that can be traced in political philosophy from John Locke to Thomas Jefferson to John Stuart Mill to John Rawls and in literature from Wordsworth, Keats, and Shelley to Emerson and Thoreau and ultimately to the mass-culture young-adult novels of Horatio Alger and their heirs in today's multimillion-dollar market for self-help books and videos.

But as Arthur Miller points out in the excerpt from the 1983 interview cited above, the American Dream is a promise that carries an inherent demand: America promises people unimpeded opportunity, and thus it demands of them that they flourish. If you fail to feel your life is flourishing, something is wrong; you need to look for a cause. People outside the American Dream—or some other cultural variation on this theme—do not feel this particular pressure: they feel lucky to survive from day to day however they can; they do not have the luxury to be concerned about thriving or flourishing. Inherent in the American Dream, however, is the same potential for despair that is inherent in Romanticism's celebration of the individual and that is a source of tragedy in both: the sense that if you do not feel you are flourishing, you are failing, and some cause needs to be found.

Tragedy always is born in hope; it is the experience of hope's betrayal. The problem with the American Dream and its promise of opportunity is that it leaves us few places to look for that betrayer; the betrayer, it says, must somehow be in ourselves, and if we look at "who we really are," we will see it there. That confrontation with the betrayer of the American Dream in ourselves is the peculiarly American form of tragedy. Even if what we confront is our own collusion with and simultaneous rebellion against the social forces that overwhelm and destroy us, the fault somehow is experienced as our own. As Christopher Bigsby says toward the end of his foreword to this anthology, a sense of abandonment and loss pervades American drama: "a sense of failure reaching down into the soul that can lead either to the tragic or the absurd." The absurd turns tragic in American theatre when characters are forced to admit, as Bigsby says, that "they are abandoned because on some level they have abandoned themselves."

* * *

Jeffery Kennedy takes up this idea in his essay on Eugene O'Neill, showing how O'Neill set out purposefully to revolutionize American theatre by transposing the themes of classical Greek tragedy into American settings and then in his last plays explored the more explicitly personal and American themes of "pipe dreams," abandonment, the impossible search for forgiveness, and the tragic collapse of the self.

Of all the essays here, Sharon Friedman's on Susan Glaspell most directly connects American tragedy to Romanticism's focus on the individual as Friedman places Glaspell's work in the context of emerging issues in feminism and the rejection of hyper-nationalism in the early twentieth century.

Jonathan Shandell's analysis of Langston Hughes's *Mulatto* begins a discussion that pervades this anthology: the pernicious complications racism introduces into the American Dream. Shandell rejects the view that Hughes's play is best understood as a study of the psychological difficulties of mixed-race individuals and sees it instead as a sociological critique, a direct challenge to racism's foundations in American beliefs and attitudes. This approach sets up an interesting juxtaposition between Shandell's essay and Werner Sollors's on Adrienne Kennedy, for Kennedy's *Funnyhouse of a Negro* is much more clearly a journey through the subjective experience of racism, the individual's personal response to the societal factors Shandell identifies as Hughes's major concern.

Jackson R. Bryer takes an in-depth look at one of Thornton Wilder's less-known plays as a way of exploring a central theme in Wilder's oeuvre: the role of God in ordering the universe and the questioning of religious faith. By focusing on Wilder's modernizing of Euripides' drama about Alcestis, Bryer explores both themes in Greek tragedy and the ways these themes were experienced by Americans in the 1940s and 1950s.

Lillian Hellman is famous for writing plays that defy easy classification into particular genres—especially the distinction between tragedy and melodrama—and Anne Fletcher makes this the center of her discussion of tragic elements in Hellman's work. Where O'Neill believed that enlightenment would arise from experiencing dramatic tragedies and set out purposefully to write them, Hellman focused on telling a good story that revealed some truth about humanity and led the audience to insight or even catharsis. Plays should be defined by their effect, not their form.

Widely recognized as the most lyrical of American dramatists, Tennessee Williams struggled with shame as much as did many of his characters. Susan C. W. Abbotson focuses on this in her discussion of Williams as a tragedian, arguing against critics who hold that Williams's plays cannot rise to the level of tragedy because of the turpitude of many of his heroes and heroines. As Abbotson points out, "Williams masterfully creates a sense of tragedy through people divided not against others but against themselves."

Stephen Marino's starting point is Arthur Miller's often-cited 1949 essay "Tragedy and the Common Man." Marino then takes Miller's explicit views on the nature of tragedy and applies them to Miller's four great plays from the 1940s and 1950s, focusing on tragedy as a depiction of challenges to a person's sense of dignity and the person's compulsion to defend that dignity. This makes Marino's essay a good background piece to the essays in this volume on African American dramatists, who also consider issues about the experience of dignity in America and for whom the basic issues Miller identifies are complicated by American racism.

Natka Bianchini takes us with Edward Albee from tragedy to the absurd and back. Broadly discussing the concept of the absurd and many of Albee's plays, she focuses on *The Goat, or Who Is Sylvia?* which Albee subtitled "Notes Toward a Definition of Tragedy." Bianchini argues that for Albee the source of both the tragic and the absurd is loneliness: people's inability to connect with one another.

For Deirdre Osborne, a British scholar with a special interest in black and women's writing globally, Lorraine Hansberry's work must be interpreted in the context of her concerns about colonialism and racist exploitation throughout the world. Osborne interprets *A Raisin in the Sun* not merely as a critique of American racism but as part of Hansberry's broader campaign as an activist for global human rights.

It is useful to take the essays on Amiri Baraka and August Wilson by Harvey Young and Sandra Shannon together, for each of these dramatists captures African American rage at racism's corruption of the American Dream. In discussing Baraka, Young, like Shandell on Langston Hughes, focuses on the societal forces of racism, discussing Clay in Baraka's play *Dutchman* as a victim of those forces despite his efforts to work within the ways they circumscribe him. In writing about Wilson, Sandra Shannon discusses Wilson's notion of the Warrior, someone who understands the way he is victimized but responds not as a victim but with rebellion. For both these dramatists, characters must understand the forces that assault them, their rebellion against those forces, and—nonetheless—the ways they have been co-opted into colluding with those forces in their own destruction.

Shannon Blake Skelton sees the American Dream and in particular its vision of the American family as the targets of Sam Shepard's plays. He argues that Shepard is not writing a critique of the American Dream and family as much as he is writing from a perspective beyond them, a kind of post–American Dream America, where the possibility of family has been destroyed by patriarchs with archaic and cataclysmal conceptions of masculinity. "The American Dream?" Shepard seems to be saying, "It's a corrupted fantasy. There no longer is a way to achieve it. Probably there never was."

In his play *Oleanna*, David Mamet directly depicts characters being victimized by external forces who then have to wonder if they are in fact colluding with those forces themselves, confronting a classic Aristotelian reversal and recognition about responsibility. Brenda Murphy discusses this idea in *Oleanna* and three other Mamet plays, exploring Mamet's comment about human freedom and options: "whichever one you choose, you're going to be wrong, and P.S., you never had a choice to begin with."

My own essay on Marsha Norman looks at the way in which the American Dream demands us to have meaningful lives and leads those of us who fail to feel we are thriving into a sense of failure and tragedy. Focusing on *'night, Mother*, I compare Jessie and her mother, Thelma, to Agamemnon and Iphigenia at Aulis, arguing that despite Jessie's suicide, the larger tragedy we see unfolding here is Thelma's, for Thelma is forced to see that Jessie's suicide condemns the absurdity and meaninglessness drift of her own life as well.

Claire Gleitman was brave to take on Tony Kushner's *Angels in America* when I asked her. Punning on Kushner's comment that "fabulousness" includes "gender-fuck," Gleitman argues that the play is a kind of "genre-fuck," moving quickly from one theatrical tone to another while constantly focusing on a tragic self-centeredness inherent in the American commitment to individualism that the Reagan era somehow made acceptable. In the end, however, as Gleitman shows, the play is about the possibility of transfiguration, the central ideal of the American Dream, and the ways in which this is linked to forgiveness, another required element if the Dream is not to become pernicious.

Suzan-Lori Parks has a strong sense of the elements of Greek tragedy. She uses them in her own plays, as Soyica Diggs Colbert shows, to depict how interactions between characters are microcosmic iterations of large historical events that shaped the African American experience. As Colbert says, "Parks's drama makes history, recalling well-known individuals, stories, and scenarios while shifting important elements of the narrative, including the figure's race or the dynamics of key historical relationships. These subtle and important changes reconfigure the shape of history through drama." For Parks, the tragedies of modern individuals reflect the tragedy of America's past.

That same theme is explored in the concluding chapter by Toby Zinman. Using a few key plays to identify and summarize central themes in the past quarter century of American theatre, Zinman discusses the way not only drama but also musicals such as *Assassins* and *Hamilton* portray the hope America promises, its betrayal, and renewal. America itself emerges as a tragic hero in her essay, "opening a wide vista on the ways drama can 'hold a mirror up to Nature,' revealing ourselves to ourselves."

This collection is intended for readers with a serious interest but perhaps little background in either the concept of tragedy or American drama. Its essays are short. Each attempts to focus a few key themes as a way of introducing a major American playwright; each is intended merely as a starting point for the reader's own explorations. All of us who worked on this book hope you find it useful.

Note

1   This belief, or course, is a fantasy that fails to recognize the power of poverty, prejudice, and mere bad luck in a human life.

References

Andreach, Robert J. (2014), *Tragedy in the Contemporary American Theatre*, Lanham, MD: University Press of America.

Bushnell, Rebecca (2008), *Tragedy: A Short Introduction*, Malden, MA: Blackwell Publishing.

Felski, Rita (2008), "Introduction," in Rita Felski (ed.), *Rethinking Tragedy*, 1–25, Baltimore, MD: Johns Hopkins University Press.

Miller, Arthur ([1949] 2016), "Tragedy and the Common Man," in *Arthur Miller: Collected Essays*, introduction by Susan C. W. Abbotson, 7–10, New York: Penguin Books. Available online: http://www.nytimes.com/books/00/11/12/specials/miller-common.html (accessed February 1, 2017).

Miller, Arthur ([1994] 2016), "About Theater Language: Afterword to *The Last Yankee*," in *Arthur Miller: Collected Essays*, introduction by Susan C. W. Abbotson, 155–72, New York: Penguin Books.

Miller, Arthur and Matthew C. Roudané ([1983] 1987), "An Interview with Arthur Miller," reprinted in Matthew C. Roudané (ed.), *Conversations with Arthur Miller*, 360–75, Jackson, MS: University Press of Mississippi. Originally published in *Michigan Quarterly Review* 24 (1985), 373–89.

Orwell, George ([1949] 1992), *Nineteen Eighty-Four*, introduction by Julian Symonds, New York: Alfred A. Knopf, Everyman's Library.

Palmer, David (2015), "Three Ways to Fail at Forgiveness: Beckett, Miller, and O'Neill," *The Eugene O'Neill Review* 36 (2): 115–49.

Poole, Adrian (2005), *Tragedy: A Very Short Introduction*, Oxford: Oxford University Press.

Wallace, Jennifer (2007), *The Cambridge Introduction to Tragedy*, Cambridge: Cambridge University Press.

Young, Julian (2013), *The Philosophy of Tragedy: From Plato to Žižek*, Cambridge: Cambridge University Press.

1

Eugene O'Neill (1888–1953)

Jeffery Kennedy
Arizona State University

"In any expression of tragic theory," Joseph P. O'Neill tells us, "two facts should be kept clearly in mind: the basic concept of tragedy differs among various authors; and tragic expression has always preceded theory" (1963: 481). As early as 1925, in the manuscript version of the foreword to his play *The Great God Brown*, playwright Eugene O'Neill wrote that he believed the theatre "should give us what the church no longer gives us—a meaning. In brief, it should return to the spirit of Greek grandeur" (quoted in Martin 2005: 138). O'Neill is considered by most scholars to be the first American playwright to truly embrace the tragic form as exemplified by the Greeks and to attempt to create an American version of it for the twentieth century. Sophus Winther, in his critical study of O'Neill, wrote, "In the final analysis, O'Neill's plays must be judged in the terms of tragedy. That is exactly what he wanted, for he held that whatever greatness a man may have his ultimate stature is measured in the terms of his ability to experience tragedy in his own life and in the life of man" (1961: 296). O'Neill attempted to fashion an American version of tragedy through many experiments that included borrowing and combining portions of existing Greek myths, attempting to emulate the Nietzschean tragic model of symbiotic Apollonian and Dionysian characters, employing various forms of stagecraft that for his time were experimental, and ultimately using his own family narrative as core material for his later tragic plays.

Winther posits that any analysis of the concept of tragedy as it finds expression in modern drama, particularly in O'Neill, must recognize that the traditional Aristotelian definition cannot be used. Though there are plots and other elements that most would consider tragic in O'Neill's early plays, by 1926 he had set out to create, in his own words, a "modern psychological drama using one of the old legend plots of Greek tragedy" (quoted in Alexander 2007: 31). Joseph O'Neill writes that O'Neill's "immediate problem was to create a modern tragic interpretation of the Greek concept of fate without benefit of the Greek gods" (1963: 483). As often was the impetus for O'Neill in his writing, he set a challenge to himself in the form of a question: "Is it possible to get modern psychological approximation of the Greek sense of fate into such a play, which an intelligent audience of today possessed of no belief in gods or supernatural retribution ... could accept and be moved by" (quoted in Clark 1947: 530). O'Neill wanted to recreate the values of Greek tradition in American drama but in a modern design. For him this meant translating the Greek notion of an external fate into the terms of modern psychology.

Brenda Murphy reminds us that while the Greek and Aristotelian axioms of tragedy clearly informed O'Neill, his literary idol was Nietzsche and his books *Thus Spoke Zarathustra* and *The Birth of Tragedy* were seminal in their influence on him. In her analysis of O'Neill's 1926 play *The Great God Brown*, Murphy shows how the play revolves around "a fundamental Nietzschean division" of Apollo, representing the more intellectual and "visionless" architect Bill Brown, driven by the new American "materialistic myth—a Success—building his life of exterior things, inwardly empty and resourceless (as expressed by Bennett Clark)" and the Dionysian artist Dion Anthony, "tortured by the division of his soul," his name a combination of Dionysius and St. Anthony; between these two they reflect "Nietzsche's idea of the self and the anti-self" (Murphy 2005: 492). For many this is a difficult Expressionistic four-act play, with the central device of the play involving the actors wearing multiple masks that show the inner and outer personas of the characters. Travis Bogard suggests O'Neill's idea to use masks may have come directly from Nietzsche, who in *The Birth of Tragedy* writes, "The essence of nature is now to be expressed symbolically; a new world of symbols is required" and later that "Dionysius *remains* the sole dramatic protagonist and ... all the famous characters of the Greek stage ... are only masks of that original hero" (Bogard 1988: 264).

In *The Great God Brown*, both men are in love with the same woman, Margaret, and though she chooses Dion over Billy, she loves him only when his mask that hides his true sensitive artistic soul is on. Later, after Dion dies, the worldly and successful Billy puts on Dion's mask, which allows him to win Margaret, but ultimately he also wants to be loved without his mask and is rejected. O'Neill later said the play conveyed "a sense of the tragic mystery drama of Life revealed through the lives in the play" (Commins 1986: 265). The play is often devoutly theological rather than driven by fully realized human characters, with the Dion character ultimately ending more Christ-like in martyrdom than truly Dionysian. It also feels subservient to the technical aspects of the art theatre it created by using masks. As a result, *The Great God Brown* may technically be a Nietzschean tragedy, but it did not fully realize what O'Neill was hoping to achieve, though he remained fond of the work for years.

It was clear to O'Neill early on that as a twentieth-century American playwright he did not have the advantage of the close relationship between drama and life that existed in ancient Athens. However, because he fully realized this dissociation and, more especially, "the disintegration of life itself in a modern mechanized culture," he desired to create a modern counterpart of the Greek theatre "to reassert the socio-religious function of an imaginative truly vibrant theatre" (Commins 1986: 265). O'Neill wrote it would be "a theatre returned to its highest and sole significant function as a Temple where the religion of a poetical interpretation and symbolic celebration of life is communicated to human beings, starved in spirit by their soul-stifling daily struggle to exist as masks among masks of the living" (1934: 166–7).

While O'Neill had used many plot elements of different Greek myths to construct his play *Desire Under the Elms* (1924), with its strong Oedipal and Freudian resonance, his most complete response to challenging himself to write an American version of a Greek tragedy came after *The Great God Brown* with a modern adaptation of Aeschylus' *Oresteia*, a trilogy based on the Greek legend of the House of Atreus. The *Oresteia* originally explored Aeschylus' tragic concept: how do you reconcile the suffering of man with divine providence? O'Neill's attempt to answer the same question resulted in *Mourning Becomes Electra* (1931). Set in New England at the end of the Civil War, it tells the story of the Mannon family, their last name a reference to the *Oresteia* character Agamemnon.

William Chase Greene wrote, "The greatest Greek drama ... rests on the interplay between fate and character, between what man cannot change and what remains within his power" (1944: 92). O'Neill appeared to be aware of this. In a letter to critic Arthur Quinn, written about a year before he began *Mourning Becomes Electra*, he wrote:

> I'm always, always trying to interpret Life in terms of character. I'm always acutely conscious of the Force behind—(Fate, God, our biological past creating our present, whatever one calls it— Mystery certainly)—and the one eternal tragedy of Man in his glorious, self-destructive struggle to make the Force express him instead of being, as an animal is, an infinitesimal incident in its expression. And my proud conviction is that it is possible—or can be—to develop a tragic expression in terms of transfigured modern values and symbols. (Quinn 1946: 199)

Mourning Becomes Electra is a trilogy of plays with the main characters, the Mannon family, fashioned completely after the House of Atreus in the *Oresteia*. The first two plays, *The Homecoming* and *The Hunted*, follow this Greek epic closely, whereas in the third play, *The Haunted*, as Frederick Carpenter has stated, O'Neill "created his own myth" (quoted in Murphy 2005: 497). In the plot of the play, Lavinia's (Electra's) father Ezra (Agamemnon) returns home from the Civil War to his unfaithful wife, Christine (Clytemnestra), who poisons him because she wants to marry her lover, Adam Brant (Aegisthus). Lavinia and her brother Orin (Orestes) murder Adam in revenge, causing Christine to respond by committing suicide, with Orin following her example, guilt-ridden by his mother's death and his incestuous involvement with Lavinia. Lavinia condemns herself to a life locked away from the world, feeling bound to the Mannon dead. "I'm the last Mannon," she cries at the end of the play, declaring that she won't go like her brother and mother, "That's escaping punishment. And there's no one left to punish me ... I've got to punish myself! Living alone ... with the dead is a worse act of justice than death or prison" (O'Neill 1931: 1053). O'Neill biographers Arthur and Barbara Gelb draw a direct line between Lavinia and O'Neill himself, with the playwright having lost his father, mother, and brother to death by the time he was writing the play. O'Neill echoed to a friend Lavinia's cry after his brother Jamie's passing, "I'm the last of the O'Neills," and like her, he lived his last years in seclusion and thematic obsession with his family (Gelb 1987: 721).

Travis Bogard notes that O'Neill struggled to find "appropriate dialogue" to match the Greek theme, writing to Joseph Wood Krutch on July 27, 1929, as he was working on *Mourning Becomes Electra*: "Oh for a language to write drama in! For a speech that is dramatic and not just conversation. I'm so strait jacketed by writing in terms of talk ... But where to find that language?" (quoted in Bogard 1988: 334) However, after rereading the entire trilogy just before it was produced, O'Neill wrote that he felt the plays had "power and drive and the strange quality of unreal reality that I wanted," and that he had achieved his goal of not resorting to the Greek convention of supernatural forces (Gelb 1987: 744). Despite the six-hour running time of the three plays, presented one after the other in a single evening, the critics of the original production lauded the work as a masterpiece. *The New York Times* critic Brooks Atkinson called it "a universal tragedy of tremendous stature—deep, dark, solid, uncompromising and grim ... heroically thought out and magnificently wrought in style and structure ... To this department, which ordinarily reserves its praise for the dead, *Mourning Becomes Electra* is Mr. O'Neill's masterpiece" (Atkinson 1931: 22). Biographer Robert Dowling writes that the play "unmistakably parallels Dostoevsky's probing into the 'Russian soul.' But in O'Neill's play, New England Puritanism is the 'soul' governing the Mannon—psychologically, historically, religiously, genetically" (2015: 383). Playwright Tony Kushner has written that "*Mourning* is a naked attempt to connect the origins of America and the origins of Western civilization and dramatic art" (2003). Dowling quotes O'Neill's later contempt for the idea of an American ability to be truly moved by a traditional Greek tragedy:

What modern audience was ever purged by pity and terror by witnessing a Greek tragedy or what modern mind by reading one? It can't be done! We are too far away, we are in a world of different values ... Our tragedy is just that we have only ourselves, that there is nothing to be purged into except a belief in the guts of man, good or evil, who faces unflinchingly the black mystery of his own soul! (Dowling 2015: 383; see also Bogard 1994: 390)

O'Neill's tragedies possess the recognition that highlights human existence: to recognize the absolute futility of humans' struggles against themselves and those that have died before them. The juxtaposition of fate and freewill establishes a certain tension and balance, as they do in all good tragedy, making this essential to the tragic circumstances in his plays. While embracing characteristics of naturalism, O'Neill "passes beyond mere defiance and determinism in his development of fate and human responsibility" (O'Neill 1963: 493). Winther believes that O'Neill's tragedy, "if it has universal appeal, deals with the fall of man from prosperity into adversity in a manner that is 'shocking' and through causes that lie within man himself in relation to the outward forces of his world." Not merely from a fatal flaw, though not necessarily without one, man is brought to his disaster by forces more powerful than he is, and this idea has been in O'Neill's plays from the beginning. "The men and women of his world are victims of a cosmic trap, cold and impersonal as steel" (Winther 1961: 298). Mary in *Long Day's Journey Into Night* says to her son Edmund, "It's wrong to blame your brother. He can't help being what the past has made him. Any more than your father can. Or you. Or I" (1956: 64). Later, when she knows that there is no escape, she thinks of her happiness as a student in the convent: "You were much happier," she says to herself. "If I could only find the faith I lost, so I could pray again." However, this cannot and will not ever happen; O'Neill makes it clear that the forces of fate have sealed her in her place of despair. Instead, her husband asks her to "Forget the past." Her answer is, "How can I? The past is the present, isn't it? It's the future, too. We all try to lie about that, but life won't let us" (1956: 87).

O'Neill's later plays get progressively balder in stating this tragic view of human fate. An example is his overtly naming what he sees as folly "pipe dreams" in *The Iceman Cometh*; here there can be no mistaking O'Neill's intent. The play's central character, Theodore

"Hickey" Hickman, a hardware salesman whose yearly arrival is anticipated as a bright light to the lost souls in Harry Hope's saloon, spends most of the play trying to "save" each of the regulars from their falsehoods, only to find none of them ultimately has the will to be saved. The play ends with them in shock as they witness Hickey's confession that he has killed the only source of love in his life, his wife Evelyn, the murder precipitated by his guilt and anger arising from her misplaced hope and continual forgiveness of his whore-mongering ways. He shouts at her corpse: "Well, you know what you can do with your pipe dream now, you damned bitch?" (1957: 241). Winther reminds us, "At the end of *The Iceman Cometh* there is no one left to summarize the story and give it meaning, for the meaning of life has been lost in Pipe Dreams. Kafka's Castle is visible on the hill, but there is no road through the tangled thicket that surrounds its base. This is the meaning of tragedy" (1961: 308).

Joseph O'Neill states that "Some critics have determined that though O'Neill's plays manifest a constant search for some redemptive element, there is never the actual discovery. Though his tragic concept passes beyond mere romantic defiance and natural determinism in expressing a tragic fall through human responsibility, it fails to achieve a human redemption and thus a complete concept of tragedy" (1963: 498). If Joseph O'Neill's statement is correct, could this be O'Neill's accommodation to accomplish his task of creating an American tragedy that will be embraced by its citizens? O'Neill clearly resists Aeschylus's *deus ex machina* endings to solve his tragic dilemmas and opts instead for a more palatable—and in some senses Freudian—approach for a modern audience that presents honest and emotional-to-the-core exposing of the causes of the tragic situation as enough, without presenting a clear path to redemption. Richard Sewall does not find this lack of redemption problematic as he feels O'Neill "explores a central arc of contemporary experience rife with tragic potential," and "transcends the limits of realism on the one hand and pathos on the other. Each reaches out toward cosmic concerns, the 'infinitude of background' without which tragedy 'dwindles to a sorrowful tale,' as Macneile Dixon once wrote." Regarding *Long Day's Journey*, Sewall sees "the wrangling Tyrones become Everyfamily, prisoners of their own temperaments;

there is no way out—except the one no one will take ... O'Neill, telling the story of his own family, sees it, too—but too late." In this sense of confession, it is as if O'Neill is saying, "This is my own story, and it is tragic." And "in the telling, in the transcendence, in the knowledge gained, [he] becomes (it might also be said) his own tragic hero." What is similar in *Long Day's Journey* to Greek drama is the pall of tragedy hanging over an entire family; nonetheless, as Sewall notes, "what O'Neill had done explicitly and imitatively in *Mourning Becomes Electra*, he here [in *Long Day's Journey*] fashions into something completely his own—a new creation" (1990: ix–x). O'Neill's new American creation fulfills his quest to develop a tragic expression in terms of modern values and achieves his goal of a modern psychological replacement of the Greek sense of fate for an audience "possessed of no belief in gods or supernatural retribution"; in other words, he believes that redemption is not required or even desired by a modern audience (Clark 1947: 530).

Sarah Churchwell, in London's *The Guardian*, wrote in a preview to the 2012 West End production of *Long Day's Journey Into Night*: "O'Neill's plays come to seem a Sisyphean endeavor, struggling up this mountain of grief; there is a real heroism in his obstinate, perpetually uphill battle to come to terms with human suffering." She quotes O'Neill saying he hoped to "convey the quality of understanding that is born only of pain and rises to perception to reach the truths of human passion. For life to be felt as noble, it must be seen as tragic."

Churchwell goes on to endorse the widely held idea that without O'Neill there would have been no Arthur Miller or Tennessee Williams, let alone David Mamet or Sam Shepard. But is this true? Did O'Neill truly influence these monumental writers? Miller once stated that O'Neill seemed "too cosmic" and "unresponsive to social realities," and also that there was nothing technical to be gained from studying his writing, with Miller instead more sympathetic to the plays of Clifford Odets that are anchored in the family. In his autobiography, *Timebends*, Miller writes that O'Neill seemed to him "the playwright of the mystical rich, of high society and the Theatre Guild escapist 'culture.'" But after he went to see *The Iceman Cometh* in 1946, while acknowledging it was an "extremely weak production," Miller changed his mind, at least about this perception he held of O'Neill's work:

I was ... struck by O'Neill's radical hostility to bourgeois civilization, far greater than anything Odets had expressed ... It was O'Neill who wrote about the working-class men, about whores and the social discards and even the black man in a white world, but since there was no longer a connection with Marxism in the man himself, his plays were never seen as the critiques of capitalism that they objectively were. (Miller 1987: 228)

In an interview in 1966, Miller said:

One thing I always respected about O'Neill was his insistence on his vision. That is, even when he was twisting materials to distortion and really ruining his work, there was an image behind it of a possessed individual, who, for good or ill, was himself ... His people are not symbolic; his lines are certainly not verse; the prose is not realistic—his is the never-never land of a quasi-Strindberg writer. But where he's wonderful, it's superb. The last play [referring to *Long Day's Journey*] is really a masterpiece. (Carlisle [1966] 1987: 105)

Miller never commented beyond this about O'Neill's family being the center of *Long Day's Journey*, yet Miller has been lauded for his insight into familial relationships, and he maintained that family relationships must be immersed in social context. Perhaps only later did Miller come to recognize—as most scholars now do—O'Neill's specific accomplishment in creating tragedies of families.

Though Tennessee Williams claimed to have detested the O'Neill plays he read in college, some of Williams's early plays are clear imitations of O'Neill, and his career was haunted by O'Neill's legacy, both because he spent a great deal of time working in Provincetown, the birthplace of O'Neill's career, and particularly because he felt threatened by critic George Jean Nathan's determination to maintain O'Neill's status as America's greatest playwright. Williams wrote O'Neill toward the end of 1946 congratulating him after reading *The Iceman Cometh*, and O'Neill responded thanking him because he'd been "down in the dumps" about the critical response to the play (Gelb 1987: 877). However, Williams's only direct comments about O'Neill came in a meeting with Arthur Gelb (see Isaac 1993), when he told him, "O'Neill forced the Broadway producers to accept his concept of native tragedy." He also said in that meeting that "O'Neill gave birth to the American theatre and died for it." In his article about O'Neill's correspondence with Miller and Williams, Dan Isaac tells us that "Years later, Williams became paranoid about the presumed rivalry between O'Neill and himself, certain that *The New York Times* was denigrating his work to ensure the exalted position of O'Neill as America's premier tragedian." In 1993, Isaac astutely observed that we are

> beginning to discover that we have developed a mature tradition of tragedy, a tradition that is as much rooted in the biblical prophetic mode that seeks justice and change, with a dash of Marxism thrown in for good measure, as it is in the Greek philosophic mode, dominated by complex causality systems that explore the interplay of necessity and chance. Eugene O'Neill, Tennessee Williams and Arthur Miller stand foremost now as our visionary spokesmen. (129–30)

Sewall in his article "Eugene O'Neill and the Sense of the Tragic" (1991) tells us that, like Melville, Shakespeare, and the Greek tragedians before him, O'Neill "was confronted by something deeply unsatisfying. It did not square with his vision of life and with his sense of the purpose of art, and in his own way, he protested. So the tragic temperament is not for the acquiescent, the timid, the dull of soul." Sewall goes on to say that the quality O'Neill perceived in Strindberg and Dostoyevsky was what American theatre did not have, quoting Dostoyevsky: "a powerful emotional ecstasy, approaching a kind of frenzy," and this is what O'Neill wanted to give his audiences (1991: 7).

However, for all his study and reading, his theatrical experiments, and his attempts to create a native tragedy for the American stage while using the Greek model as guide, it is striking that, in the end, the American tragedies O'Neill most fully realized used as plot and character his own complex and misbegotten family. Perhaps more astonishingly, O'Neill could not possibly have known for certain that his would be the kind of tragedy that America ultimately would embrace as its greatest. He wrote and lived in isolation most of the time, particularly in the second half of his career, and in the 1940s he was considered by many to be finished with nothing more to contribute. His masterpiece *Long Day's Journey Into Night* was not produced until almost three years after his death in 1953, and yet it is this play that many other major American playwrights, both his contemporaries and those to follow, would admire and be challenged by in terms of tragic form, particularly Tennessee Williams, Arthur Miller, Edward Albee, Sam Shepard, August Wilson, and Tony Kushner. Kushner writes: "O'Neill's great forebear is not Shakespeare ... but Aeschylus. O'Neill reaches in past the skin and the viscera and operates directly with the bones. He doesn't garden and landscape and cultivate and harvest; he shifts tectonic plates" (2003). After Kushner's play *The Intelligent Homosexual's Guide to Capitalism and Socialism with a Key to the Scriptures* premiered in New York in 2011, Margaret Spillane wrote in *The Nation* that the play "lives at the intersection of the garrulous family dramas of Eugene O'Neill and Arthur Miller" (2011). David Finkle wrote of this same production that "The drama might be categorized as a dysfunctional family drama—that old American staple—but only if the same can be said of Eugene O'Neill's *Long Day's Journey Into Night* or Edward Albee's *Who's Afraid of Virginia Woolf?* That's right, it's the latest in a welcome line of apotheoses of dysfunctional family dramas" (2011).

O'Neill's tragic legacy is felt most strongly not by stopping at moments throughout his career—specific plays that are the results of his questioning and testing the elasticity of what could be portrayed on the American stage—but in viewing the sweep of the arc of his writing and where that ultimately led: to the depth of the portrayal of his own humanity and that of his tortured family. Sewall, in the preface to the third edition of *The Vision of Tragedy*, speaking of both O'Neill and Miller, writes,

> We no longer need read these plays in critical detachment. Personalities stand here, as, indeed, they have from The Poet of Job on down, only now they can be documented. To sense the living playwright in the play is to find ... our perceptions sharpened, our own very selves made more alive, even ... our involvement in the tragic quest strengthened, perhaps confirmed. (1990: vii)

In 1940, O'Neill wrote to critic and friend George Jean Nathan about a new play he was writing: "It's a deeply tragic play, but without any violent dramatic action. At the final curtain, there they still are, trapped within each other by the past, each guilty and at the same time innocent, scorning, loving, pitying each other, understanding and yet not understanding at all, forgiving but still doomed never to be able to forget" (Bogard 1994: 506–7). In 1941, O'Neill wrote a note to his wife Carlotta when he gave her the finished script of Long Day's Journey Into Night as a present on their twelfth wedding anniversary. It reads in part:

> Dearest ... I give you the original script of this play of old sorrow, written in tears and blood ... I mean it as a tribute to your love and tenderness which gave me the faith in love that enabled me to face my dead at last and write this play—write it with deep pity and understanding and forgiveness for *all* the four haunted Tyrones. (O'Neill 1956: 7)

Sewall describes a lecture he once heard titled "What Aristotle Left Out," and what the lecturer, a priest, "found missing, or undeveloped" in Aristotle, Sewall notes, was what O'Neill put into his note to Carlotta: "the blood, the tears; love, understanding, forgiveness." This suggests an important point about Long Day's Journey: "With this play, O'Neill's career comes full circle. He had started with men of flesh and blood—his shipmates, often bloody in a quite literal sense—and he had found in that riotous crew the very qualities he speaks of to Carlotta: pity, understanding, forgiveness." Sewall outlines how O'Neill followed his early work with experimentation, with Greek, biblical, Freudian, and sociological themes, and with technical devices and asides. "Then, in this climactic play, he comes back to where he started: the simple, direct dramatization of a life situation he knew all too well—his own. He rides no theory; there is no experimentation: He 'tells this tale'—and we are left to make of it what we can" (Sewall 1991: 9).

In his 1930 acceptance speech upon receiving the Nobel Prize in Literature, Sinclair Lewis declared that Eugene O'Neill

> has done nothing much in American drama save to transform it utterly, in ten or twelve years, from a false world of neat and competent trickery to a world of splendor and fear and greatness, you would have been reminded that he has done something far worse than scoffing—he has seen life as not to be neatly arranged in the study of a scholar but as a terrifying, magnificent, and

often quite horrible thing akin to the tornado, the earthquake, the devastating fire. (Lewis 1930)

Not long after his first Broadway play, *Beyond the Horizon*, opened in 1920, which some recognize as his first tragedy, O'Neill said, "To me the tragic alone has that significant beauty which is truth. It is the meaning of life—and the hope. The noblest is eternally the most tragic" (quoted in Gelb and Gelb 1987: 5). All O'Neill had produced in the long arc of his writing culminated and integrated into his greatest work at the *end* of his career, something not true of almost any other twentieth-century American playwright who now is gone from us. In the end he left us with perhaps his most tragic work as well, nobly written to be filled with the "beauty which is truth," and in doing so, with the deepest part of himself.

References

Alexander, Doris (2007), "Mourning Becomes Electra," in Harold Bloom (ed.), *Eugene O'Neill*, Blooms Modern Critical Views, updated edition, 31–57, New York: Infobase.

Atkinson, Brooks (1931), "Strange Images of Death in Eugene O'Neill's Masterpiece," *The New York Times*, October 27: 22. Available online: https://partners.nytimes.com/library/theater/102731oneill-electrahtml (accessed January 8, 2017).

Bogard, Travis ([1972] 1988), *Contour in Time: The Plays of Eugene O'Neill*, revised edition, New York: Oxford University Press.

Bogard, Travis and Jackson R. Bryer (eds.) (1994), *Selected Letters of Eugene O'Neill*, New York: Limelight.

Carlisle, Olga and Rose Styron ([1966] 1987), "The Art of Theatre II: Arthur Miller, An Interview," *The Paris Review* 10: 61–98, reprinted in Matthew Roudané (ed.), *Conversations with Arthur Miller*, 85–111, Jackson, MS: University Press of Mississippi.

Churchwell, Sarah (2012), "Eugene O'Neill, Master of American Theatre," *The Guardian*, March 30. Available online: http://www.theguardian.com/stage/2012/mar/30/eugene-o-neill-master-american-theatre (accessed January 8, 2017).

Clark, Bennett H. (1947), *European Theories of the Drama, with a Supplement of the American Drama*, revised edition, New York: Crown.

Commins, Dorothy (ed.) (1986), *Love, Admiration and Respect: The O'Neill-Commins Correspondence*, Durham, NC: Duke University Press.

Dowling, Robert M. (2015), *Eugene O'Neill: A Life in Four Acts*, New Haven: Yale University Press.

Finkle, David (2011), "First Nighter: Tony Kushner's Intelligent Homosexual's Guide ... Continues Genius Display," *Huffington Post*, May 5, updated July 5. Available online: http://www.huffingtonpost.com/david-finkle/first-nighter-tony-kushne_1_b_858324.html (accessed January 8, 2017).

Gelb, Arthur and Barbara Gelb (1987), *O'Neill*, enlarged edition, New York: Harper & Row.

Greene, William Chase (1944), *Moira: Fate, Good, and Evil in Greek Thought*, Cambridge, MA: Harvard University Press.

Isaac, Dan (1993), "Founding Father: O'Neill's Correspondence with Arthur Miller and Tennessee Williams," *The Eugene O'Neill Review*, 17 (1/2): 124–33. Available online: http://www.jstor.org/stable/29784493 (accessed January 8, 2017).

Kushner, Tony (2003), "Eugene O'Neill: The Native Eloquence of Fog," *Times Literary Supplement*, December 18. Available online: http://www.hotreview.org/articles/nativeeloquence.htm (accessed January 8, 2017).

Lewis, Sinclair (1930), "The American Fear of Literature," Nobel Lecture, December 12. Available online: http://www.nobelprize.org/nobel_prizes/literature/laureates/1930/lewis-lecture.html (accessed January 8, 2017).

Martin, Ronald E. (2005), *The Languages of Difference: American Writers and Anthropologists Reconfigure the Primitive 1878–1940*, Newark, DE: University of Delaware Press.

Miller, Arthur (1987), *Timebends: A Life*, New York: Grove Press.

Murphy, Brenda (2005), "Tragedy in the Modern American Theatre," in Rebecca Bushnell (ed.), *A Companion to Tragedy*, 488–504, Malden, MA: Blackwell.

O'Neill, Eugene ([1931] 1988), *Mourning Becomes Electra*, in Travis Bogard (ed.), *Eugene O'Neill: Complete Plays 1920–1931*, 887–1054, New York: Library of America.

O'Neill, Eugene (1934), "Memoranda on Masks," in George Jean Nathan (ed.), *American Spectator Yearbook*, 159–67, New York: Frederick A. Stokes.

O'Neill, Eugene (1956), *Long Day's Journey Into Night*, New Haven: Yale University Press.

O'Neill, Eugene (1957), *The Iceman Cometh*, New York: Vintage Books.

O'Neill, Joseph P. (1963), "The Tragic Theory of Eugene O'Neill," *Texas Studies in Literature and Language* 4 (4): 481–98. Available online: http://www.jstor.org/stable/40753603 (accessed January 8, 2017).

Quinn, Arthur Hobson ([1927] 1946), *A History of the American Drama*, vol. 2: *From the Civil War to the Present Day*, New York: Irvington.

Sewall, Richard B. (1990), *The Vision of Tragedy*, 3rd edition, New York: Paragon House.

Sewall, Richard B. (1991), "Eugene O'Neill and the Sense of the Tragic," in Richard F. Moorton Jr. (ed.), *Eugene O'Neill's Century: Centennial Views on America's Foremost Tragic Dramatist*, 3–16, Westport, CT: Greenwood Press.

Spillane, Margaret (2011), "Tony Kushner's Intellectual Homosexuals," *The Nation*, April 27. Available online: http://www.thenation.com /article/tony-kushners-intelligent-homosexuals (accessed January 8, 2017).

Winther, Sophus Keith (1961), *Eugene O'Neill: A Critical Study*, 2nd edition, New York: Russell & Russell. Available online: http://www .eoneill.com/library/winther/contents.htm. See Chapter 12, "O'Neill and Modern Tragedy" (accessed January 8, 2017).

2

Susan Glaspell (1876–1948)

Sharon Friedman
New York University

Ever since early reviews, critics have pondered the "surprise" element in Susan Glaspell's work ("Woman Satirizes" 1918): her twists on conventional plot lines and her range of styles and genres—the sentimental novel with unsentimental conclusions, character-driven plays with absent protagonists, farce, satire, expressionist theatre—even within the same play. *Trifles* (1916), her most well known play, is a one-act that begins as a murder mystery and turns into a "modernist revenge tragedy" (Makowsky 1999: 53) when two women discover that an isolated and silenced, prairie farm wife has countered abuse. Glaspell draws on all these theatrical modes to dramatize conflicts that emerged with cultural and political shifts during the early decades of the twentieth century. Although she often is cited for her Pulitzer Prize-winning drama *Alison's House* (1930), her most innovative playwriting took root in the experimental Provincetown Players (1915–1922), which she cofounded with George Cram Cook.

We hear in her plays written for the Provincetown the discourses of modernism, feminism, psychoanalysis, socialism, eugenics, and a retort to nativism and the heightening of American nationalism during the crisis period of the First World War. It is not surprising, then, to discern a tragic dimension in some of her stylistically hybrid dramas composed during these turbulent times. As theorists have argued, tragic drama seems to emerge during periods of social upheaval and changing beliefs and values (Wallace 2007: 8, 75), or a profound "social reorganization" that heightens "self-consciousness" and impels individuals to "draw ... old relations into question" (Rosslyn 2000: 6), and for some to transgress the murky boundaries between freedom and necessity.

Two of Glaspell's full-length plays, *The Verge* and *Inheritors*, both produced in 1921, though starkly different stylistically and thematically, render their protagonists' struggle with shifting cultural norms in a "tragic mode" as Rita Felksi has theorized this term. Acknowledging the "hybrid mixed qualities of genres," Felski resists the categorical definitions of tragedy as a "text's overall defining structure," or even the generalizing worldview implicit in the philosophical "idea of the tragic ... forged in the crucible of German Romanticism" with its claims to the "pathos and horror of human existence." Felski sees the "tragic mode" as denoting "a selective group of features" in texts of "various forms and guises" with "formal particulars" that she calls the "shape of suffering" (Felski 2008: 14, 2). Protagonists grapple with "the ineluctable power of social forces or unconscious desires," test "the limits of our own agency," encounter "the inevitability of conflict [or] the constant possibility of acting badly or wrongly," or confront "incompatible goods" (Felski 2008: 9, 12). Situating Glaspell's use of the tragic mode historically as well as aesthetically, I also take my cue from classicist Simon Goldhill who urges us to historicize the terms by which we define "the tragic" and to "pay due attention to the specific socio-political context" of not only ancient drama but also later developments within the genre, "while recognizing the drive toward a transhistorical truth both in the plays' discourse and in the plays' reception" (Goldhill 2008: 61).

Clearly, Glaspell's drama in no way resembles Aristotelian form, with its linear development of conflict, a reversal of fortune and the concomitant recognition of the forces at play by the tragic protagonist, noble though imperfect, willing or compelled to transgress constraints upon her or his actions, and erring in judgment, often due to circumstance and a lack of knowledge at crucial junctures in the plot. And although Glaspell's questing figures seem to evoke the more philosophical sense of tragedy that Felski has described as "a painful and irrevocable schism between the individual and the world in which he finds himself stranded" (Felski 2008: 2), the world is very much with Glaspell's protagonists—mostly women. They struggle with a range of issues within and beyond the home—the home being the prevalent setting of modern American tragedy. Her characters suffer the isolation from home and community that accompanies their oppositional stance. Claire Archer in *The Verge* rejects all boundaries—fixed inheritable forms, gender roles, and moral precepts, in her spiritual quest. Madeline Morton in *Inheritors* commits an act of civil disobedience that severs her relationships with those who love her. Although these characters differ in terms of the source of their discontent and their transgressions, their actions resonate with the feminisms of the period as they deviate markedly from prescribed gender norms in plots that turn tragic as tensions within and between characters move toward catastrophic ends.

Claire, the scientist/artist of *The Verge*, is Glaspell's most radical character. She is psychically imprisoned at the same time that she struggles toward freedom from tradition that we associate with modernity. Her goals are boundless, and it is only this boundlessness that she seeks to preserve. The play begins as a comedy of manners surrounding a woman who slowly but surely turns the witty repartee into a debacle. The setting of Acts 2 and 3 morph into an expressionist and symbolist rendering of her subjectivity as Claire pursues autonomy and what she calls "otherness" and "outness" in her effort to smash existing forms in her botanical experiments and in her personal relationships. She spends much of the play in her greenhouse, which has become her home. The greenhouse has the aura of a laboratory, its temperatures carefully controlled, its atmosphere refined. When not in the greenhouse, she retreats to a tower, seeking escape from the demands and expectations of others—husband, sister, daughter, and lover. Struggling to break free of deceptions and refusing to accommodate herself to stagnant norms, Claire remains isolated and alienated.

Through her plants, Claire experiments with life. She attempts to create hybrid forms that never have existed before and that will continue to reproduce in unpredictable ways, much like Glaspell's hybrid dramas. The scenario develops around the flowering of her latest botanical creation, Breath of Life, symbol of Claire's own quest. When the plant breaks through its old form into new life, Claire tries to emulate it, spiritually and psychically, as she crosses over the verge of the familiar and transcends into the unknown. Her struggle, however, turns tragic, culminating in murder and madness as she strangles the man who would protect her from "fartherness" and what he views as self-destruction.

To be sure, many scholars note the European influences in this work, the Nietzschean or Dionysian rapture in Claire's exhortations (Bigsby 1987: 22; Carpentier 2006: 46; Ozieblo 2000: 186), or the resonance with Strindberg's projected correspondence between the human and plant world (Bigsby 1987: 19–20; Gainor 2001: 144) and Maeterlinck's vision of "a theatre in which the soul took precedence over the material, and dramatic action centered on conflicts within the self and marked by no external action" (Ben-Zvi 2005: 96–7). Furthermore, we hear the strains of modernism, defined by Irving Howe as a "turn from truth to sincerity, from the search for objective law to a desire for authentic response," in Claire's desperate attempts to find a new language and new patterns of living that would disarticulate stagnant ideas lodged in language and shatter any stable meanings (Howe [1967] 1970: 9).

Glaspell seems equally inspired by her Romantic predecessors to value subjectivity and the prerogative of the individual to ignore mundane limits in creating the terms of her reality. In her discussion of romantic tragedy and its legacies, Jennifer Wallace points to the rebellion of alienated individuals against society and the "psychological retreat into the private [and alternative] world of the imagination" where "desire is central for self-assertion and political resistance ... and yet desire itself is forbidden," crushed by social convention (Wallace 2007: 63, 65). Goethe's *Faust* (1808) sells his soul for an "alternative experience" and Byron's *Manfred* (1816) becomes an outlaw hero, "impervious to society." Ibsen is heir to these legacies, and in *The Verge* I hear echoes of his dramas of artist heroes asserting a "creative will" in seeking "freedom of the imagination"—for example, the Master Builder Solness and his muse Hilda (Wallace 2007: 65–7). The ambitious Solness, though fearful of heights, has built a tower, and Hilda urges him to climb to the top, from which he falls literally and metaphorically.

Unlike Solness, however, Claire is devoid of a muse, and she takes this journey alone as she suffers the consequences of enacting her vision. Although she surrounds herself with men—husband, lover, friend—she dismisses them as obstacles to her pursuits. Without compunction, she sleeps with her husband's guest and rejects both of them for a male soul mate who ultimately disappoints her. They appear dispensable, if not interchangeable, in their adoration of this unobtainable woman. Writing in the *New Republic* in 1921, Stark Young pointed out her objectification by her admirers: "she is something connected with their dreams and their short flights from the daily actual" (quoted in Moses and Brown 1934: 253). Free as she might seem, however, Claire's expression of her sexuality is defined and constrained by the needs of the men, expressed in their varying discourses on Claire's allure.

The most traditional character is Claire's husband, Harry. Although amused by her clever ways, he is alarmed when she appears to move beyond ingenuity to genius, and he connects his trepidations to his view of an appropriate role for women. From Harry's perspective, Claire's botanical experiments violate the "feminine instinct" to nurture and to grow, and instead manifest conventionally masculine goals: to create and, if necessary, to destroy.

Claire's lover, Dick, a high modernist, fails to comprehend her vision and to establish an intimate bond beyond an illicit affair. An artist lost in abstraction, he can only appreciate the formal properties of something new. When Claire creates a plant that is unique in form but cannot regenerate itself, Dick does not understand why Claire wants to destroy it. She responds: "And you think I'll stop with that? Be shut in—with different life—that can't creep on? It's hard to get past what we've done. Our own dead things—block the way" (77). For Dick, Claire's charm emanates from her style and novelty, her deviation from expectations of womanhood that excite Dick more than any substantive meaning she gives to her actions.

Ironically, Tom, Claire's soul mate, becomes her greatest torment. Fearful that their earthly love would destroy the spiritual bond between them, he is threatened by her expression of sexuality. Her candor in speaking of her desire resonates with the new psychology and a feminism that sought to undermine the traditional dichotomy between spirituality and sexuality (Heller and Rudnick 1991: 5). Her quest for another kind of spiritual union mocks the solipsism in his vision and the sexual repression of this spiritual seeker expressed in the language of the courtly lover who worships from afar ("You rare thing untouched"). Resisting containment, whether in the form of protection or the consummation of her desire with one who might hold her back, she flails against him. In an earthy metaphor that parodies the exalted images of the beloved, Claire expresses her basest desires: "I'd rather be the steam rising from the manure, than be a thing called beautiful!" (99). In her desperate effort to resist Tom's protective embrace, Claire strangles him to death, singing, haltingly at first, the hymn, "Nearer My God to Thee," taught her from an early age. Rather than seeking redemption, she seems to claim for herself the godlike role of creator/destroyer.

Claire's most blatant transgression against her prescribed womanly role is her rejection of her daughter, Elizabeth. Raised by Claire's responsible sister Adelaide, Elizabeth has been educated in a respectable school for girls and, according to Claire, "prepared to take her place in life." Claire is profoundly alienated by her daughter's smug complacency and her blank acceptance of the fixed order of things. She sees Elizabeth as the manifestation of her own thwarted growth, the turning back of her flowering to its old form.

Most critics agree that *The Verge* is Glaspell's most experimental work in terms of character, genre, and staging. Using the theatrical devices of symbolism and expressionism, she renders Claire's tragic quest psychologically in stage environments that signify attempts at transcendence but also seclusion—the greenhouse and the tower. The stage directions indicate: *"This is not a greenhouse where plants are being displayed, nor the usual workshop for the growing of them, but a place for experiment with plants, a laboratory"* (58). Claire Archer does not tend her garden, she experiments with it. The only object illuminated by the shaft of light is a *"strange plant"* with *"twisted stem"* and a *"brilliant blossom."* At the back of the stage is a *"strange vine"* that arrests the viewer rather than pleases, though to the astute eye, it might reveal the *"form of a cross."* The leaves are at once *"repellent and significant."* Both the set and its symbolic images of the blossom and the vine suggest metaphors for the transformation of Claire's identity from an object of beauty to a subject that might repel its beholder in defying expectations. Of course, the potential for martyrdom in defying authority is also present in the sign of the cross.

Claire's tower also signifies her attempt to transcend the mundane world, to escape from the intrusion of others, particularly the "neurologist" brought in by the family to set her straight—but also isolation and enclosure. The play's expressionist set design by Cleon Throckmorton, one of the first on the American stage, clearly renders Claire's psychological entrapment. It is described as a *"thwarted tower"*: *"Thought to be round but does not complete the circle. The back is curved, then jagged lines break from that; and the front is a clear bulging window in a curve that leans. The whole structure is as if given a twist by some terrific force—like something wrung"* (78).

Like the stem of Claire's flower, the tower is twisted by some unidentified force, but not of Claire's doing. The shape of its circular form is incomplete and interrupted by uneven and harsh lines. It is not difficult to see the analogy between the architecture of this wrenched structure and Claire's thwarted development. The bulging window that leans forward in a curve appears to have accommodated the desperate need of the viewer within to see beyond the scope of its frame. Claire, however, does not look out. As the stage directions tell us, she is seen through this *"huge ominous window as if shut into the tower."* Although she has transformed the private spheres of her life, she remains isolated and entrapped.

The array of contextual frameworks—scientific (the eugenics movement, botanical experimentation) philosophical, and psychoanalytic—employed by scholars to interpret Claire's quest suggests the complexity and intertextuality of Glaspell's vision in rendering a woman who painfully feels her bounds as she moves toward the margins of rationality. As already noted, Bigsby discusses the influences of Strindberg and Nietzsche on the theme of the "radical restructuring of the sensibility" and the "drive to attain a new level of being" even if it means "madness and ... extinction in order to break out of the banality of forms," as Claire seeks the "flow" that can never be articulated in language (Bigsby 1987: 22–3). As soon as Claire speaks, she finds her "words going into patterns." Furthermore, Gainor provides extensive documentation related to medical, cultural, and literary discourses on hysteria and psychoanalysis prevalent in the early twentieth century, especially concerning women who do not adhere to prescribed roles, and she notes the "gendered significance" of Claire's psychosis (Gainor 2001: 151).

Whether we view the debacle of madness and murder in the concluding act as Claire's symbolic though macabre victory over her constraints or as a sign that her unrelenting quest destroys any hope of transcendence, even at the cost of intimacy and destruction of the lives around her, we cannot view her desires and frustrations in simply transhistorical terms—as the philosophical schism between the individual and the world she inhabits, or as a kind of Faustian desire for knowledge of the unseen, or even as the tragedy of an exceptional woman crushed by convention. The particular upheaval in gender relations in America during the early twentieth century informs the articulation of her frustration. Her vision of a future beyond established patterns in behavior and language appears in the discourses of the feminists of the period, the "mood of experimentation" and "open-endedness" that Liza Maeve Nelligan identifies as this "period of metamorphosis." As Nelligan explains, the suffrage victory in 1920 (a year before the production of *The Verge*) "liberated" feminists who had long attempted to analyze women's oppression beyond their exclusion from the political system. For some, this signaled a movement away from their primary definition as women to their identification as "autonomous individuals with unique attributes and desires" though not without feeling the loss of community among women, seen in earlier Glaspell works (Nelligan 1995: 91–3).

To be sure, Glaspell presents her audiences with a would-be heroic but ultimately disturbing character who raises "uncomfortable questions about the consequences of a 'radical individualism'" (Nelligan 1995: 92). However, she also presents a question that tragedy has posed for centuries: "to what extent is the individual responsible for his or her own fate?" John Northam writes: "Exploration is needed because although man [*sic*] acts on the assumption that he is free to choose, he comes into conflict with powers in the universe [divine, cosmic, societal] over which he has no ultimate control. There is no fixed or clear demarcation between freedom and necessity" (Northam 1965: 92–3).

Other theorists, such as Raymond Williams and Terry Eagleton, take a political and cultural view of tragic conflict and connect the exploration of freedom in tragedy to real world suffering beyond the solitary quest of the exceptional individual. Writing about tragedy in modernity, Felski evokes Terry Eagleton to argue that

> only with freedom does the tragic gulf between desire and realization become possible. While this freedom may be far from absolute, modern history extends the promise of self-actualization to an ever-widening circle of persons, thereby multiplying the opportunities for human agency, miscalculation, and error, while simultaneously underscoring the painful schism between

incandescent dreams and insurmountable social circumstance. (Felski 2008: 9)

It might well be that the specter of increased freedoms for women opened not only a space for increased frustration but also the need to voice it.

Gainor describes the "groundswell of feminist response" to *The Verge* within Glaspell's own community. Members of the Heterodoxy Club, a discussion group composed of women artists, writers, and professionals, responded with a "collective fervor" (Gainor 2001: 167–8) that we associate with tragic catharsis. First described by Aristotle as purgation through pity and fear, catharsis has been theorized by countless thinkers over the centuries to include the expulsion of anxieties and guilt over unseemly desires and actions through witnessing the suffering of a protagonist with whom we on some level identify. If we agree that tragedy is determined not only by the protagonist's action but also by its effect upon the audience, the ardent reception by the women of Heterodoxy foreshadows the intensity of response among feminists in the 1970s who brought renewed attention to this play, opening up new questions about the significance of Claire's desires and the tragic fall in which she is both agent and victim.

My second example of a Glaspell play in which she casts her protagonist's conflicts in a tragic mode is *Inheritors*, also from 1921, a family saga of pioneer settlement in a developing nation. When a member of the youngest generation commits an act of civil disobedience, the family drama morphs into a problem play around the issue of what it means to be an American. Unlike Claire's boundary-defying spiritual quest in *The Verge*, the young Madeline Fejevary Morton's exploration of freedom from prescribed norms is defined in explicitly political terms shaped by the social crisis of intensifying American nationalism and xenophobia during the years surrounding the First World War. Madeline is first presented to us as a lively co-ed responding reflexively to the suppression of a campus protest. Gradually, she rises to engage a serious ethical dilemma, but not without suffering the agonizing loss of family, her place in the community, and her freedom when she confronts irreconcilable choices implicit in the social forces bearing down on her young life. The spiraling of seemingly innocent actions into crisis begins to feel inevitable even when we are aware that she still has a choice.

The compromises of democratic freedoms that engulf Madeline in 1920 seem to unfold through a myriad of agencies—individuals, institutions, and belief systems.

The scenario of this four-act play traces the three-generation trajectory of a family that in the spirit of inclusion has founded a college for the children of midwestern farmers. Act 1 provides the back story, tracing the intersecting lives of two neighbors who together realize this dream of building a college upon the hill: Silas Morton, a farmer with a tract of land won from Native Americans, and his neighbor, the educated nobleman Felix Fejevary, a refugee from the Hungarian War of Independence against Austria in 1848. Set on the Morton farm in 1879 in the midst of a July 4th celebration, the first act constitutes Glaspell's backward glance at moments of national pride interspersed with ambivalence about the means of achieving a unified nation and an American identity. The patriotic reminiscences among the characters quickly reveal the moral and political tensions of the expanding nation in the late nineteenth century. Talk of dishonest dealings with the "Indians" is followed by the younger generation's discourse on social Darwinism to justify the claims of white men to the land, theorizing that individuals and races alike are engaged in a struggle for existence that leads inexorably to domination and hierarchy in society. Fejevary Jr.'s racism here foreshadows the jingoism of "100 per-cent American" that he espouses later in the play when he assumes his privileged place in the community as banker, president of the board of trustees of Morton College, and friend to State Senator Lewis, chairman of the state appropriations committee.

In the later acts set in 1920, Madeline, the granddaughter of both Morton and Fejevary (their children have married), becomes the play's tragic protagonist when she attempts to reclaim the democratic principles of the college in the midst of nationalist loyalties fostered by the First World War. The slogan "100% American" threatened freedom of expression for those opposed to the war as well as the lives of immigrants thought hostile to the country's interests. As a young student at the college, Madeline defends not only a conscientious objector to the war but also the right of Hindu students (referred to by Senator Lewis as "the foreign element") to protest colonialism in India as well as the college's refusal to intervene in the government's decision to deport them. Deportation was the sword held over those who were seen as fomenting rebellion. In this case, the Hindu students protesting British colonialism were perceived as incendiary revolutionists and a threat to America's alliance with England. As Linda Ben-Zvi reminds us, during this period opponents of the war confronted the Espionage Act, which placed tight restrictions on political expression (Ben-Zvi 2005: 285, 288–9).

Madeline emerges as the inheritor not only of her grandfathers' aspirations but also of the conflicts between democratic values and repressive politics in their shared history. In the final scene, we witness her labored decision to abandon her family, confront prison, and become an exile in her own country, the latter a familiar trope of the tragic protagonist. Envisioning incarceration, she inscribes, with yardstick and chalk, the narrow dimensions of the prison cell that awaits her. As she "walks its length," the gesture becomes chilling. Walling herself up like a modern-day Antigone, she, too, resists her uncle's entreaties that she use his influence to avoid punishment by acquiescing to the state. Situated in the early twentieth century, however, Glaspell's young coed turned enemy of the people anticipates Arthur Miller's tragedy of the "common man" whose "revolutionary questioning of the stable environment is what terrifies" (Miller 1949).

The stable environment in this modern American tragedy includes not only the state but also family and community. Wallace notes that in its American context, tragedy focuses on the family house:

> enclosed, private spaces and upon the very boundaries themselves which protect or shut off these places ... but these boundaries [are also] a means of exploring the relationship between the private family and the wider society, the connections between the small group of people witnessed by us on stage and the imagined wider society beyond those walls ... [and] the theatre itself (Wallace 2007: 75–6)

It is worth noting that Kenneth MacGowan's 1921 review of *Inheritors* reports that the play was attended by the United States Marshal of New York, "to see if the stories of its 'un-Americanism' were true enough to justify its suppression or amendment" (quoted in Gainor 2001: 113). In *Inheritors*, spectators do not need to imagine the wider society; it is just beyond the door of Madeline's homestead—on campus, in the statehouse, and the prison.

We see these agonizing decisions in the college's intimidation of Professor Holden. He eventually acquiesces to the college's demand for his silence after he had supported his student, Fred Jordan, the conscientious objector, and publicized Fred's poor treatment in prison. Holden's reasons lie in his personal responsibilities and his love for his family. He needs to retain his position in order to care for his sick wife, and his decision points up the agonizing quandary that Madeline's relative freedom forces on her: because she lacks Holden's financial responsibilities, she must confront her ability to make a different choice. However, she too must give up her powerful ties to family and their profound need for her. Madeline confronts her own sacrifice when she turns her back on the aunt who has been a mother to her after her own mother's death and abandons her father whose needs, disappointments, and self-absorption threaten to consume her.

Madeline struggles, as do many tragic protagonists, not only with reconciling competing choices but also comprehending their ramifications, including her exile from family and community. It is telling that in the final scene of the play Glaspell incorporates Madeline's bereaved and defensive father's insularity as a contrapuntal motif to his daughter's act of civil disobedience on behalf of others. Ira Morton cuts himself off from the community, obsessed with creating a breed of perfect corn, fearful that others' plots will contaminate his—clearly a metaphor for the social engineering associated with eugenics movements of the period as well as anti-immigrant sentiment in the name of nationalism. His daughter, however, comes to the recognition that although she will be isolated in prison, the "world is a—moving field. Nothing is to itself" (156). Her metaphor of a world perpetually changing and shifting ground, where nothing remains stagnant or isolated, might very well represent Glaspell's response to the alienated and ultimately destructive character Claire in *The Verge* as well as to those who imprison Madeline. That Glaspell gives this tragic choice and recognition to a young woman raises the stakes for the community that silences her.

The issues dramatized in *The Verge* and *Inheritors* seem particularly timely in our cultural moment—almost a century after these plays were written—as we upend gender binaries, defy essentialist notions of inheritance in genetic or cultural terms, and contemplate what it means to be an American in a global context and in polarizing debates about citizenship and immigration laws. These seemingly topical issues take on tragic dimension not only when we consider the anguish of those who defy social norms and repressive laws, both off-stage and on, but also when we witness Glaspell's protagonists confront what Felski calls the "role of the incalculable and unforeseeable" in tragedy, when the "consequences of their actions ... deviate disastrously from the expected and hoped for" (11). As spectators, we might not immediately sense the impending crisis building gradually in these stylistically hybrid dramas. However, the shattering final scenes impel us to experience the plays retrospectively and to see the inexorable will in the protagonists' desire to shape their worlds at all costs.

References

Ben-Zvi, Linda (2005), *Susan Glaspell: Her Life and Times*, Oxford: Oxford University Press.

Bigsby, C. W. E. (ed.) (1987), "Introduction," in C.W.E. Bigsby (ed.), *Plays by Susan Glaspell*, British and American Playwrights Series, Cambridge: Cambridge University Press.

Carpentier, Martha C. (2006), "Apollonian Form and Dionysian Excess in Susan Glaspell's Drama and Fiction," in Martha C. Carpentier and Barbara Ozieblo (eds.), *Disclosing Intertextualities: The Stories, Plays, and Novels of Susan Glaspell*, DQR Studies in Literature 37, 35–50, Amsterdam: Editions Rodopi.

Felski, Rita (2008), "Introduction," in Rita Felski (ed.), *Rethinking Tragedy*, 1–25, Baltimore, MD: Johns Hopkins University Press.

Gainor, J. Ellen (2001), *Susan Glaspell in Context: American Theatre, Culture, and Politics, 1915–1948*, Ann Arbor, MI: University of Michigan Press.

Glaspell, Susan ([1921] 1987a), "Inheritors," in C. W. E. Bigsby (ed.), *Plays by Susan Glaspell*, 103–57, British and American Playwrights Series, Cambridge: Cambridge University Press.

Glaspell, Susan ([1921] 1987b), "The Verge," in C. W. E. Bigsby (ed.), *Plays by Susan Glaspell*, 57–101, British and American Playwrights Series, Cambridge: Cambridge University Press.

Goldhill, Simon (2008), "Generalizing About Tragedy," in Rita Felski (ed.), *Rethinking Tragedy*, 45–65, Baltimore, MD: Johns Hopkins University Press.

Heller, Adele and Lois Rudnick (1991), "Introduction," in Adele Heller and Lois Rudnick (eds.), *1915, The Cultural Moment: The New*

Politics, the New Woman, the New Psychology, the New Art, and the New Theatre in America, 1–13, New Brunswick, NJ: Rutgers University Press.

Howe, Irving ([1967] 1970), "The Culture of Modernism," in Irving Howe (ed.), *Decline of the New*, 3–33, New York: Harcourt, Brace & World. Originally published in *Commentary*, November 1, 1967. Available online: https://www.commentarymagazine.com/articles/the-culture-of-modernism/ (accessed January 26, 2017).

Makowsky, Veronica (1999), "Susan Glaspell and Modernism," in Brenda Murphy (ed.), *The Cambridge Companion to American Women Playwrights*, 49–65, Cambridge: Cambridge University Press.

Miller, Arthur (1949), "Tragedy and the Common Man," *The New York Times*, February 27. Available online: http://www.nytimes.com/books/00/11/12/specials/miller-common.html (accessed January 26, 2017).

Nelligan, Liza Maeve (1995), "'The Haunting Beauty from the Life We've Left': A Contextual Reading of *Trifles* and *The Verge*," in Linda Ben-Zvi (ed.), *Susan Glaspell: Essays on Her Theatre and Fiction*, 85–104, Ann Arbor, MI: University of Michigan Press.

Northam, John (1965), "Ibsen's Search for the Hero," in Rolf Fjelde (ed.), *Ibsen: A Collection of Critical Essays*, 91–108, Englewood Cliffs, NJ: Prentice-Hall.

Ozieblo, Barbara (2000), *Susan Glaspell: A Critical Biography*, Chapel Hill, NC: University of North Carolina Press.

Rosslyn, Felicity (2000), *Tragic Plots: A New Reading from Aeschylus to Lorca*, Studies in European Cultural Transition 9, Farnham, Surrey: Ashgate Publishing.

Wallace, Jennifer (2007), *The Cambridge Introduction to Tragedy*, Cambridge: Cambridge University Press.

"Woman Satirizes Woman's Honor" (1918), *The Herald*, May 22.

Young, Stark ([1921] 1934), "Susan Glaspell's *The Verge*," in Montrose J. Moses and John Mason Brown (eds.), *The American Theatre As Seen by Its Critics, 1752–1934*, 252–55, New York: Norton.

3

Langston Hughes
(1902–1967)

Jonathan Shandell
Arcadia University

Playwright, poet, essayist, and fiction writer Langston Hughes is a singular voice in American letters whose writings survey a national landscape scarred by centuries of racial oppression. In Hughes's literary sensibility, consciousness of the suffering, victimization, and waste associated with white hegemony in the United States often is mirrored by humor, optimism, and a sense of the ironic. Surveying the totality of this writer's varied works, R. Baxter Miller argues, "Tragicomedy unifies the literary art of Hughes' entire oeuvre. Tragedy and comedy mark the formal range of his literary creativity as well as his perception of human life" (Miller 2015: 100).

A broad tonal range is visible within Hughes's writings for the stage. A few brief and varied examples from his several dozen dramatic works can illustrate. The play *Don't You Want to Be Free?* (1938)—a stage chronicle of "Negro history from Africa to America" that was perhaps Hughes's most popular play among black audiences—begins with the foreboding sight of "*a lynch rope* ... [that] *hangs at the back, center, throughout the entire performance, and serves as a symbol of Negro oppression.*" The prop gets put to its designed use for an on-stage lynching. Nonetheless, the play rises out of this dark scene toward a triumphant finale in which an entire integrated cast sings, together in solidarity with audiences:

Oh, who wants to come and join hands with me?
Who wants to make one great unity?
Who wants to say, no more black or white?
Then let's get together, folks,
And fight, fight, fight! (Hughes 2002a: 569–70)

Hughes's one-act *Soul Gone Home* (1936) starts with a mother grieving over her child's dead body: "Oh, Gawd! Oh, Lawd! Why did you take my son from me? ... He was all I had! ... Ronnie, say something to me! Son, why don't you talk to your mother? Can't you see she's bowed down in sorrow?" Her lamentation is cut short when the corpse reanimates, sits up, and grants her request. "I wish I wasn't dead, so I *could* speak to you. You been a hell of a mama! ... First time you ever did cry for me, far as I know," he says to her, setting off a squabble between the living and the dead over who's to blame for the boy's troubled upbringing (Hughes 2002a: 267). The subsequent exchange is lighthearted and irreverent but taps into painful truths about urban poverty and its toll on African American family life.

Similarly, the sketch *Mother and Child: A Theatre Vignette* (1936) confronts a terrifying social situation through a comic lens. The play centers on a gossipy group of African American ladies in a small Ohio town discussing the latest scandal. The situation they discuss is a serious one—the recent birth of a black child to a white married woman, the product of an interracial extramarital affair—with violent repercussions likely to ensue. "They liable to burn our Negroes' houses down ... Anything's liable to happen. I'm as nervous as can be ... I ain't nervous, I'm *scared*," the women confide to one another, fearing a violent backlash from white locals. Hughes concludes the conversation, however, with a sardonic twist: we soon learn that these women have gathered for a meeting of the "Ladies' Missionary Society for the Rescue of the African Heathen." The Society's white "Madam President" tries to silence the chattering: "Will you ladies *please* be quiet? What are you talkin' 'bout back ther, anyhow?" "Heathens, daughter, heathens," is the ladies' rejoinder. "They ain't in Africa, neither!" (Hughes

2002a: 276, 277). Their subtle skewering of white moral hypocrisy counterbalances the terrifying image of an impending race riot. All in all, no matter how directly his dramas evoke the painful reality of racism in the United States, Langston Hughes's indomitable optimism and playfulness often are waiting in the wings.

The genre label "tragedy" fits more naturally on only a handful of Hughes's dramatic works. *Emperor of Haiti (Troubled Island)* (1936), for example, dramatizes the historic rise and fall of Haitian revolutionary Jean-Jacques Dessalines. *Front Porch* (1938) centers on a young African American girl from a solidly middle class family who falls in love against her mother's wishes with a labor organizer and ultimately perishes in heartache. The tragedy for which Hughes is best known is his first full-length play and his only one to find success on the commercial stage: *Mulatto: A Play of the Deep South* (written in 1930; first performed on Broadway, 1935). Hughes's most widely influential drama, *Mulatto* offers direct and profound connections to the wider sweep of American tragedy.

The play's title aligns it squarely with the genealogy of the "tragic mulatto," prominent in US culture since the eighteenth century. Both African American and white American authors have employed the archetype of the tragic mulatto to speak to the complications surrounding mixed-race identity within the brutal realities of white supremacy. Hughes invokes it in several of his writings: particularly in the poems "Mulatto" and "Cross," as well as in the short story "Father and Son" (a fictionalization of the play *Mulatto*). The stage version of *Mulatto* centers on Robert Lewis: child of plantation owner Colonel Thomas Norwood and his black housekeeper/ mistress Cora Lewis. Robert's struggles with the ramifications of his mixed parentage bring about tragic results: suicide by way of patricide. Thus Robert aligns with Sterling Brown's description of the "tragic mulatto" figure as "the anguished victim of divided inheritance [who] must therefore go down to a tragic end" (1969: 145).

Critical responses to *Mulatto* tend to highlight Robert's psychological division and inner anguish as the engine of tragedy. Brooks Atkinson's original review in *The New York Times* speaks of the "tragic confusion of the people whose blood is half black and half white" (1935: 25). Richard K. Barksdale proclaims, "there is no doubt that Hughes had intended to probe ... the vitiating aftereffects of miscegenation ... [and] was primarily interested in the emotional stress and psychological insecurities of children born of forced interracial liaisons" (1986: 193). Germain Bienvenu, emphasizing what he sees as the protagonist's "intracaste prejudice" against fellow African Americans, describes Robert as a doomed hero "who seeks whiteness over blackness ... this futile, lifelong attempt is what makes Hughes's mulatto tragic" (1992: 352). Such interpretations of *Mulatto* are not completely off base, but typify what Elinor Fuchs describes as "the immediate (and crippling) leap to character and normative psychology" in the interpretation of dramatic narratives (2004: 5). By tunneling into the protagonist's psyche in search of tragic resonance, such interpretations lose sight of the larger societal forces that Hughes illuminates in the play and thus minimize the playwright's wider social critique.

My reading of *Mulatto* more closely follows that of Harry J. Elam and Michele Elam, who reject a tendency to fixate on "the mixed-race figure as an icon of private neurosis." Following that critical approach, I will demonstrate how Hughes turns the "tragic mulatto" narrative on its head and will extend Elam and Elam's reading of *Mulatto* as "a 'surrogate historical text'" (Elam 2009: 87, 88). From such a vantage point, Hughes's play looms as a searing condemnation of the racial caste system of the United States and fits squarely in a tradition of social criticism that includes the works of Eugene O'Neill, Clifford Odets, Arthur Miller, August Wilson, and Suzan-Lori Parks.

Commentators who write of Robert's inner anguish are engaged in a purely speculative enterprise of psychoanalysis. Never once in the play does Robert speak or act in a way that seems uncertain, equivocal, or hampered by anxiety. In this regard, the theatrical character departs somewhat from its literary counterpart. In his short story "Father and Son," Hughes ascribes to Robert a "self-pity of bewildered youth," and says that he is "never homesick for the plantation—but he did wish sometimes that he had a home, and that the Colonel would treat him like a son" (Hughes 2002b: 137). No such longings appear on stage. From his first bold entrance through the front door of the house (a point of entry that Colonel Norwood forbids the "darkies" on his plantation to use), Robert is a paragon of self-assurance. "Bring out the cookies and lemonade," he proclaims. "*Mister* Norwood's here! ... isn't this my old man's house? Ain't I his son and heir? (*Grandly, strutting around.*) Am I not Mr. Norwood, Junior?" (Hughes 2002a: 31).

Robert poses these rhetorical questions in direct defiance of his father and the white supremacist logic that would deny him access not only to the front door and to the Norwood family name but also to fundamental rights of free movement, self-determination, and equal protection. Robert's aggressive driving into town and his protest against unfair treatment at the local post office—actions reported by Colonel Norwood's bigoted neighbor and friend Fred Higgins—reinforce the portrait of a man confident in himself and insistent upon respect from others. Higgins, Norwood, and all of white society might see Robert as "one yellow buck [who] don't know his place" (25), but such a pronouncement says nothing about Robert, and everything about the oppressive Southern racial caste system against which he struggles.

When he first confronts Colonel Norwood in Act 1, Robert does not shrink before white authority, but *"draws himself up to his* [father's] *full height,"* stares him down, and then *"walks proudly out the front way"* (35–6). He faces his father with equal bravado in Act 2, telling him defiantly, "I'd like to kill all the white men in the world" (39). Such a bold pronouncement radiates forward three decades to the angry defiance of Clay (the protagonist of Amiri Baraka's *Dutchman*) and other revolutionary characters created in the Black Arts Movement. When Colonel Norwood raises his pistol at Robert, the young man physically overpowers his father, squeezing his throat *"until his body grows limp"* (40). At that moment, the Colonel symbolically becomes "all the white men in the world," and Robert achieves his imagined revenge against them. This act, of course, will become his undoing; a lynch mob is now inevitable. But there is no psychic anguish in Robert's repudiation of the dehumanizing logic of white supremacy. He steadfastly rejects his own marginalization, not (as some critics have argued) himself or his own blackness. Thus, Hughes's tragedy takes root not in a private psychological experience of a divided consciousness, but as a direct indictment of the absurdities of an oppressive racial essentialism.

In defending himself against his father, rather than yielding to subjugation, Robert affirms his "inherent unwillingness to remain passive in the face of what he conceives to be a challenge to his dignity, his image of his *rightful* status" as a human being and lawful citizen of the United States. The deaths of both Mister Norwoods are the direct and inevitable "consequence of [Robert's] total compulsion to evaluate himself justly," even as the world enforces cruel injustice upon him. Here I apply to *Mulatto* phrases from Arthur Miller's seminal essay "Tragedy and the Common Man" (1949), which articulates a vision of tragedy that Langston Hughes deployed decades before Miller theorized it. Far from the stereotypically tortured "tragic mulatto," Robert is an ancestor to Willy Loman: a "common man" thrashing against immovable social obstacles in a "battle to secure his rightful place in the world" (Miller 1949).

And what of Robert's "intracaste prejudice," as Bienvenu calls it: his apparent yearning for whiteness and his antipathy toward blackness in himself, his family, and his community? Robert does at one point call his brother William "a rabbit-hearted coon" (32) and also slurs the African American men who fail to come to his aid at the post office as "dumb jigaboos" (34). When his mother, Cora, tries to cool his hot-headed rebellion by telling him, "you ain't white," he snaps back, "And I'm not black, either" (35). These pronouncements might seem to suggest that Robert has internalized the ideology of the plantation to the point of self-loathing, but here, too, an analytical shift away from the individual and toward the social reveals more of Hughes's true purpose. When Robert speaks of wanting to "act like my white half, not my Black half" (32), I see his proclamation not as evidence of psychological confusion but as a protest against the rules of his society. His struggle is political, not personal.

In the backstory of *Mulatto*, Robert spends six years studying in Atlanta and traveling with his college's football team. The experience transforms his sense of how he should act toward others. "I've learned something," he tells his brother William, "seen people in Atlanta, and Richmond, and Washington ... *real colored people* who don't have to take off their hats to white folks or let 'em go to bed with their sisters" (32). His invocation of "real colored people" is telling of how this proud young man aspires to live: emancipated from the prevailing white standards of real personhood. On the plantation, however, Robert knows well that asserting his full autonomy requires *acting* like a white man acts. He must distance himself from the subservience that his brother, mother, sister, and other "darkies" have adopted. To do so is not to yearn for whiteness nor to recoil from his own blackness, but to insist upon real personhood using the only basis the world of the plantation affords him: his patrimony. Critics err in seeing Robert's total compulsion toward justice for himself as psychological insecurity or a "hyper-elitist stance" (Bienvenu 1992: 347) against his own kin. Robert detests neither blackness nor black people; he simply rejects what the social order of the rural Jim Crow South forces black people to become.

When Robert tells Colonel Norwood, "I'm not a nigger, Colonel Tom. I'm your son" (39), he is not expressing filial longing for a father's love but delivering an indictment of US history. Decades of white oppression, bigotry, exploitation, and rape have given birth to a schizoid society that denies real people their innate humanity. Facing his fate within such a world, Robert chooses suicide over dehumanization. His choice expresses neither self-loathing nor despair but rather clear-headed rebellion. By killing himself, Robert solidifies his victory over the lynch mob, denying blood-thirsty whites the grotesque retribution they yearn to enforce on a "yellow buck [who] doesn't know his place" (25). His suicide evokes the noble self-slaughter of Shakespeare's Cleopatra, Brutus, or Cassius—the choice of self-inflicted death over dishonor at the hands of a disdainful enemy.

The spiritual foundation of Robert's tragic heroism is illuminated in remarks by August Wilson from a 1988 interview:

Since the first Africans set foot on the continent there has been a resistance. The people who look around to see what the society has put out for them, who see the limits of their participation, and are willing to say, "No, I refuse to accept this limitation that you're imposing on me"—that's the warrior spirit. (Wilson 2006: 78)

It is this spirit of defiance—not a haze of confusion, nor self-loathing, nor private neurosis—that motivates the tragedy of *Mulatto*. Noble in its aspirations and tragic in its consequences, the "warrior spirit" animates the play's call to resist—to death, if necessary—injustice and oppression. It is a call that resonated within Hughes's era and still speaks evocatively to our own.

References

Atkinson, Brooks (1935), "Race Problems in the South the Theme of 'Mulatto,' a 'New Drama' by Langston Hughes," *The New York Times*, October 25: 25. Available online: http://query.nytimes.com/

mem/archive-free/pdf?res=9F06E4D91F3DE53ABC4D51DFB667838E
629EDE (accessed December 30, 2016).

Barksdale, Richard K. (1986), "Miscegenation on Broadway: Hughes's
Mulatto and Edward Sheldon's *The Nigger*," in Edward J. Mullen
(ed.), *Critical Essays on Langston Hughes*, 191–99, Boston: G. K. Hall.

Bienvenu, Germain (1992), "Intracaste Prejudice in Langston Hughes's
Mulatto," *African American Review* 26 (2): 341–53.

Brown, Sterling (1969), *Negro Poetry and Drama and the Negro in
American Fiction*, New York: Atheneum.

Elam, Harry J. and Michele Elam (2009), "Blood Debt: Reparations in
Langston Hughes's *Mulatto*," *Theatre Journal* 61 (1): 85–103.

Fuchs, Elinor (2004), "EF's Visit to a Small Planet," *Theater* 34 (2): 5–9.

Hughes, Langston (2002a), *The Collected Works of Langston Hughes*,
vol. 5, *The Plays to 1942: "Mulatto" to "The Sun Do Rise*," Leslie
Catherine Sanders with Nancy Johnston (eds.), Columbia, MO:
University of Missouri Press.

Hughes, Langston (2002b), *The Collected Works of Langston Hughes*,
vol. 15, *The Short Stories*, R. Baxter Miller (ed.), Columbia, MO:
University of Missouri Press.

Miller, Arthur (1949), "Tragedy and the Common Man," *The New York
Times*, February 27. Available online: https://www.nytimes.com/
books/00/11/12/specials/miller-common.html (accessed December 30,
2016).

Miller, R. Baxter (2015), *The Art and Imagination of Langston Hughes*,
Lexington, KY: University of Kentucky Press.

Wilson, August (2006), *Conversations with August Wilson*, Jackson
R. Bryer and Mary C. Hartig (eds.), Jackson, MS: University of
Mississippi Press.

4

Thornton Wilder
(1897–1975)

Jackson R. Bryer
University of Maryland

In considering how to approach the subject of Thornton Wilder and tragedy, one is struck, as one so often is in reading and researching Wilder, by how difficult it is to categorize the man or his work simply or definitively. A prime example of this dilemma can be found in his personal life: Wilder was the most sociable of men, with friends all over the world and from all walks of life; yet, in May 1962, nine days after attending a White House dinner where he reveled in the company of the President and Mrs. Kennedy, as well as—among many others—Robert Penn Warren, Robert Lowell, Tennessee Williams, Isaac Stern, George Balanchine, Anne Morrow Lindbergh, and Saul Bellow, he got into his Thunderbird convertible, bound for the desert Southwest. At the top of a hill, the car stalled at a sign that read "Douglas, Arizona," whereupon Wilder spent the next twenty months in a town of 10,000 residents where he knew no one and where no one knew who he was (Niven 2012: 653–6).

A similar contradiction exists with Wilder's writing. His work frequently has been dismissed as the literary equivalent of Norman Rockwell's *Saturday Evening Post* covers. Sinclair Lewis, in accepting the 1930 Nobel Prize for Literature, praised Wilder for "dream[ing] of old loves ... and eternal romances" (Lewis 1930: 12), and F. O. Matthiessen criticized him for creating "a too facile world of the imagination" and for not struggling "with the actual" but rather turning "too gracefully away" (Matthiessen 1930: 213). Although these assessments date from 1930—and it can be argued that in more recent years critics have tended to see Wilder's work in more nuanced ways—the misconception of Wilder that these two observations suggest too frequently persists. In fact, Wilder's writing can be seen—and seems to have been intended by its author to be seen—as conveying a far darker view of life, one that in many respects often verges on tragedy.

Noting that it is "a work which cannot be ignored merely because it is popular," Arthur H. Ballet, in "*Our Town* as a Classical Tragedy," has shown persuasively how Wilder's most famous work can be viewed as following the major precepts of classical Greek theatre: "like its Greek predecessors, *Our Town* [1938] is concerned with the great and continuing cycle of life; out of life comes death and from death comes life" (2000: 76). Ballet points specifically to the Stage Manager as equivalent to the classical chorus in that both "represent the observing community"; to "the classical simplicity of the setting," which "avoids realism of time and place" and permits the play's "larger applications"; and to Emily, "a tragic figure of enormous dimensions" who, in her death, "gains the true ability really to see and understand" (2000: 77, 82). But if one looks at the Wilder play that is explicitly modeled on a classical tragedy, the far less well-known *The Alcestiad* (1955), and his comments on it, one also can discern Wilder's view of the differences between the ancient Greeks and ourselves and bring new insights into a discussion of Wilder and tragedy.

Although he famously wrote, "I am not an innovator but a rediscoverer of forgotten goods and I hope a remover of obtrusive bric-a-brac" (Wilder 1997: 688), and despite the fact that he was intimately conversant with all genres of world literature, in particular the drama from the Greeks and Romans to his contemporaries, Wilder's only direct commentary on classical tragedy is an essay on Sophocles' *Oedipus Rex*, written in 1939 as an introduction to Francis Storr's translation but not published until 1955. In it Wilder maintains that Sophocles' play "presents a number of aspects which were more impressive to the Greeks than they are to us," chief among these being "its religious force ... the shudder and awe induced by the presence of the numinous, by the *tremendum* of religious experience" (Wilder 1997: 710–11). Wilder here is asserting what long has been acknowledged to be true: Greek audiences responded to these plays with different assumptions about the forces that lay behind human behavior from those modern audiences are willing to accept.

While this short piece is his one direct statement about classic tragic drama, Wilder's exposure to and familiarity with the genre began early and persisted throughout his life—and one example of the form seems particularly to have preoccupied him: the story of Alcestis. It was, according to his sister Isabel, "a benign insistence in his inner consciousness, that hidden storehouse which is an author's source and springboard." She traces the origins of his fascination with Alcestis to young Thornton, age seven or eight, "reading or being read to from Bullfinch's *The Age of Fable*" and then shortly thereafter, when his family moved to Berkeley, California, to his frequent attendance at plays by Aeschylus, Sophocles, and Euripides put on by the University of California's Classics Department. His interest was sustained through classes at Oberlin College with his favorite professor, the distinguished classicist Charles H. A. Wager; his postgraduate eight months at the American Academy for Classical Studies in Rome; and through his teaching during the 1930s at the University of Chicago, where he often taught the classic dramatists in translation. The original date of Wilder's essay on Sophocles, 1939, is also significant because, again according to his sister, it was in the summer of that year that his long fascination with classical tragic drama and the story of Alcestis in particular culminated in his intensive work on his own version of the myth, *The Alcestiad*. He had begun thinking about the play at least a year earlier, but work on *Our Town* and *The Merchant of Yonkers*, his first two full-length Broadway plays, had intervened (1998b: 154–8).

As the Second World War approached, Wilder turned away from *The Alcestiad* and focused instead on another project he had been working on simultaneously, one more appropriate for a world facing its second international conflict in two decades: *The Skin of Our Teeth*. The latter opened in New York in November 1942 as Wilder, now a captain in the Air Force, was departing for deployment overseas. At this point, he refocused on *The Alcestiad* and took the manuscript with him. Two years later, near Boston awaiting his discharge, all his manuscripts were lost. Undaunted, armed with a three-day pass, he went to the Boston Public Library and, in Isabel Wilder's words, "drowned himself once more in the Golden Age of Greece" (Wilder 1998b: 156). He began to reconstruct *The Alcestiad* from memory, a task he continued for seven months, before abandoning it once again, because, as he explained in a February 1947 letter to June and Leonard Trolley, "my ideas about life had changed and I felt it to be sentimental" (Wilder 2008: 453). He would not return to the project until almost a decade later.

In 1954, the Edinburgh Festival presented a production of Wilder's *The Matchmaker*, his reworking of *The Merchant of Yonkers*, and, based on its success, commissioned a new play from him for the following season. For this assignment he turned again to *The Alcestiad*, which received its world premiere in August 1955 under the title *A Life in the Sun*, which his sister notes the producers felt would have more "box-office appeal" (Wilder 1998b: 161). The play was not received favorably by the critics, and Wilder withdrew its English rights and again revised it, adding a satyr play, the one-act *The Drunken Sisters*, to the previously written three-act drama. This revised version was successfully performed in a German translation in 1957 and 1958, but an English version of *The Alcestiad* was not published until 1977, two years after Wilder's death, and the play did not receive a professional production in the United States until August 1984 when it was presented at the Ohio Theatre in Cleveland (English 2013: 350). Since then, it has occasionally been staged at American universities, but it remains one of Wilder's least-produced and lesser-known works, although his dedication to it extended over twenty-five years and includes an opera version, for which Wilder wrote the libretto and Louise Talma the music. The relevance of *The Alcestiad* to any consideration of Wilder and tragedy is apparent.

In Euripides' *Alcestis* (438 BCE), King Admetus is told by the god Apollo that he can avoid death if he finds someone else who will die in his place. His relatives and friends all refuse to sacrifice themselves, but his wife Alcestis agrees, leaving their children with him. Shortly after her death, the hero Heracles unexpectedly arrives, and Admetus decides not to upset his guest by mentioning his wife's death; but when Admetus's father, Pheres, arrives to offer condolences, Admetus, angry at his father, who he believes should have taken Admetus's place in death because he had lived a full life and because as a parent he should have wanted to save his son's life, charges Pheres with murdering Alcestis. Pheres' counterargument is that a parent's obligation to his children is not the same when they are adults as when they are young and that his love for his own life is as justifiable as Admetus's is for his. When Heracles learns of Alcestis's self-sacrifice, he vows to repay Admetus's hospitality by going to the underworld and bringing her back—which he does.

As classicist Mary C. English has noted, Euripides "is purposely vague about the motivating forces behind Alcestis's decision" and Admetus also is a puzzling figure: it is unclear whether he is worthy of Alcestis's self-sacrifice. Similarly, it is unclear whether Heracles' action in restoring Alcestis to life is motivated by his appreciation of the king's hospitality or by the king's desire to regain his wife, especially because when Heracles returns with Alcestis, Admetus, who has promised not to take a second wife, initially accepts her as a new bride before she is revealed to be Alcestis (English 2013: 336). Using Wilder's 1939 essay on *Oedipus Rex* as an answer to the questions posed by English, we can assume that Euripides' audience would not have been troubled by these vagaries of motivation but simply would have accepted them as the inexplicable will of the gods, in Wilder's words "the numinous," the "*tremendum* of religious experience."

Wilder's choice of a title, *The Alcestiad*, suggests his intention to differentiate his play from Euripides'. Wilder divided his version into three acts; Euripides' *Alcestis* consists of a prologue and seven scenes. Nevertheless, as Helmut Papajewski has argued, the structure of Wilder's version "has a kind of classical quality." Papajewski notes, "The action of each [act] is divided from the others by the span of twelve years, thus assuring the play a kind of classical homogeneity." Each act observes the unity of time. A night watchman—who, like the Stage Manager in *Our Town*, resembles the chorus in classical tragedy—opens each act. The play has a classical symmetry: the first and third acts, both of which concern the dispute between Apollo and Death, are built around Alcestis's decision to sacrifice herself, which occurs in the middle of the second act, so that the entire play is "centered on the person of Alcestis" (Papajewski [1965] 1968: 152–3).

But it is in Wilder's deviation from his classical model that we may be able to see most clearly how his vision of tragedy differs from that of the Greeks. If we accept that classical tragedy is, in the words of the Chorus in Jean Anouilh's version of *Antigone*, "restful" because "nothing is in doubt and everyone's destiny is known" (Anouilh [1942] 1962: 788), Wilder deliberately set out in *The Alcestiad*, as English puts it, to redefine "Greek tragedy in contemporary terms" (2013: 337). One way he did so was by explicitly questioning what Euripides left unexplored.

In his program note for the play's premiere in 1955, Wilder remarked that the Greek classics "seem at first glance to be clear enough"; but "on closer view many of them ... give the impression of having been retained down the ages because they are ambiguous and puzzling." Among the ambiguities and puzzles he found in the story of Alcestis, he singled out two: although "we are told that Apollo loved Admetus and Alcestis ... how strangely he exhibited it" and "why should divine love impose on a devoted couple the decision as to which should die for the other?" By adding, in a third act depicting events not present in Euripides' play, a depiction of Alcestis reduced to slave status in the palace of the tyrant who succeeded her husband after murdering him, Wilder also posed the question, why "should the omnipotent friend [Apollo] permit some noble human beings to end their days in humiliation and suffering?" (Wilder 1998b: 168).

In Wilder's play, Alcestis's motivation is a complex, contemporary, and ambivalent combination of her earthly love for her husband and her religious devotion to Apollo. She wants to devote her life to worshipping Apollo and is convinced to marry Admetus, whose love for her is clear, only when the seer Tiresias appears and reveals that Apollo will take on the appearance of a common shepherd and live in the palace. In Wilder's Act 2, unlike in Euripides' play, Admetus is unaware that he can avoid death. When a message from Delphi arrives indicating that his life can be spared if someone will die in his place, many volunteer but Alcestis prevails because she asserts that only she does it out of love—"This is work of love" (Wilder 1998b: 201). But is this love for Admetus or for Apollo? Euripides' Alcestis declares that she dies because of her love for her husband and because she likes the idea of a wife who would die for her husband, but Wilder mingles Alcestis's love for Admetus with her devotion to Apollo and clearly wants his audience to ponder the resulting ambiguity. Wilder also changes Heracles' motivation for bringing Alcestis back from the underworld. In *The Alcestiad*, he does so because, as he explains, "I once came near to Alcestis in violence, in brutish violence," but "some god—intervened in time, to save her and to save me. Alcestis forgave me. How can that be? How can any man understand that?" (Wilder 1998b: 218).

As a result of these changes, Admetus is a much more sympathetic figure because Alcestis plans her sacrifice without his knowledge and her death sentence is not imposed by her husband and because Alcestis is depicted as selfless and forgiving. Isabel Wilder, recognizing the effect of these changes her brother made to Euripides' original, asserts that they deepen "the characterizations and relationship of husband and wife, enriching the bare outlines of the legend for our twentieth century understanding" (Wilder 1998b: 159). Nonetheless, English maintains that Wilder also "accentuates the *mysterium* of the divine by not clarifying why exactly Alcestis is restored: does Apollo simply love the couple so much that he wants to reunite them or does he have something else in store for Alcestis?" (English 2013: 339).

That "something else" may well be explained by Wilder's third act, which, as mentioned above, departs entirely from Euripides' original, taking place twelve years after Alcestis's resurrection and depicting her as enslaved by the tyrannical new ruler, Agis, who murdered Admetus and seized the throne. Alcestis's son Epimenes and his friend Cheriander return from exile intent on avenging Admentus's death and overthrowing Agis, who has been weakened by the death of his own beloved daughter, but Alcestis dissuades them and even consoles Agis on the death of his child. Both actions reveal Wilder's intention to make her a more sympathetic, complex, and human character. At act's end, Alcestis is left with Apollo, who assures her that her life is not over and that she will have "grandchildren and the grandchildren of grandchildren ... beyond all counting." When she asks, "Whom do I thank for all the happiness?" he replies, "Those who have loved one another do not ask one another that question" (Wilder 1998b: 242).

The play ends there but the questions Wilder poses linger; despite Apollo's reassurances, his interventions have not resulted in entirely positive outcomes: Alcestis's sacrifice for her husband did not prevent his being deposed by Agis, and her resurrection did not shield her from suffering after her husband's death. While he was working on the play, Wilder wrote in his journal, "If I cannot find a theatrical way of throwing doubt even on the visible participation of Apollo in our action I am writing a *mysterium* which assumes the personified divinity. And such a play I do not wish to write" (Wilder 1985: 190). But, as we saw above, English views the play as more ambivalent: "On the one hand, *The Alcestiad* inspires hope that faith in the divine can shepherd us through life's obstacles; on the other hand, there remains a tragic side to Alcestis, who, after all she has endured, still lacks a clear and definitive relationship with the solar divinity" (2013: 340). In his 1955 program note, Wilder calls his play "a comedy about the extreme difficulty of any dialogue between heaven and earth" and cites Kierkegaard on the "misunderstandings that result from the 'incommensurability of things human and divine'" (Wilder 1998b: 168).

Elsewhere, Wilder wrote that he hoped to compose the play "in such a way that we would never be certain that the Supernatural was, truly speaking, hovering—nay, existing; to devise every sign and message and intrusion of the Other in such a way that it could be interpreted as accident, delusion, mirage: 'Some say it thundered; others that a god spoke'" (Wilder 1985: 229). Put another way, he asked, "Could I mould [*sic*] the story in such a way that it left in doubt whether the Supernatural had spoken to men or whether men had had sublime promptings which they immediately ascribed to the Supernatural?" (Wilder 1985: 187).

In writing his version of classical tragedy, then, Wilder introduced skepticism and ambivalence where for the ancients there was no doubt, introduced questions where there had been certainty. As Papajewski puts it, Wilder transformed "a tragedy of classical antiquity ... into a drama of martyrdom. Pain, agony, and farewell are the tormenting experiences by which a surer knowledge is attained, a knowledge that includes the possibilities of bridging the gulf between God and man" (Papajewski [1965] 1968: 174). In David H. Porter's assessment, its "most significant classical debt is the fact that while it begins and ends with the gods, it leaves us above all with an expanded understanding of the human condition" (Porter 1985: 149). In Wilder's own words, he did not want to write "a 'beautiful' saint's legend"; instead he aimed for "puzzling ambiguity" and a play in which "all must be wider, newer, crazier" (Wilder 1985: 190).

In a 1967 letter to John R. Tibby, Wilder revealed one possible explanation for his ambivalence about "the *tremendum* of religious experience" and his consequent impulse to complicate his version of classical tragedy by depicting his major characters in *The Alcestiad* as human beings rather than simply as playthings of the gods. He explains to Tibby that his father, along with the fathers of his college classmates Robert Hutchins and Henry Luce, "were very religious, very dogmatic Patriarchs" who "preached and talked cant from morning til night—not because they were hypocritical but because they knew no other language ... They thought they were 'spiritual' ... They had no insight into the lives of others—least of all their families ... We're the product of those (finally bewildered and unhappy) Worthies" (Wilder 2008: 645–6). He had said much the same to his Yale professor Chauncey B. Tinker forty years earlier: "isn't there a lot of New England in me ... All that bewilderment as to where Moral Attitude begins and where it shades off into mere Puritan Bossiness" (Wilder 2008: 219). His handling of his material in *The Alcestiad* also is evident in a 1928 letter to his ex-student John A. Townley in which he quoted Chekhov: "The business of literature is not to answer questions, but to state them fairly" (Wilder 2008: 226). Calling Wilder's play "the most significant interpretation" of the Alcestis story in "modern world literature," Käte Hamburger asserts that its "dominant idea ... is that ... in the end all remains enigmatic" ([1962] 1969: 108, 112).

Wilder's letter to Townley was in response to the latter's queries about his former teacher's recently published novel *The Bridge of San Luis Rey* (1927). There Wilder juxtaposes the belief of Brother Juniper that the collapse of a bridge in Peru and the loss of five lives cannot be anything other than "a sheer Act of God," that, in Russell Banks's words, "the apparently accidental collapse of a bridge" has "a divine purpose" against what the investigation of the lives of those five killed people reveals: again quoting Banks, "any one of us could have been on that bridge when it collapsed" (Wilder 1998a: xii–xiii), supporting the idea that the tragedy was a random occurrence. Wilder explained to an interviewer in 1953, "the central idea of the work ... stems from friendly arguments with my father, a strict Calvinist" (Bryer 1992: 59). Wilder's reworking of classical tragedy in *The Alcestiad* is thus very much of a piece with his other work with respect to this ambivalence about the divine element in human affairs. He acknowledged the connection in a 1945 letter to Sibyl Colefax when he said of *The Alcestiad*, "the whole play must be subtended by one idea, which is not an idea but a question (and the same question as the Bridge of San Luis Rey!)" (Wilder 2008: 434).

Like many brought up in a strict, religious home, Thornton Wilder wrestled all his life with the conflicting influences it left on him. He demonstrates a skeptical view of the "religious force" assumed by the Greeks that he refers to in his 1939 essay on *Oedipus Rex* and replaces it with an assertion of the ambivalent or the inexplicable. This can be seen in *Our Town* when Emily asks the Stage Manager if "any human beings ever realize life while they live it?—every, every minute?" and the Stage Manager replies, "The saints and poets, maybe—they do some" (Wilder 1997: 207), thus linking the divine and the human, albeit with the significant reservation contained in the word "some."

Similarly, in his 1948 novel *The Ides of March*, which others have noted reads almost like a play with its alternating voices couched in letters, he explained that his intention was contained in its epigram, only slightly mistranslated from Goethe's *Faust*: "Out of man's recognition in fear and awe that there is an Unknowable comes all that is best in the explorations of his mind" (Wilder [1948] 2003: ix). For Wilder, it is the unexplained and the unknowable that lie behind the tragic occurrences in human lives.

There is another respect in which Wilder's reworking of classical tragedy in *The Alcestiad* echoes his concerns in his other work. In a 1929 letter to Norman Fitts, he identified the subject of his books to date—which at that point included the novels *The Cabala* (1926) and *The Bridge of San Luis Rey* (1927) and a collection of one-act plays, *The Angel That Troubled the Waters* (1928)—as "what is the worst thing that the world can do to you, and what are the last resources one has to oppose to it. In other words: when a human being is made to bear more than [a] human being can bear—what then?" (Wilder 2008: 240). Although he was not to begin work on *The Alcestiad* for almost a decade after writing this, the topic clearly still preoccupied him when he began that play, as it does in his later novels and in his two most famous works for the stage, *Our Town* and *The Skin of Our Teeth*.

One can further assert that, in calling *The Alcestiad* in his 1955 program note "a comedy about a very serious matter" (Wilder 1998b: 168), he was identifying the mixture of comedy and seriousness, of dark and light, that characterizes many of Wilder's plays, as well as much of his other writing. That mix, in turn, was also based on his conviction that, ultimately, there is no definitive explanation for human behavior and for the tragedies that befall us. How else can one reconcile what is often misconstrued as the merely nostalgic and optimistic tone of much of Wilder's work with his belief, expressed in a 1928 interview with André Maurois, that "all human beings are unhappy—in varying degrees … They are solitary, they are consumed with desires which they dare not satisfy; and they wouldn't be happy if they did satisfy them, because they are too civilized" (Bryer 1992: 14). Or how can we reconcile the madcap doings in his 1942 play *The Skin of Our Teeth* with its author's assertion, in a 1962 interview, that its theme is Sabina's line, "This is a wicked world, and that's the God's truth" (Bryer 1992: 96)? The play's ambivalence lies in Sabina's observation that—despite the bleak reality that she expresses tearfully to Mr. Antrobus, "Oh, the world's an awful place, and you know it is"—Mr. and Mrs. Antrobus's "heads are full of plans and they are as confident as the first day they began" (Wilder 1997: 281, 284). Even Emily's famous line in *Our Town*, "Oh, earth, you're too wonderful for anybody to realize you," usually read as a hopeful comment, can just as easily be seen as a despairing one, especially when it is juxtaposed with Emily's lines that immediately follow: "I should have listened to you. That's all human beings are! Just blind people!" (Wilder 1997: 207). And, in *The Matchmaker*, the farce is interrupted by Dolly's comment, "there comes a moment in everybody's life when he must decide whether to live among human beings or not—a fool among fools or a fool alone" (Wilder 1997: 363).

Contrary to much popular consensus, there certainly is a dark side to Thornton Wilder; he saw life and its tragedies clearly in all their complexity and resisted simple explanations for them. Ultimately, he is far from simply an optimist. He celebrated the willingness of human beings to survive in a harsh and cruel world, their ability to marshal the "last resources" he referred to in his letter to Norman Fitts; but he was certainly familiar with and willing to depict the tragic.

References

Anouilh, Jean ([1942] 1962), *Antigone*, trans. Lewis Galantière (1946), in Haskell M. Block and Robert G. Shedd (eds.), *Masters of Modern Drama*, 781–99, New York: Random House.

Ballet, Arthur H. (2000), "*Our Town* as a Classical Tragedy," in
    Thomas Siebold (ed.), *Readings on "Our Town,"* 74–82, San Diego:
    Greenhaven Press.
Bryer, Jackson R. (ed.) (1992), *Conversations with Thornton Wilder*,
    Jackson, MS: University Press of Mississippi.
English, Mary C. (2013), "*The Alcestiad*: Wilder and the
    'Incommensurability of Things Human and Divine,'" in Jackson R.
    Bryer and Lincoln Konkle (eds.), *Thornton Wilder: New Perspectives*,
    334–59, Evanston, IL: Northwestern University Press.
Hamburger, Käte ([1962] 1969), *From Sophocles to Sartre: Figures from
    Greek Tragedy, Classical and Modern*, trans. Helen Sebba, New York:
    Frederick Ungar.
Lewis, Sinclair (1930), "Text of Sinclair Lewis's Nobel Prize Address at
    Stockholm," *The New York Times*, December 13.
Matthiessen, F. O. (1930), "Figures in a Dream," *New Freeman*, May 10:
    212–13.
Niven, Penelope (2012), *Thornton Wilder: A Life*, New York:
    HarperCollins.
Papajewski, Helmut ([1965] 1968) *Thornton Wilder*, trans. John Conway,
    New York: Frederick Ungar.
Porter, David H. (1985), "MacLeish's *Herakles* and Wilder's *Alcestiad*,"
    Classical Journal 80 (2): 145–50.
Wilder, Thornton (1985), *The Journals of Thornton Wilder: 1939–1961*,
    Donald Gallup (ed.), New Haven: Yale University Press.
Wilder, Thornton (1997), *Collected Plays & Writings on Theater*, New
    York: Library of America
Wilder, Thornton ([1927] 1998a), *The Bridge of San Luis Rey*, New York:
    Harper Perennial.
Wilder, Thornton (1998b), *The Collected Short Plays of Thornton Wilder*,
    vol. 2, New York: Theatre Communications Group.
Wilder, Thornton ([1948] 2003), *The Ides of March*, New York: Harper
    Perennial.
Wilder, Thornton (2008), *The Selected Letters of Thornton Wilder*, Robin
    Gibbs Wilder and Jackson R. Bryer (eds.), New York: HarperCollins.

5

Lillian Hellman (1905–1984)

Anne Fletcher
Southern Illinois University

"If you believe, as the Greeks did, that man is at the mercy of the gods, then you write tragedy. The end is inevitable from the beginning. But if you believe that man can solve his own problems and is at nobody's mercy, then you will probably write melodrama". This epigraph, attributed to Lillian Hellman in her obituary in *The New York Times* (July 1, 1984), encapsulates critical debate over Hellman's plays and genre. Enigmatic in death as she was in life, the playwright's remark tells us little about how she herself categorized her works. Indeed, Hellman eschewed classifications like tragedy, melodrama, or well-made play, declaring, "I don't like labels and isms. They are for people who raise or lower skirts because that's the thing you do for this year" (Hollander 1965: 5) and on another occasion stating, of dramatic form, in this case the well-made play, "I don't think it's any more important than what meal you eat" (Gardner 1986: 115). In yet another instance, when asked about melodrama in general and *The Little Foxes* in particular, the playwright responded, "it's a meaningless word unless one is using it as a put-down" (Albert 1986: 175). And another time, she concluded, "form doesn't matter" (Lehmann 2016: 8). Lillian Hellman's ambivalence toward genre makes investigating the tragic possibilities in her plays an enticing proposition.

Definitions of *tragedy*, traced, of course, to Aristotle's comments on the subject in his *Poetics,* vary—twisted and tweaked across centuries to mesh with the tenor of the times. Colloquial usage points to the word "tragedy" as expressing varying degrees of sadness, as in "tragic accident." Both Hans-Thies Lehmann and Terry Eagleton find this use problematic with regard to theatre. Some academicians focus specifically on suffering, violence, victimization, and the impact of the tragic action on others. There appears to be no "one size fits all" definition for the term. For Lehmann, "tragic experience is tied to the theatre" (2016: 8); for Eagleton, "tragedy turns on a number of distinctions ... between fate and chance, free will and destiny, inner flaw and outer circumstances, the noble and the ignoble, blindness and insight, historical and universal, the alterable and the inevitable, the truly tragic and the merely piteous, heroic defiance and ignominious inertia" (2003: 21). Arthur Miller's essay "Tragedy and the Common Man" (1949), written shortly after *Death of a Salesman* opened on Broadway, expanded notions of classical tragedy to apply to the average person, relating to his contemporary audience and ennobling the more proletarian protagonist's struggle. George Steiner in *The Death of Tragedy* (1961) pointed to the demise of classical tragedy in the modern world, questioning the continued relevance of commonly espoused attributes of tragedy, such as *hubris* (pride), *hamartia* (missing the mark or making a mistake), *peripeteia* (reversal of fortune), *anagnorisis* (recognition), and *catharsis* (purging). Arthur Miller believed that pathos diminished tragedy, claiming the pathetic character is one who "has fought a battle he could not possibly have won" (1949). But the tragic in Hellman's works often stems from *pathos* where, despite the presence of overpowering fate and inevitability, the dialectic between the production and the audience incites the experience of tragedy as an emotional response. Hellman's ability to create this emotional experience may be the key to understanding her plays and their reception.

Despite Katherine Lederer's admonition that *The Children's Hour* (1934) was a *first* play and that Hellman's successive pieces have been unfairly compared to this initial work (1979: 28), *The Children's Hour* hints at issues of form, style, and genre that permeate Hellman's oeuvre. From its first productions, reviews and advertisements have characterized the play as a tragedy, but how efficacious is this concept in exploring what Hellman actually is doing?

Structurally, *The Children's Hour* is akin to Henrik Ibsen's middle plays with its inclusion of social issues and to French nineteenth-century well-made plays with its implementation of a *clou*, the small object upon which the action turns: in *The Children's Hour*, the stolen bracelet. The play exhibits elements of melodrama, like aborted action(s), what-if moments, the teeter-totter or punch/counterpunch scenes in which fundamentally good characters vie with others who appear inherently bad, and strong curtains. Hellman deftly dangles the possibility that the teachers might win until the highly charged, courtroom-like scene at the close of Act 2 when, fearful of Mary, Rosalie confesses. The good/bad dichotomy extends itself beyond Mary's apparent evil and into the protagonists' self-evaluations. Martha goes so far as sarcastically to call herself and Karen "bad people," and after she confesses that she loves Karen, she uses the word "guilty" (Hellman 1942: 78–9). By the play's conclusion, both Karen and Martha have inscribed negative images on themselves.

The piece well may be viewed as tragedy, not in Karen's idea of "sick, high, tragic people" (Hellman 1942: 73) but, rather, in quasi-Aristotelian terms. Both the working-class teachers and the wealthy Mrs. Tilford experience Aristotelian falls, and Mary's lie affects the future fortunes of almost every character in the play—and arguably of the community beyond. The persecution and ostracizing to which Martha and Karen are subjected as consequences of rumors and lies lend universality to the piece. A Hegelian analysis might pit Karen and Martha against the Tilford character(s) in an Antigone-versus-Creon paradigm. Mrs. Tilford's change of mind might be seen as an Aristotelian reversal and recognition, although we learn of her transformation only through Hellman's clunky *scène à faire*, the well-made play's obligatory scene, grafted on at the play's conclusion. The playwright, in fact, considered eliminating the scene for the 1952 revival she directed but came to the conclusion that the task would involve unravelling the entire structure of the play, so she left Mrs. Tilford's visit to Karen intact.[1] *The Children's Hour*'s worldview is narrow, and spirituality, let alone religion or an objective, universal moral order, figures little in the play. It concerns itself, rather, with socially constructed taboo. Karen does refer to "sin" (1942: 78) but as a wrongdoing in the culture of this community, not in a religious or objective sense.

When famed feminist critic Jill Dolan reviewed the 2011 London production of *The Children's Hour* starring Kiera Knightly and Elisabeth Moss, she queried, "Why now?" and does not use the word "tragedy" in her blog. She does, however, reference how Mrs. Mortar's failure to cut her alleged stage tour short and return to the States to testify on the teachers' behalf "seals Martha and Karen's fate." She also asserts the inevitability of Martha's "destiny," which "sadly, can't be changed," and she describes Ellen Burstyn's performance in the role of Mrs. Tilford as demonstrating "both the hubris of those who think they know what's right and true and the devastating downfall of those who can't buy their way back into blamelessness" (Dolan 2011). *The Children's Hour* exhibits many tragic elements. At the play's conclusion, every character suffers; some (perhaps all) have been victimized by others. Martha is dead; Karen and Joe are no longer together; Mrs. Tilford must bear the burden of raising the pathological Mary alone; and Mrs. Mortar is deprived of a home and must find a way to live without the benevolence of others. Karen is left onstage, alone. There are violent elements within the play as well: Mary's psychological and physical bullying of Rosalie and the other girls, and Martha's suicide (Ellsworth 2014). Dolan concludes her review, "*The Children's Hour* winds up being a terrific, compelling, and even relevant production ... I'm still surprised by how moving I found the production" (Dolan 2011). Here Dolan expresses the audience's experience of tragic catharsis, an experience Hellman was a master of creating regardless of the genre in which her plays are classified.

Unlike *The Children's Hour*, Hellman's second Broadway play, *Days to Come* (1936), her only overtly political or "strike" play, was a dismal failure. Hellman admits to the play's weakness (Hellman 1942: ix), which emanates from the playwright's desire to center on a conflict between good and evil, the underpinning of melodrama. The play is included in this analysis of Hellman's vision of tragedy because of a telling line: "All the things we know were there to know a long time ago" (Hellman 1979: 145) uttered by the play's protagonist, Andrew Rodman—words that capture the play's tragic essence. The Rodman family members suffer the ramifications of their past actions. Throughout the play, they embrace deception and self-delusion in a manner that presages characters created later by Tennessee Williams. Their actions, informed or unwitting, are reprehensible, from Julie's long-standing extramarital affair with her husband's friend to Andrew's hiring of strikebreakers, which leads to the murder of a worker's child. But like Williams's characters, they are trapped in the confines of their upbringing, their pasts— their own skins. While Hellman fails to balance her focus on the Rodman family's relationships with the story of class struggle and the workers' strike, once the final scene is reached, we see how the play's action was "inevitable from the beginning"—in Hellman's view, a hallmark of tragedy.

After the short and unsuccessful run of *Days to Come*, Hellman regained her stride with *The Little Foxes* (1939). Although she was pleased with the play's critical and box office success, she remained baffled—as she had been by the response to Mary in *The Children's Hour*—by how the Hubbard family, with the exceptions of Birdie and Alexandra, was perceived as intrinsically evil. In the case of the fragile Williamsesque Birdie, Hellman states that she "had meant people to smile at, and to sympathize with, the sad, weak Birdie, certainly I had not meant them to cry." With Alexandra, the playwright intended to "half-mock" her own youth (1973: 180). Humor and irony were meant as vital underpinnings for the play, yet *The Little Foxes* often is produced as a handily crafted well-made play or melodrama, while a few critics discuss it as tragedy. Reviewing Ivo van Hove's off-Broadway production in 2010, Ben Brantley declares the play is "as ominously predetermined as Greek tragedy," and Glenda Frank suggests, "the black servants who are critical observers, emerge from their background roles like a Greek chorus." Bob Hoover, reviewing a 2009 Pittsburgh production, identifies the Hubbards as a "fatally flawed family." In her 2015 review of the Goodman Theatre production, Catey Sullivan concludes that the "ensemble captures the cruelty, pathos, and tragedy of the Hubbard clan with blazing impact." Generally, however, beginning with Brooks Atkinson's review of the play's premier (1939), in which he called it "contrived" and alluded to Arthur Wing Pinero, "melodrama" is the moniker most applied to *The Little Foxes*, with numerous references to its characters as villains or as evil.

Regina Giddens, the scheming Hubbard sister who stands by idly—or, rather, intentionally—as her dying husband grasps for his medication, is central to the play, but her brothers rival her in maliciousness and greed. That these characteristics are perpetually attributed to the Hubbards in this play and in *Another Part of the*

Forest points to the shortcoming of a frequently applied element in definitions of tragedy, in particular that stemming from earlier critics like A. C. Bradley whose analysis of Shakespeare's tragic heroes includes the infamous "fatal flaw," or, as he calls it, "trait" (Bradley [1904] 1991: 37). This misinterpretation of the Greek notion of *hamartia*, an image from missing the mark in archery or metaphorically of making a mistake, misleads commentators into searching for a singular character defect and discourages fully developed characterizations in production, moving toward the black-and-white, good/evil dichotomy of melodrama. Labeling Hellman's plays as melodramas follows this train of thinking.

   Another Part of the Forest (1946) was written as a prequel to *The Little Foxes* as part of an intended trilogy harkening back to Aeschylus's *Oresteia* and O'Neill's *Mourning Becomes Electra*. Again here Hellman's play generally is referred to as melodrama. Surprisingly, reviewers seldom explore Marcus Hubbard's fascination with Aristotle or the play's Greek revival setting and how these aspects of the play nod to classical tragedy. In *Understanding Lillian Hellman*, Alice Griffin and Geraldine Thorsten briefly reference Hubbard's interest in the classics as well as his "sin" and the "dark, unshakable curse" on the family. However, they conclude that "the audience feels no pity for those who end badly" in the play, identifying as sympathetic only Hubbard's long-suffering wife, Lavinia, who might achieve her goal of founding a school for black children (1999: 42–3). In fact, Griffin and Thorsten remark on her courage in the face of adversity: her husband perpetuates the "myth" that she is insane while she, as the only character aware of his impropriety during the Civil War, holds the key to exposing his chicanery. Their analysis points to Lavinia's function as, perhaps, a tragic heroine.

   Griffin and Thorsten praise Hellman for *Another Part of the Forest*'s "taut" construction and note how the play's action is confined to a pivotal forty-eight hours in the Hubbard's lives. While they do not make this connection, it is interesting to contemplate ways in which Hellman's condensed time frame and the play's single setting might, as a subtle meta-theatrical exercise, constitute a modern adaptation of tenets of Neoclassicism.

   The Autumn Garden (1951) is looser and more meandering— more Chekhovian in structure—than Hellman's other plays, and like the Russian playwright's work, it defies genre. In contrast to

The Children's Hour, *The Little Foxes*, and *Another Part of the Forest*, *Garden* relies not on the requisite villains and heroes of melodrama, nor on the dramatic falls of the people of tragedy, but rather supports itself on the slow self-immolation of characters who singularly and as a composite have no one to blame but themselves for the outcome. The play's tragedy is comprised of lost hopes and aspirations, individual and collective. Reflecting *Garden*'s autumnal setting, its characters in a last burst of sunshine look to the past, hope for the future, but end in decay.

Building on ideas developed by David Magarshack in his biography of Chekhov, Marvin Felheim suggests that the characters in *The Autumn Garden* serve in essence as their own chorus, providing moral judgments. Hellman, he says, in this play "lets her characters alone to act out their destinies." The characters find themselves "caught in the essential tragedy, the tragedy of life." Felheim finds both pity and terror in the play, "but they are not for the singular, noble (no matter how representative) individual, the Hamlet or the Lear; the pity and terror are spread out, they are for all. Pity and terror have been democratized." Because the play is crafted in prose, not in the heightened language of poetry, Felheim finds its "tragic intensity" and the "tragic nobility" of character and situation "less magnificent" than in poetic dramas but not in a pejorative way; in fact, he concludes that "the kind of drama we have in *The Autumn Garden* is the only kind which makes for modern tragedy" (Felheim 1960: 193–5).

Hellman premiered *Toys in the Attic* (1960) more than a quarter century after her first play, *The Children's Hour*. As in *The Autumn Garden*, the focus is not on melodrama's fight between good and evil but on the characters' internal, subterranean struggles. In an article coupling *Garden* and *Toys*, Júnia De Castro Magalhães Alves discusses Hellman's blend of milieu, character, and lyrical dialogue to create "mood plays." Hellman's Bernier sisters in New Orleans recall Chekhov's Prozorovs in *Three Sisters*: they long for adventure beyond their stultifying existence. Hellman herself was fully aware of the connection; she had edited a collection of Chekhov's letters in 1955.

Here again, while critics generally do not identify the play as tragedy, they acknowledge powerful tragic elements within it. In his review of the McCarter Theatre's 1978 revival, Mel Gussow states that Julian's "fate has already been charted" (1978: 12).

Ginia Bellafante, commenting on Austin Pendleton's acclaimed 2007 production, notes how it "falls to Anna to embody the play's fatalism ... she doesn't express resignation so much as inhabit it," and, Bellafante adds, Pendleton finds the "seed of redemption" in the piece.

Suffering in *Toys in the Attic* is precipitated by secrecy, social deviance, self-delusion, and life lies: a sister experiences sexual longing for her brother, a white woman ends a clandestine affair with her black employee. The tragic in Hellman's dramas intensifies when the wounds are self-inflicted.

As an examination of Lillian Hellman's plays and their reviews elucidates, seeking a solid definition of tragedy weaves an intricate and frequently confusing web. Generally accepted tragic elements reoccur in Hellman's works: notions of inevitability; reversal of fortune; in some cases, recognition. In production, the plays incite what might be called "performative pathos," even catharsis. That Jill Dolan responded to the pathos (and tragic elements) of *The Children's Hour* more than three-quarters of a century after Hellman wrote it—and after all the changes in cultural values and perspectives that have occurred in that time—is testimony to that particular play's insight and power. Ultimately, as Hellman said, perhaps genre "doesn't matter." Whether their endings are predictable, or the characters' fates "inevitable," regardless of genre, Lillian Hellman's plays endure. They continue to engage live audiences in their portrayals of violence, victimization, and suffering. Characters grapple with their pasts and present circumstances, some with dignity, others with indignation, ruthlessness, or despair, and, as Andrew states at the conclusion of *Days to Come*, "it seems almost right that it should be this way" (Hellman 1979: 148).

Note

1   Even earlier than the revival, in her "Introduction" to *Four Plays,* Hellman explains: "The play probably should have ended with Martha's suicide; the last scene is tense and over-burdened. I knew this at the time, but I could not help myself. I am a moral writer, often too moral a writer, and I cannot avoid, it seems, that last summing-up" (1942: vii–ix).

References

Albert, Jan (1986), "Sweetest Smelling Baby in New Orleans," in Jackson R. Bryer (ed.), *Conversations with Lillian Hellman*, 165–78, Jackson, MS: University Press of Mississippi.

Alves, Júnia De Castro Magalhães (1984), "Miss *Hellman's mood* plays: *The Autumn Garden* and *Toys in the Attic*," *Research Gate*, December. Available online: https://www.researchgate.net/publication/287930114_Miss_Hellman's_mood_plays_The_Autumn_Garden_and_Toys_in_the_Attic (accessed January 4, 2017).

Atkinson, Brooks (1939), "Tallulah Bankhead Appearing in Lillian Hellman's Drama of the South, 'The Little Foxes,'" *The New York Times*, February 16. Available online: https://timesmachine.nytimes.com/timesmachine/1939/02/16/94678969.html?pageNumber=23 (accessed January 4, 2017).

Bellafante, Ginia (2007), "Polishing the Silver as Family of Cannibals Licks its Chops," *The New York Times*, January 16. Available online: http://www.nytimes.com/2007/01/16/theater/reviews/16toys.html (accessed January 4, 2016).

Bradley, A. C. ([1904] 1991), *Shakespearean Tragedy: Lectures on "Hamlet," "Othello," "King Lear" and "Macbeth*," New York: Penguin Classics.

Brantley, Ben (2010), "A Dysfunctional Family, Greedy with 'the Gimmes,'" *The New York Times*, September 21. Available online: http://www.nytimes.com/2010/09/22/theater/reviews/22foxes.html?pagewanted=all&_r=0 (accessed January 4, 2017)

Dolan, Jill (2011), "*The Children's Hour*," *The Feminist Spectator*, March 17. Available online: http://feministspectator.princeton.edu/2011/03/17/the-childrens-hour/ (accessed January 4, 2017).

Eagleton, Terry (2003), *Sweet Violence: The Idea of the Tragic*, Malden, MA: Blackwell Publishing.

Ellsworth, Shari (2014), "Directing Lillian Hellman's *The Children's Hour* for Today's Society and Its Contemporary Relevance: A Professional Problem Dissertation" (diss., Texas Tech University). Available online: https://ttu-ir.tdl.org/ttu-ir/handle/2346/58907 (accessed January 4, 2017).

Felheim, Marvin (1960), "*The Autumn Garden*: Mechanics and Dialectics," *Modern Drama* 3 (2): 191–5.

Frank, Glenda (2010), "An American Family," *New York Theatre Wire*. Available online: http://www.nytheatre-wire.com/gf10101t.htm (accessed January 4, 2017).

Gardner, Fred (1986), "An Interview with Lillian Hellman," in Jackson R. Bryer (ed.), *Conversations with Lillian Hellman*, 107–23, Jackson, MS: University Press of Mississippi.

Griffin, Alice and Geraldine Thorsten (1999), *Understanding Lillian Hellman*, Columbia, SC: University of South Carolina Press.
Gussow, Mel (1978), "Lillian Hellman's 'Toys in the Attic' Revived," *The New York Times*, March 4: 12. Available online: http://www.nytimes.com/1978/03/04/archives/lillian-hellmans-toys-in-the-attic-revived.html (accessed January 4, 2017).
Hellman, Lillian (1942), *Four Plays by Lillian Hellman*, New York: The Modern Library.
Hellman, Lillian (1973), *Pentimento*, Boston: Little, Brown and Company.
Hellman, Lillian (1979), *Six Plays by Lillian Hellman*, New York: Vintage Books.
Hollander, Anne and John Marquand (1965), "Lillian Hellman: The Art of Theater No. 1," *The Paris Review* 33: 1–19. Available online: http://www.theparisreview.org/interviews/4463/the-art-of-theater-no-1-lillian-hellman (accessed January 4, 2017).
Hoover, Bob (2009), "'Little Foxes,' 'Glengarry' leave viewers wanting more," *Pittsburgh Post-Gazette*, November 21. Available online: http://www.post-gazette.com/ae/theater-dance/2009/11/21/Little-Foxes-Glengarry-leave-viewers-wanting-more/stories/200911210149 (accessed January 4, 2017).
Lederer, Katherine (1979), *Lillian Hellman*, Boston: Twayne Publishers.
Lehmann, Hans-Thies (2016), *Tragedy and Dramatic Theatre*, trans. by Erik Butler, New York: Routledge.
"Lillian Hellman, Playwright, Author, and Rebel, Dies at 77" (1984), *New York Times*, July 1. Available online: http://www.nytimes.com/learning/general/onthisday/bday/0620.html (accessed January 4, 2017).
Miller, Arthur (1949), "Tragedy and the Common Man," *The New York Times*, February 27. Available online: https://www.nytimes.com/books/00/11/12/specials/miller-common.html (accessed January 4, 2017).
Steiner, George ([1961] 1996), *The Death of Tragedy*, New Haven: Yale University Press
Sullivan, Catey (2015), "The Goodman Theatre Dusts Off a Classic with Lillian Hellman's Southern Gothic," *Theatre Mania*, May 18. Available online: http://www.theatermania.com/chicago-theater/reviews/the-little-foxes-goodman-review_72936.html (accessed August 16, 2016).

6

Tennessee Williams (1911–1983)

Susan C. W. Abbotson
Rhode Island College

Writers growing up in the first half of the twentieth century still had an intrinsic sense of the divine that colored their belief systems, whatever religiosity they claimed or disclaimed. The weakening of such beliefs as the twentieth century progressed seemed to necessitate a change in how tragedy might be written beyond the classical design. Dramatists needed it to mean more than a sad occurrence, but how to achieve this without a belief in fate or the divine? Eugene O'Neill, in his exploration of man's relationship to God, clearly had none of those qualms, and Thornton Wilder portrays an almost Victorian divine sensibility through his Stage Manager, who calmly watches over the restricted lives of humanity and translates life into a grander scheme. Even Arthur Miller, despite his declared secularism, reflects profound Judaic beliefs throughout his work and in his innate rejection of absurdist principle. It is perhaps harder for those of the next generation, such as Edward Albee or David Mamet, who, despite their humanistic impulses, see little to denote meaning in the ways people live their lives. All of these playwrights create their own version of tragedy, but with his discomforting view of religion and belief in the inevitable, Tennessee Williams offers an interesting bridge between the old and the new.

Though often overlooked or even denied as a writer of tragedy, Williams may be the American dramatist most suited to the role.

While Williams only occasionally refers to any of his plays as tragedies,[1] there is clearly a tragic aspect to much of what he wrote, despite what several critics have asserted. Robert Heilman, for example, narrowly suggests, "a recurrent Williams problem [is] a lack of tragic stature" in characters who instead display "a limitedness or weakness that is not the raw material of tragic life" (1977: 34). Walter Kerr complained, "Mr. Williams seems capable of [tragedy] but not yet ready to reach for it" (1959: 1–2). John Gassner asserted that Williams was not truly serious about the conventions of tragedy (1960: 228–31), and Leda Bauer declared that Williams's work is "devoid of any significance, cosmic, social or political" (1951: 34). John Von Szeliski suggests that Williams is too pessimistic and sexually fixated to be tragic, and his works are generically unsuited to tragedy as they are too full of dread (1966: 203–11). But as William Sharp insisted, it is wrong to dismiss him as a mere "sensation monger" for "Williams is a writer of tragedy; that is, he is seriously concerned with man's attempt to solve conflicts (psychological, emotional, and intellectual) within him. The particular conflict that most concerns Williams is the struggle between what man feels he is or ought to be and what society says he is or ought to be" (1962: 161, 160).

From the start there have been those who saw Williams's tragic potential. In a 1948 *Life* article, Lincoln Barnett asserted that Chekhov and Williams both deal with "the isolation of human beings and their tragic inability to understand one another" (1948: 116). Reflecting on the character of Blanche DuBois, Brooks Atkinson insisted, "Her agony is no less poignant than the suffering of Oedipus Rex, the victim of whimsical Greek gods with malign dispositions. To tell the truth, the fate of Blanche DuBois purges and terrifies me more deeply than the fate of Oedipus Rex. His gods never threaten me, but her gods are hard at work under a democratic constitution and they speak English" (1948: 1).

While there remains dissension over whether or not a play such as *A Streetcar Named Desire* is truly tragic, the cause of this may be in the vision of the critics rather than the play itself. Elia Kazan, after first reading and subsequently directing it both for stage and film, certainly saw it as a tragedy and Britton J. Harwood (1977: 104–15), Leonard Berkman (1967: 249–57), and Signi Falk

(1978: 53–62) all concurred, but each focused on the plot, viewing Blanche's "rape" as the climax of the play. Such opinions position Blanche as a moth caught in the flame rather than the monster she sees herself as being. As Felicia Londré suggests, the play's crisis cannot occur so early if Blanche is its protagonist, as that would make her far too passive a figure for the remainder of the play. Thus, Londré insists that the actual climax takes place in the final scene "when (as the active agent of her destiny) [Blanche] finds a way to salvage her dignity" (1977: 61). This seems more likely, but as Anne Fleche asserts, "closure" for Williams was "always just next door to entrapment," and Blanche escaping into madness should not be considered "purifying" and should not be viewed as a comforting or positive denouement (1997: 100, 106).

Blanche as tragic heroine *is* a monster of the likes of Shakespeare's Richard III. The "dream" of Belle Reve is no happy dream of a better, more affluent past, but the nightmare of what Blanche did to her young husband, Allan. She cruelly rejected him because of his sexuality and caused him to kill himself. It is a nightmare from which she never can be released, though she might take any series of streetcars in her attempt to flee. As Williams wrote in an earlier play, *At Liberty* (1941), which contains many seed ideas for both *The Glass Menagerie* and *A Streetcar Named Desire*, "The past keeps getting bigger and bigger at the future's expense" (2011: 271). Blanche's past eventually overwhelms her and destroys any chance of a future. Her final exit is no transcendence over the banalities of Stanley and his crew but a descent into madness as she is led to what would have been, in the 1940s, the putative hell of a mental asylum. As Jacqueline O'Connor has suggested, "insanity awaits [Williams's] women almost as often as death awaits Shakespeare's tragic heroes" (1997: 30). Williams's tragic protagonists all must live under the constant threat of displacement and/or destruction.

Williams frequently portrays his characters as exiles forced to live in environments incompatible to their natures, such as Amanda Wingfield in her claustrophobic, rundown St. Louis apartment, or Blanche DuBois on a day-bed in her sister's steamy New Orleans' love-nest. They are depicted as having fallen from real or imagined heights—Amanda's Blue Mountains or Blanche's Belle Reve—or simply from a former respectability, such as Alma Winemiller from her father's rectory to picking up strangers on a park bench. Usually, new social orders have pushed them out—but that has happened in most cases before the play even begins, and is not the thrust of the drama. Williams is more interested in the tragedy that follows such tragedy: not the protagonist getting caught but vainly trying to escape once trapped.

Williams's dramas are fraught with images of attempted escape. Each of the men in *The Glass Menagerie*—the father, Tom, and Jim—flies from that stifling apartment; almost the entire cast of *Camino Real* struggle to board the Fugitivo airplane; Blanche dreams of Shep Huntleigh's yacht; and poor Ben Murphy, trapped in his office in *Stairs to the Roof*, is mocked by Mr. E. for his naive belief in the possibility of escape in this world.

Williams depicts escape in different ways. First, there is the physical kind of escape via a literal fire-escape as in *The Glass Menagerie*, lighting out for the West in *Vieux Carré*, or running into the wastelands as in *Camino Real* or *The Red Devil Battery Sign*. Then there are escapes from the restrictions of social expectation or involvement, such as Alma's embrace of drugs and promiscuity, or Flora Goforth's removal of herself into a cushioned world of wealth in *The Milk Train Doesn't Stop Here Anymore*. And of course Williams also frequently depicts the potential psychological refuge of insanity, as grasped by Blanche, Zelda (*Clothes for a Summer Hotel*), Lucretia (*Portrait of a Madonna*), Mark (*Bar of a Tokyo Hotel*), Joanie (*A House Not Meant to Stand*), or for a time Catherine in *Suddenly Last Summer*. Unable to bear "the whips and scorns of time" these characters try to flee, but escape is never lasting, for Williams and his characters are unable to run away from who they are or their pasts. As his semi-autobiographical self, Tom, in *The Glass Menagerie* understood: "Oh, Laura, Laura, I tried to leave you behind me, but I am more faithful than I intended to be" (2000: 465). Like the ancient mariner, Tom must return each night to share with a listening audience the albatross-like guilt from which he never can be free; it is a burden from which he never truly can run away as he cannot escape his past or himself.

Williams's whole life is filled with an unrequited desire to escape—his guilt over not preventing his sister Rose's lobotomy, his guilt over his own socially and religiously condemned sexuality, and his guilt over not always being the successful writer he so craved to be. The character of Lord Byron in *Camino Real* seems a rare exception to this motif of the inability to escape. Byron leaves the Plaza easily, declaring his intent to "*Make Voyages!—Attempt them!*—there's nothing else" (2000: 797). But too few of us can make the voyages of Lord Byron; it is too fearful a proposition. Most of us choose nothing. Byron's ability to grasp freedom may be because he is based upon a real person who refused to be limited in his life. It is noticeable that while Kilroy appears to follow him away from the Plaza at the close of the play, he does so with a figure from fiction, Don Quixote, and not an actual person—which suggests that their potential for escape is similarly fictive. As Williams told Lincoln Barnett, "Every artist has a basic premise pervading his whole life, and that premise can provide the impulse to everything he creates. For me the dominating premise has been the need for understanding and tenderness and fortitude among individuals trapped by circumstance" (Barnett 1948: 116). The most we can hope for is a temporary relief—the possible catharsis that comes from the momentary kindness of strangers, or from the aftermath of violent acts, both physical and mental.

There is a network of imagery running throughout Williams's drama, much of it darkly violent that depicts, as Henry Schvey has suggested, "sacrifice and martyrdom," two key elements of tragedy and ones that underpin what Schvey correctly identifies as Williams's "tragic conception of life" (2011: 74–5). His tragic protagonists must suffer, and they are in full agreement with this fate.

Like Aristotle, Williams believed that watching violence enacted, and even hearing about it second-hand, can lead to a cathartic release (Williams 1978: 110). His first published short story, "Vengeance of Nitocris," depicted macabre violence and potential mental disability, with a Pharaoh torn to pieces by a mob, those who caused this murder later drowned en masse, and a final suicide by fire. Such hysteria and violence became keynotes in Williams's work. Neal A. Lester points out how the dramas in *27 Wagons Full of Cotton and Other One Act Plays* (1953) are filled with "adultery and sexual violence, brother-sister incest, crimes of passion, bestiality, lesbianism, and mental strain" (1998: 2–3). This seems the very stuff of Greek tragedy rather than Williams simply being out to shock. Williams links his characters' fates to their crimes, for as Francesca Oglesby Hitchcock explains, "Punished for their sexual desires, Williams's characters are raped, castrated, blowtorched, cannibalized, mutilated, murdered, or driven to madness" (1998: 163).

Many of his characters have connections to archetypal classical myths and Greek drama, from the offstage, often obscene mutilation of a variety of transgressors (Sebastian in *Suddenly Last Summer*, the title character of *Gnädiges Fräulein*, Val in *Orpheus Descending*, or Chance Wayne in *Sweet Bird of Youth*), to the echoes of Persephone (*The Glass Menagerie*), Phaedra, Artemis, and Aphrodite (*Cat on a Hot Tin Roof*), Venus, Oedipus, and Jocasta (*Suddenly Last Summer*), Orpheus and Aphrodite (*Kingdom of Earth*), Oedipus and Antigone (*Night of the Iguana*), Dionysius (*The Rose Tattoo*), or Orpheus and Eurydice (*Battle of Angels/Orpheus Descending*). He also includes a series of Adonises from Stanley Kowalski (*A Streetcar Named Desire*) and Chance Wayne (*Sweet Bird of Youth*) to Christopher Flanders (*The Milk Train Doesn't Stop Here Anymore*) to capture both the male and female gaze. He smoothly integrates these into his own personal symbolism, which turns many of these classical *doppelgängers* darker than the originals on which they were based.[2]

While many of Williams's characters might echo mythical archetypes, they are contemporized by a deeper sense of humanity and a far more muted possibility of greatness or triumph. The impact on Williams's work of his problematic relationship with his sister Rose and his lifelong guilt over what he viewed as his selfish abandonment of her is inescapable. Her ghostly presence haunts more plays than *The Glass Menagerie*, and as Michael Paller suggests, "The past and Rose have become Williams's jailers, have been his jailers for a long time," as he becomes trapped by his connection to the sister who had been trapped. Rose is forever represented in those characters driven insane by the demands of a society that simply cannot accept them, and she becomes a cypher for Williams himself. As Paller concludes, "His very deep love acquired shades of resentment and even hatred, which through guilt, bound him ever closer to Rose, until escape became impossible" (2002: 88, 90).[3]

Just like Oedipus, most of Williams's heroes and heroines search for an uncomfortable truth, and for them (just as for Oedipus) it will be a truth that ultimately destroys rather than uplifts, but it is a truth from which they cannot hide. Crippled by their own shame and guilt, they come to understand that they are doomed to walk this earth alone. As Williams once wrote, "My greatest affliction ... is perhaps the major theme of my writings, the affliction of loneliness that follows me like a shadow, a very ponderous shadow too heavy to drag after me all of my days and nights" (quoted in Anguelov 2012). As Williams has Val declare in *Orpheus Descending*, "We're all of us sentenced to solitary confinement inside our own skins, for life" (1971a: 271).

George Niesen has already pointed out the paradoxical nature of Williams's artist figures who are deeply creative *and* destructive and through their sensitivity all too often bring death on others (1977: 463), and Jacqueline O'Connor relates this to Williams's connection to the specter of madness—"the need to create art can be the source of both mental anguish and salvation"—that for Williams can "provide a means of keeping madness at bay" (1997: 70). So Williams writes at full tilt to keep his own life together, but the specters are always present, threatening to break through.

Williams's tragic dimension certainly draws on antiquity and is frequently embellished, as Aristotle directed, by music and spectacle, but it also draws on more modern considerations of that term. Offering a combination of the Aristotelian unities of place and action,[4] with a desire for cathartic action through violence and large emotion, mixed with Arthur Miller's tragedies of the common man, Williams adds his own unique twist. His plays are filled with tragic heroes, frequently balanced between guilt and/or insanity, and the biggest tragedy in their lives is not that they are nobly striving to correct a wrong, or that they even have committed a wrong, but that in a profoundly hostile world, they are largely unable to find the supportive kindness or love they need simply to survive. The even darker understanding that follows this is that it is these characters' own selves that prevent this.

As I have written elsewhere, "Williams's life can be read as a romantic quest with himself at the center as the flawed and misunderstood hero" (2010: 39). It is also, given Williams's awareness of human nature and assessment of his own self, a quest doomed to failure. The quest is to find comfort and acceptance in the world, but as Blanche explained, "I have always depended upon the kindness of strangers," and therein lies the rub. A passing respite might arrive through the attentions of a stranger, but once fully known, Williams's heroes always will be cruelly rejected because they are intrinsically rotten in the eyes of the larger society, and even more importantly in their own eyes. "For Williams," I have suggested, "while love and survival were definite goals for both himself and his more sympathetic characters, they were goals that he felt, in reality, were ultimately unobtainable" (2010: 38).

In Williams's mind, "Guilt is universal ... Hence guilty feelings, and hence violent aggressions, and hence the deep dark despair that haunts our dreams, our creative work, and makes us distrust each other" (Williams 1978: 109). Williams presents this sense of spiritual decay as a contamination rampant in the world in a physical sense, and at its heart lies the true pollution against which Williams struggles: homosexuality. In *Auto-Da-Fé* (Act of Faith), one of the short plays in *27 Wagons Full of Cotton*, he has Eloi, the unbalanced son of a domineering mother, burn a photograph of homosexuals, then the house, and finally himself, to eliminate such contamination! This is a pattern that will repeat: the attempt to eradicate one's own sin in the eradication of the self.

John Clum has pointed out the "connection between disease/ugliness and homosexual desire" in Williams's short story "Hard Candy," and acknowledges the resonance of such homophobic imagery throughout Williams's work (2010: 232). Williams, despite coming out of the closet, was never entirely comfortable with his own sexuality, always portraying his homosexual characters as predatory, self-hating, and doomed. As I have pointed out, Williams "never advocated for gay rights or described being homosexual as a happy condition because for him, growing up in a country that predominantly viewed homosexuality as a perversion or pathological abnormality, it could not be" (2010: 50). As Nancy Tischler suggests, "Brick simply can't acknowledge the homosexual tendency within himself because he accepts the world's judgment upon it" (1961: 214). As he explains to his father, "Don't you know how people *feel* about things like that? How *disgusted* they are by things like that" (2000: 948). It is a disgust Williams himself could not escape however much he reveled in his sexual conquests.

The solitary, sleazy homosexual Baron de Charlus from *Camino Real* speaks of his way of life as "corruption" and tells Kilroy, "The eyes are the windows of the soul, and yours are too gentle for someone who has as much as I to atone for" before he gets carted away in a barrel by the Streetcleaners, destroyed by his own wickedness (2000: 773–4). Sebastian from *Suddenly Last Summer* runs to the top of the town in what can only be seen as an act of self-immolation rather than toward the safety of the docks.[5] He is torn apart and eaten by the very boys on whom he had preyed. Homosexual couples are portrayed in a similarly negative fashion, usually with an older or more experienced man trying to take advantage of a younger one, and the specter of disease frequently present as a telling metaphor for the way in which Williams could not help but view such relationships.

In *Vieux Carré*, we watch the diseased painter Nightingale push himself on the Writer, for which he will soon die alone of tuberculosis. In *Small Craft Warnings*, Quentin, a self-hating gay screenwriter of sex movies, currently on the downslide, with a face described as *"burned thin by a fever that is not of the flesh"* (1971b: 160), picks up Bobby, a young man on a bicycling trip open to sexual exploration. Upset and confused over Bobby's indifference to his money and desire for affection, Quentin beats a hasty retreat, leaving Bobby to Leona, whose young gay brother, we learn, died of pernicious anemia. Frank Rich describes August (a grown-up version of the Writer from *Vieux Carré*, and a cipher again for Williams himself) in *Something Cloudy, Something Clear* as a "predatory tiger" as he stalks the terminally ill and sexually inexperienced dancer, Kip (1981: C3). Kip will die of a brain tumor, and August writes a poem asking God to end his own life before he gets jaded. Death is the only release for such conflicted individuals.

And Williams does not limit his depiction of characters corrupted by cancer or fatal tumors to homosexuals, as evidenced by King del Rey (*Red Devil Battery Sign*), Lot (*Kingdom of Earth*), Flora Goforth (*Milk Train*), Big Daddy (*Cat on a Hot Tin Roof*), Jane (*Vieux Carré*), or Jabe Torrance (*Orpheus Descending*), for this metaphor expands to include all those who have in a sense kept secrets and taken unfair advantage of someone else and must suffer as a result. Yet Williams has sympathy even for these rotten and rotting individuals, mostly because he sees himself as no different from them in his personal obsessions and desires.

The "goat-song" sacrifice of archetypal tragedy is the noble hero being martyred by the stern hands of fate. In more modern times, while heroes may have less stature, they nevertheless are meant to be enviable on some level for a willingness to sacrifice themselves for something they see as greater than their individual lives. But Williams offers us characters whose sacrifice has none of that sense of greater good, and yet they still demand our interest and sympathy. Schvey describes these as "a new order of tragic [heroes] for our age"—characters who do not follow an older tragic mold of exhibiting hubris or stature, but are notable for their "human weakness and vulnerability" (2011: 77).

Most of Williams's characters are from the pool of common humanity that Arthur Miller insisted should be the matter of modern tragedy (1949: 1, 3). They are truck drivers, a local sports reporter, travelling singers, teachers, a tourist guide, salesmen, and impoverished and tortured artists. They rarely are intelligent, respectable, or even likable, though they are by and large, distinctly American. What they also are are needy and guilt-ridden, desperate for the warmth of another human being, but reluctant to inflict their unworthy selves on that person. For Williams the simple act of living in America with its homegrown morality (based on its religious upbringing) was a tragic experience: what he saw as the "tragedy of Puritanism. That is life in America" (1978: 26). This belief is what makes him not just a writer of tragedy but a writer of specifically American tragedy. For him America was a place where "we love and betray each other in not quite the same breath but in two breaths that occur in fairly close sequence" (1978: 51). This dynamic was to him intrinsically American, given the contradictions of a set of religiously motivated pilgrims (caught between reverence of life and a disgust of whatever they held sinful) who arrived in the country to avoid persecution and ended up persecuting so many of its natives.

When the Greeks initially conceived of tragedy, a fundamental necessity seemed a belief in gods, fate, or at least some kind of divinity at the helm. Williams, partially raised and certainly supported by his Episcopal grandparents, maintains a dark thread of religious belief throughout his work. I suspect it lies at the basis of his self-rejection because of his, to him, indefensible homosexuality. In New Orleans, where Williams most likely had his first homosexual encounters, he pointedly explains how he "found the kind of freedom I had always needed. And the shock of it against the Puritanism of my nature has given me a theme, which I have never ceased exploiting" (Leverich 1995: 285): the tragedy of a man divided not against others but against himself.

Notes

1   Williams describes *Cat on a Hot Tin Roof* as a tragedy that follows classical rules with its unity of time and place and "magnitude of theme" in *Memoirs* (1975: 213). He also subtitled *Auto-da-fé* "a tragedy in one-act" and the pair of surreal one-acts *The Gnädiges*

Fräulein and *The Mutilated* were grouped under the title *Slapstick Tragedy*, but these are rare examples.

2   For extended discussions of such tropes, see Hethman (1965), Moritz (1985), Garcia (1988), and Barberà (2006).

3   Though not the first, Paller's essay is the most thorough consideration of the relationship between Williams and his sister and the ways in which she haunts his work in characters ranging from a "damaged, lost girl" to a "chattering, unwanted nuisance" (2002: 80).

4   The unity of time is more rarely observed by Williams than those of place and action, since for Williams, time tends to be too fluid to be restricted to a single day. As Arthur Miller suggested through the title of his autobiography *Timebends*, Williams also viewed time as a mutable bridge connecting the past, present, and future, and not something that could be viewed as strictly chronological.

5   In the movie version they even show Sebastian lying on an old stone altar as the boys attack.

References

Abbotson, Susan C. W. (2010), "Tennessee Williams on America," in Brenda Murphy (ed.), *Critical Insights: Tennessee Williams*, 38–57, Hackensack, NJ: Salem Press.

Anguelov, Zlatko (2013), "Tennessee Williams," Virtual Writing University, University of Iowa. Available online: https://www.writinguniversity.org/writers/tennessee-williams (accessed January 8, 2017).

Atkinson, Brooks (1948), "Everything Is Poetic," *The New York Times*, June 6: sec. 2, 1. Available online: http://query.nytimes.com/mem/archive-free/pdf?res=9A07E1D9153BE33BBC4E53DFB0668383659EDE (accessed January 8, 2017).

Barberà, Pau Gilabert (2006), "Literature and Mythology in Tennessee Williams's *Suddenly Last Summer*: Fighting against Venus and Oedipus." Available online: www.publicacions.ub.edu.

Barnett, Lincoln (1948), "Tennessee Williams," *Life* 24 (February 16): 116

Bauer, Leda (1951), "American Tragedy," *Theatre Arts* 35: 34–5.

Berkman, Leonard (1967), "The Tragic Downfall of Blanche DuBois," *Modern Drama* 10: 249–57.

Clum, John M. (2010), "'Something Cloudy, Something Clear': Homophobic Discourse in Tennessee Williams," in Brenda Murphy (ed.), *Critical Insights: Tennessee Williams*, 226–45, Hackensack, NJ: Salem Press.

Falk, Signi (1978), *Tennessee Williams*, revised edition, Boston: Twayne Publishers.

Fleche, Anne (1997), *Mimetic Disillusion: Eugene O'Neill, Tennessee Williams, and U.S. Dramatic Realism*, Tuscaloosa, AL: University of Alabama Press.

Garcia, A. Gómez (1988), *Mito y realidad en obra dramatica de Tennessee Williams*, Salamanca: Ediciones University de Salamanca.

Gassner, John (1960), *Theatre at the Crossroads*, New York: Holt.

Harwood, Britton J. (1977), "Tragedy as Habit: *A Streetcar Named Desire*," in Jac Tharpe (ed.), *Tennessee Williams: A Tribute*, 104–15, Jackson, MS: University Press of Mississippi.

Heilman, Robert B. (1977), "Tennessee Williams: Approaches to Tragedy," in Stephen S. Stanton (ed.), *Tennessee Williams*, 16–34, Englewood Cliffs, NJ: Prentice Hall.

Hethman, Robert (1965), "The Foul Rag-and-Bone Shop of the Heart," *Drama Critique* 8 (3): 94–102.

Hitchcock, Francesca Oglesby (1998), "The Milk Train Doesn't Stop Here Anymore," in Philip C. Kolin (ed.), *Tennessee Williams: A Guide to Research and Performance*, 158–65, Westport, CT: Greenwood Press.

Kerr, Walter (1959), "*Sweet Bird of Youth*, by Tennessee Williams," *New York Herald Tribune*, May 17: sec. 4, 1–2.

Lester, Neal A. (1998), "27 Wagons Full of Cotton and Other One Act Plays," in Philip C. Kolin (ed.), *Tennessee Williams: A Guide to Research and Performance*, 1–12, Westport, CT: Greenwood Press.

Leverich, Lyle (1995), *Tom: The Unknown Tennessee Williams*, New York: Norton.

Londré, Felicia (1977), "A *Streetcar* Running Fifty Years," in Matthew Roudané (ed.), *The Cambridge Companion to Tennessee Williams*, 45–66, Cambridge: Cambridge University Press.

Miller, Arthur (1949), "Tragedy and the Common Man," *The New York Times*, February 27, sec. 2: 1, 3. Available online: https://www.nytimes.com/books/00/11/12/specials/miller-common.html (accessed January 8, 2017).

Moritz, Helen (1985), "Apparent Sophoclean Echoes in Tennessee Williams' *Night of the Iguana*," *Classical and Modern Literature* 5: 305–14.

Niesen, George (1977), "The Artist against the Reality in the Plays of Tennessee Williams," in Jac Tharpe (ed.), *Tennessee Williams: A Tribute*, 463–93, Jackson, MS: University Press of Mississippi.

O'Connor, Jacqueline (1997), *Dramatizing Dementia: Madness in the Plays of Tennessee Williams*, Bowling Green, OH: Bowling Green State University Press.

Paller, Michael (2002), "The Escape That Failed Tennessee and Rose Williams," in Ralph Voss (ed.), *Magical Muse: Millennial Essays on*

Tennessee Williams, 70–90, Tuscaloosa, AL: University of Alabama Press.

Rich, Frank (1981), "Play: Adapted Memoirs of Tennessee Williams," *The New York Times*, September 11: C3. Available online: https://www.nytimes.com/books/00/12/31/specials/williams-cloudy.html (accessed January 8, 2017).

Schvey, Henry I. (2011), "The Tragic Poetics of Tennessee Williams," *Études Anglaises* 64 (1): 74–85.

Sharp, William (1962), "An Unfashionable View of Tennessee Williams," *Tulane Drama Review* 6: 160–71.

Tischler, Nancy (1961), *Tennessee Williams: Rebellious Puritan*, New York: Citadel.

Von Szeliski, John (1966), "Tennessee Williams and the Tragedy of Sensitivity," *Western Humanities Review* 20: 203–11.

Williams, Tennessee (1971a), *The Theatre of Tennessee Williams*, vol. 3, New York: New Directions.

Williams, Tennessee (1971b), *The Theatre of Tennessee Williams*, vol. 7, New York: New Directions.

Williams, Tennessee (1975), *Memoirs*, New York: New Directions.

Williams, Tennessee (1978), *Where I Live: Selected Essays*, New York: New Directions.

Williams, Tennessee (2000), *Plays 1937–1955*, New York: Library of America.

Williams, Tennessee (2011), *The Magic Tower and Other One Act Plays*, New York: New Directions.

7

Arthur Miller (1915–2005)

Stephen Marino
St. Francis College
and *The Arthur Miller Journal*

Arthur Miller always found himself in the middle of controversy—sometimes on purpose, often inadvertently. He caused considerable discussion with an essay he wrote shortly after the Broadway premiere of *Death of a Salesman* on February 10, 1949, in which he responded to critics' concerns about whether the play should be considered a tragedy. Viewed in light of Greek and Shakespearean tragedy, critics wondered whether tragedy was possible any longer in twentieth-century America: Could Willy Loman or any modern character possess the qualities associated with a classical tragic hero? The chief drama critic of *The New York Times*, Brooks Atkinson, led those who saw the play's tragic dimensions. In his review, he wrote that Miller "conveys this elusive tragedy in terms of simple things ... Chronicler of one frowsy corner of the American scene, he evokes a wraith-like tragedy out of it that spins through the many scenes of his play and gradually envelops the audience" (1949: 27).

On February 27—not quite three weeks after *Salesman*'s premiere—Miller threw himself into the public debate by publishing

"Tragedy and the Common Man," a controversial essay that challenges Aristotelian and Renaissance principles of tragedy and remains one of the most important commentaries on the tragic hero in modern drama. He rejects the notion that tragedy is an archaic form that chronicles the fall only of high figures, declaring that the "common man is as apt a subject for tragedy in its highest sense as kings were." Like Aristotle in the *Poetics*, Miller considers the effect of the tragic hero's action on the audience; however, rather than grounding the audience's response in feelings of pity and fear or their understanding of the hero's *hamartia*, Miller posits that "The tragic feeling is evoked in us when we are in the presence of a character who is ready to lay down his life, if need be, to secure one thing—his sense of personal dignity." Miller then considers great classical tragic heroes using this lens, seeing each of them as an individual "attempting to gain his 'rightful' position in his society." Willy Loman never is mentioned here, but the implication is clear: Willy too is this kind of tragic hero, a tragic hero for modern America ([1949a] 1996: 4).

Miller further maintains that Aristotelean *hamartia*, the misguiding possession of a tragic flaw, is not limited to the lofty. Tragic flaws are not a variety of weaknesses of character; rather, this particular flaw exists only when a character is passive against a "challenge to his dignity." Thus, tragedy is "the consequence of a man's total compulsion to evaluate himself justly." Miller rejects the idea that tragedy is pessimistic; he views people's struggles to achieve their humanity and dignity as optimistic ([1949a] 1996: 4, 6).

One month later, Miller clarified his view of tragedy as optimistic in an essay in *The New York Herald Tribune*, making a clear distinction between the tragic and the pathetic. Both tragedy and pathos stimulate "sadness, sympathy, identification and even fear," but tragedy is distinguished by delivering knowledge or enlightenment to the audience, knowledge that pertains to the "right way of living in the world." For Miller, "tragedy is the most accurately balanced portrayal of the human being in his struggle for happiness" ([1949b] 1996: 9, 11).

In the "The Urgency of Tragedy Now," the introduction to the 2014 special edition of *PMLA*, Helene P. Foley and Jean E. Howard consider how "twentieth century playwrights torque the structures and conventions of tragedy to invent new configurations of it" (619). Arthur Miller's vision of tragedy was formed at the University of Michigan, where as an English major he was exposed to the Greek tragedians, Shakespeare, German Expressionism, and early modern playwrights, such as August Strindberg and Henrik Ibsen. He also read one-act protest plays about miners and stevedores and was moved by the social-protest work of Clifford Odets. After winning the Hopwood Award at Michigan for his first play, *No Villain*, Miller took the playwriting class of Kenneth T. Rowe, who taught him the "dynamics of play construction" in the classical mode (Miller 1987: 227). In essays produced throughout his career,[1] Miller acknowledged the influence of Ibsen, O'Neill, Shaw, and Wilder. In Miller's autobiography, *Timebends*, he says that seeing Tennessee Williams's *A Streetcar Named Desire* allowed him to speak "full throat" as a playwright (Miller 1987: 182). Consequently, Miller's vision of tragedy represents—in theory and practice—his unique amalgam of Aristotle's *Poetics*, English Renaissance tragedies, and the dramas of the late nineteenth and early twentieth century that feature middle and working-class protagonists.

Miller's reputation rests mainly on the four great plays he wrote at the start of his career: *All My Sons* (1947), *Death of a Salesman* (1949), *The Crucible* (1953), and *A View From the Bridge* (one-act version, 1955; two-act version, 1956), and much of the discussion of these plays still centers on questions about the nature of modern American tragedy. The protagonist in each of these plays meets a "challenge to his dignity" and consequently acts in "total compulsion to evaluate himself justly." In these plays, Joe Keller, Willy Loman, John Proctor, and Eddie Carbone initiate the action that ultimately results in their tragic downfall, but each is thrust into circumstances he did not create. For Miller, the forces of modern society play as powerful a role as the gods, fate, religion, and human frailties did in Greek and Renaissance tragedy. Miller also insists that all tragedy is about the "birds coming home to roost" (Carroll 1989: 12; Miller [1999] 2016: 294): that past actions have present consequences. In Miller's plays, the tragedy often has roots in the past, and what we witness on stage are the characters' struggles with the present consequences of those past actions.

All My Sons, Miller's first Broadway hit, illustrates this structure. The drama focuses on Joe Keller, a small factory owner, finally forced to confront his legal and moral crime of knowingly manufacturing defective airplane parts during the Second World War, which resulted in the deaths of twenty-one pilots. Joe denied his part in the event—which occurred three years earlier—by blaming his business partner, who has been in jail for the crime, while Joe has gone on to continue his successful business. The play dramatizes the unraveling of this cover-up. When Joe ultimately is forced to confront the ramifications of his crime for his family, society, and particularly the dead pilots—whom he finally recognizes as "all my sons"—he kills himself. According to Miller, *All My Sons* is "designed to bring a man into the direct path of the consequences he has wrought" (Miller [1957] 1996: 130).

All My Sons is complicated because Joe Keller not only creates the circumstance—the manufacturing of the parts—that ends in tragedy for him, but he and his wife, Kate, also create an illusion of social respectability that belies their crime and cover-up. This false atmosphere is Joe's attempt to respond to what he perceived as an assault on his dignity—his reputation—when he was accused and arrested. His pride at walking down the street on the day he was acquitted—the court paper exonerating him in his pocket—is his continued denial of his responsibility, a denial so self-deluding that he fails to realize that many of his neighbors are wise to the "fast one" he pulled to get out of jail by blaming his partner. Neighbor Sue Bayliss professes disdain for the Keller's reputation as "The Holy Family."

When confronted by his son Chris after the cover-up is revealed, Joe rationalizes his action by blaming economic forces: the pressure of running a successful business, the threat of being shut down if the faulty manufacturing process were discovered. He explains to Chris, "I did it for you" (Miller [1947] 2010: 77), seeing his action as being driven by his fully justified desire to fulfill the American Dream of financial success for his family

Joe's ultimate awareness of his responsibility comes only when a letter is revealed that Joe's son Larry, a Second World War pilot, wrote before he purposely crashed his plane in shame after learning of his father's company's involvement with the faulty engine parts. Understanding that responsibility leads to accepting different kinds of consequences in different ways, Joe acknowledges that the Second World War pilots were "all his sons," and the only way he can accept social responsibility for his crime is by going to jail. However, he has declared to Kate that there is nothing greater—nothing more important to him—than his relationships with his sons. "If there is something bigger than that, I'll put a bullet in my head" (Miller [1947] 2010: 83), which is exactly what he does as he now confronts both Larry's and Chris's rejection.

Many tragedies end in the protagonist's self-punishment for past transgressions, and in suicide Joe Keller joins this group. Jail would redress his poor judgment and social irresponsibility, but it would not redeem his lost dignity—his new-found sense of shame and disappointment in himself as he confronts the ways he has betrayed the people he valued most: his sons, Larry and Chris. It is the confrontation with that shame—a deep, personal sense of the ways he has betrayed his own dignity—that kills him.

In his masterpiece *Death of a Salesman*, Arthur Miller created a character whose every action—in the past and present—is a reaction to what he perceives as assault on his dignity. Alfred R. Ferguson in "The Tragedy of the American Dream in *Death of a Salesman*" maintains that the play "dramatizes the tragic life and death of the American Dream. Willy Loman, the salesman of the story, is the American Dream personified" ([1978] 2006: 187). The drama depicts the last days in Willy's life, a life where he has spent thirty-six years as a traveling salesman pursuing the success that the American Dream promises only to find that personal satisfaction, a sense of self-worth, and economic security have eluded him. The play depicts the moments when Willy looks back over his life and confronts this failure. Perhaps this is why audiences and readers continue to identify with Willy: the assault that Willy perceives on his dignity is an assault on all who identify with the American Dream.

The actions that cause Willy's ultimate downfall occur years before the play begins, but are reenacted crucially in his imaginings: his salesmanship inspired by Dave Singleman, his decision not to go with his brother Ben to Alaska, Biff's great success as a high school football player and his discovery of Willy with the woman in the Boston hotel room. Are we to see Willy's tragedy as the pathetic demise of a small man, a man who perverted his dreams, or is Willy the fateful victim of American economic forces and pernicious ideals? Our attraction to Willy is our identification with his desperation to justify his life, to achieve some dignity and "not crawl into his grave like an old dog" (Miller [1949] 1976: 56).

John Proctor in *The Crucible* often is viewed as the most heroic of Miller's tragic figures because of his stand against the injustices of the Puritan theocracy in the Salem witch hunt—but Proctor is complicated, a prime example of Miller's fascination with questions of personal character and the inconsistencies between public and private behavior. Proctor has committed adultery with a teenage serving girl, Abigail Williams, betraying his wife, Elizabeth, and exacerbating the tension in their marriage. When he seeks to make a stand against the Puritan court, he feels himself morally unworthy of such heroism: living with secret sin and shame, he sees himself as a moral fraud. Like Willy Loman, he is both the victim of forces he cannot control and the maker of his own collapsing dignity.

In "Proctor, The Moral Hero in *The Crucible*," Sydney Howard White makes a strong case that Proctor is the first clearly recognizable tragic hero in Miller's canon. White asserts that the most important aspect of Miller's definition of tragedy is the protagonist's "discovery of the moral law." According to White, Miller's tragic heroes are compelled to judge themselves according to a set of moral convictions that drive them to go against a wrong in society; their tragedy is their defeat in that conflict. Miller's dramas redefine tragedy as "predicaments of the man of determined action in modern life" (White [1970] 1997: 148). Proctor is exactly this type of dramatic character, one who reacts against injustice and defends the most important characteristic of Miller's tragic hero: his sense of personal dignity. But unlike Joe Keller and Willy Loman, Proctor ultimately is concerned with more than merely his own dignity. He dies defending not only himself but also the dignity of all the other innocent victims of the Puritan court's brutal hypocrisy. This gives his tragedy a broader dimension than the downfalls of the heroes of Miller's earlier plays.

White also stresses that Miller's truly tragic hero must discover and defend some truth, which he feels Joe Keller and Willy Loman do not. He argues that Joe kills himself not to defend a moral truth but because he has violated one, and Willy remains deluded throughout *Salesman*. Willy's son Biff, White suggests, is the character who makes moral discoveries and who should be seen as the hero of the play. In a similar way, White argues, Proctor should be seen as a tragic hero for modern times, despite being a seventeenth-century farmer. As an allegory for McCarthyism, *The Crucible* focuses moral issues that continue in modern times, particularly, to use Miller's own words, how "the sin of public terror divests man of conscience" (quoted in White [1970] 1997: 150). Proctor discovers his moral vision and maintains his conscience—and thus his dignity—to become the quintessential Miller tragic hero. At play's end, Proctor's recognition is total: he recognizes and acts to rectify his personal flaws, his flaws as a husband, his flaws as a Christian, and most importantly, the flaws of an unjust society.

Unlike some of Miller's earlier plays, *A View from the Bridge* had a long gestation. In 1947, after his success with *All My Sons*, Miller became intrigued by the Italian immigrant culture of the Brooklyn docks after he learned about Pete Panto, a young longshoreman who had challenged the corruption of the powerful Mafia leadership of the seaman's union and then mysteriously disappeared. Miller was fascinated by Panto's heroism. As he investigated this story, he heard another about a longshoreman who had informed to the Immigration Bureau on two brothers to break up the relationship between one of them and his niece. Not only did the informer become a pariah, local gossips claimed he had been killed by one of the brothers. In the essay "On Social Plays" (1955), which he wrote as an introduction to the published, one-act version of *Bridge*, Miller explained that when he first heard the tale, he thought he had heard it before as "some re-enactment of a Greek myth" ([1955] 1996: 67). To Miller, the story seemed millennia old and almost the work of fate.

Eddie Carbone is another puzzling Miller protagonist.[2] Like Joe Keller, Willy Loman, and John Proctor, he is responsible for actions that have devastating familial and even societal consequences, but even at the end of the play he is much less self-aware than these earlier Miller heroes, particularly with regard to the play's central focus: his desire for his niece, Catherine. Audiences are shocked and appalled by much of what Eddie refuses to see: that his feelings for Catherine are borderline incestuous; that he ignores his wife, Beatrice, in ways that are abusive; that his attack on Rodolpho's masculinity may contain homoerotic motives; and that his snitching to the immigration authorities is not motivated by an honorable concern for Catherine's well-being but by embittered jealousy and vengeance.

Functioning like a Greek chorus, the play's narrator, the lawyer Alfieri, judges Eddie to be "as good a man as he had to be in a life that was hard," but Alfieri goes on later to explain that a passion "had moved into [Eddie's] body, like a stranger" (Miller [1956] 2010: 18, 39). Eddie's passion outweighs his reason to the point where he refuses to admit its existence and danger even when it is pointed out to him by both Alfieri and Beatrice (Miller [1956] 2010: 43, 77). When Alfieri suspects that Eddie is about to call the immigration authorities, he warns him that the tightknit, Italian community of the Brooklyn docks will punish him viciously as an informer. Eddie has seen before how informers are punished; nonetheless, he places the call. Eddie even seems unable to understand how questionable his insulting kissing of Rodolpho in their fight seems to other people. Eddie merely insists that he wanted to prove to Catherine that Rodolpho "ain't right" (Miller [1956] 2010: 60).

The best way to understand Eddie is in the context of the cultural codes of his Sicilian-American immigrant culture in the Red Hook section of Brooklyn in the mid-1950s. Donald P. Costello has analyzed what he calls Eddie's "circles of responsibilities" (1993: 443): self, family, society, the universe. The play shows Eddie's violation of the cultural and moral codes that govern each of them. Certainly much of the audience's reaction to Eddie's actions arises out of what we judge as the immorality of his violation of cultural codes. His borderline incest with his niece and informing on his wife's cousins doom him in his society, and he is cast out. Nonetheless, he is reacting to a perceived assault on his dignity when Marco accuses him publicly of snitching; what he fails to see is that it is a dignity he himself has besmirched.

Like much of Western literature, tragedy historically has tended to tell the stories of men. Miller has been criticized for his focus on males in his plays and his relegation of women to background roles. However, recent critics have examined the power and influence of female characters and the intersection of masculine and feminine roles and identities in Miller's conception of tragedy. While assaults on women's senses of dignity are not central to Miller's plays, women are essential to men's sense of dignity here, affirming or even bestowing it. Women restore order to the chaos the males create so that the plays end not in despair but in hope—fulfilling Miller's requirement that tragedy be optimistic, not pessimistic. This optimism fulfills Miller's demand that tragedy deliver knowledge or enlightenment to the audience. As the restorers of order, women often are the last characters to speak in many Miller plays, providing closure to the tragic events.

When Arthur Miller wrote *All My Sons*, his working title was *The Sign of the Archer* because his original idea was to center the action on Kate Keller's obsession with astrology. The play became a father-son saga, but Kate remained central to the action. Her friendliness, concern, and infectious warmth are a veneer for her collusion with Joe. Kate is a controlling force over Joe and Chris, a threatening power to be reckoned with. When she tells Joe at the end of Act 1 to "Be smart" (Miller [1947] 2010: 43), it is a powerful command. Kate cannot save Joe, but she seeks to restore order at the end of the play by commanding her son Chris to "Live" (Miller [1947] 2010: 91)—perhaps hoping to help him to preserve the dignity that Joe did not deserve.

Linda's role in *Salesman* has prompted much debate. Janet Balakian maintains she clearly is a figure who typifies the marginalization of women. She functions to support Willy in his massive dreams, but also provides an essential stability as Willy pursues his vision of the American Dream. Linda shows knowledge of the "complex social factors that have dehumanized" Willy when she tells her sons that Howard Wagner has taken away his salary (Balakian 1995: 122). Charlotte Canning agrees, maintaining that Linda is vital to Willy as his "foundation and support," while he nonetheless asserts a condescending control over her that he cannot have in business. For Canning, Linda has vital dramatic importance as the character who points to the universally human elements in Willy's experience. Without her "Attention must be paid" speech, Willy would be merely an undistinguished failure unable to achieve his dreams rather than a tragic hero who embodies something fundamental about our shared humanity (Canning 1995: 73).

Linda's most significant speech is in the "Requiem" at Willy's grave. Miller structured the scene to give each major character a voice in expressing the meaning of Willy's life and death. Charley declares, "A salesmen has got to dream"; Biff that "The man didn't know who he was"; and Happy that Willy "had the only dream a man can have—to come out number one." Linda, however, speaks the final words of the play. Declaring, "We're free, we're free" (Miller [1949] 2010: 139), she gives dignity to Willy's struggle for happiness in his pursuit of the American Dream.

Similarly, in *The Crucible* Elizabeth Proctor plays a crucial role in John Proctor's coming to understand how his sense of sin and guilt impedes his ability to see himself as good. Elizabeth is a crucial catalyst in helping Proctor to find his moral compass and the innate goodness of his "name." In Act 4, Elizabeth urges, "But let none be your judge. There is no higher judge under heaven than Proctor is ... It is a good man" who defies the injustice of the Puritan theocracy. Her final words of the play publically proclaim Proctor's dignity and bring closure to his tragedy when she says to Hale: "He have his goodness now" (Miller [1953] 1976: 137, 145).

In *A View from the Bridge*, Beatrice wields a strength that belies her role as a subservient Sicilian housewife. A mediator who controls much of the action, she is particularly adept at reading the tension among Eddie, Rodolpho, and Catherine, and the sources of Eddie's sexual estrangement. She is the first character to understand the responsibility she, Catherine, and Eddie all share in the tragedy: "Whatever happened we all done it" (Miller [1956] 2010: 75). With this remark she admits her and Catherine's place in the ensuing tragedy, but at the play's end both women keep the dramatic focus on Eddie by calling out his name, returning to him the dignity he so desperately feared Marco had taken away. In reaction, Eddie calls, "My Bea" (Miller [1956] 2010: 137), indicating their reconciliation and his recognition of the tragedy he has caused all of them.

Although Miller's fame rests primarily on these four plays from the 1940s and 1950s; his career lasted nearly sixty years until his death in 2005. It is intriguing to see how he altered his tragic vision as he remained prolific but his plays generally failed to be acclaimed, at least in the United States. Miller continued his interest in themes from the early works: challenges to dignity, the ways the present emerges from the past, and the paradox of denial. But in plays from the 1960s—*After the Fall, Incident at Vichy,* and *The Price*—he began exploring his characters' psychological complexity more fully than before, where he saw their responses to cultural demands and stresses as the source of their tragic downfalls. This psychological exploration continued into his works in the 1990s, such as *The Ride Down Mt. Morgan, The Last Yankee, Broken Glass,* and *Mr. Peters' Connections.*

Some critics claim these more psychological dramas fail to be tragedies because acceptance of responsibility and consequences no longer results in death as punishment. Often characters in these later plays are brought to the verge of death, as in *Incident at Vichy* or *Broken Glass*, but Miller's changed vision perhaps is expressed best by Lyman Felt in *The Ride Down Mt. Morgan* when he shouts: "Life! Life! Fuck death and dying!" (Miller 1991: 110–11). The characters in these plays still struggle for self-knowledge and forgiveness—which for Miller seems to be endemic to the human condition—but their situations seem less desperate than those of the characters in the earlier plays.

Whatever differences there may be between Miller's early and later works, the core concern he identified at the heart of the human condition and that formed the basis of his vision of tragedy remains consistent not only throughout his own plays but also in the works of other major American dramatists. Minnie Wright, Emily Webb, Blanche Dubois, the four haunted Tyrones, George and Martha, Troy Maxson, Shelly Levene ... which of these is not responding to assaults on his or her dignity? Which does not demand to be recognized in a rightful place in society? Which does not desire to be evaluated justly?

Notes

1   Although Arthur Miller's reputation derives largely from his famous plays, he also wrote fiction, reportage, and screenplays. As an essayist he discussed theatre and hot-button political and social issues. In the introduction to the original edition of Miller's *Theatre Essays,* Robert Martin asserted that Miller was the most significant dramatist-essayist since George Bernard Shaw (1996: 20).

2   For an expanded discussion of Eddie's character, see Marino (2013).

References

Atkinson, Brooks (1949), "At the Theatre," *The New York Times,* February 11: 27. Available online: https://timesmachine.nytimes.com /timesmachine/1949/02/11/85634870.html?pageNumber=27 (accessed January 15, 2017).

Balakian, Jan (1995), "Beyond the Male Locker Room: *Death of a Salesman* from a Feminist Perspective," in Matthew C. Roudané (ed.), *Approaches to Teaching Miller's "Death of a Salesman,"* 115–24, New York: Modern Language Association of America.

Canning, Charlotte (1995), "Is This a Play about Women? A Feminist Reading," in Steven Centola (ed.), *The Achievement of Arthur Miller: New Essays,* 69–76, Dallas: Contemporary Research Press.

Carroll, James and Helen Epstein (1989), "Seeing Eye to Eye," *Boston Review* 14 (February): 12–13.

Costello, Donald P. (1993), "Arthur Miller's Circles of Responsibility: *A View from the Bridge* and Beyond," *Modern Drama* 36: 443–53.

Ferguson, Alfred R. ([1978] 2006), "The Tragedy of the American Dream in *Death of a Salesman,*" *Thought* 33: 83–98, reprinted in Steven R. Centola and Michelle Cirulli (eds.), *The Critical Response to Arthur Miller,* 185–99, Critical Responses in Arts and Letters 45, Westport, CT: Praeger.

Foley, Helene P. and Jean E. Howard (2014), "The Urgency of Tragedy Now," *PMLA* 129 (4): 617–34.

Marino, Stephen (2013), "Commentary on *A View from the Bridge,*" in Enoch Brater (ed.), *A Student Handbook to the Plays of Arthur Miller,* 157–204, London: Bloomsbury.

Martin, Robert A. (1996), "Introduction to the Original Edition," in Robert A. Martin and Steven R. Centola (eds.), *The Theatre Essays of Arthur Miller,* xix–xliii, New York: Da Capo Press.

Miller, Arthur ([1947] 2010), *All My Sons,* Toby Zinman (ed.), London: Methuen Drama.

Miller, Arthur ([1949] 1976), *Death of a Salesman,* New York: Penguin Books.

Miller, Arthur ([1949a] 1996), "Tragedy and the Common Man," *The New York Times,* February 27, Sec. 2: 1, 3, reprinted in Robert A. Martin and Steven R. Centola (eds.), *The Theatre Essays of Arthur Miller,* 3–7, New York: Da Capo Press. Available online: http://www.nytimes.com/books/00/11/12/specials/miller-common.html (accessed January 15, 2017).

Miller, Arthur ([1949b] 1996), "The Nature of Tragedy," *The New York Herald Tribune,* March 27, Sec. 5: 1–2, reprinted in Robert A. Martin and Steven R. Centola (eds.), *The Theatre Essays of Arthur Miller,* 8–11, New York: Da Capo Press.

Miller, Arthur ([1953] 1976), *The Crucible,* New York: Penguin Books.

Miller, Arthur ([1955] 1996), "On Social Plays," reprinted in Robert A. Martin and Steven R. Centola (eds.), *The Theatre Essays of Arthur Miller,* 51–68, New York: Da Capo Press.

Miller, Arthur ([1956] 2010), *A View From the Bridge,* Stephen Marino (ed.), London: Methuen Drama.

Miller, Arthur ([1957] 1996), "Introduction to the *Collected Plays*," reprinted in Robert A. Martin and Steven R. Centola (eds.), *The Theatre Essays of Arthur Miller*, 113–74, New York: Da Capo Press.

Miller, Arthur (1987), *Timebends: A Life*, New York: Grove Press.

Miller, Arthur (1991), *The Ride Down Mt. Morgan*, New York: Penguin.

Miller, Arthur ([1999] 2016), "*The Price*—The Power of the Past," reprinted in *Arthur Miller: Collected Essays*, introduction by Susan C. W. Abbotson, 291–5, New York: Penguin Books.

White, Sydney Howard ([1970] 1997), "Proctor, The Moral Hero in *The Crucible*," in *The Merrill Guide to Arthur Miller*, Columbus, OH: Charles E. Merrill. Reprinted in Thomas Siebold (ed.), *Readings on Arthur Miller*, 148–51, San Diego: Greenhaven.

8

Edward Albee (1928–2016)

Natka Bianchini
Loyola University Maryland

A half-century ago, Raymond Williams declared that the word "tragedy" has been "persistently and perhaps viciously misused" (1966: 14). This is not surprising when one considers that the genre is more than twenty-five centuries old, and theorization about its principles stretches back at least to Aristotle and his *Poetics*. Our task in this anthology is to consider tragedy in modern American drama through the words and stories of our most articulate and successful dramatists. I take as my starting point Williams's notion that there is no such thing as universal tragedy. Tragedy and tragic theory can be interpreted only through a careful consideration of particular societal conventions and institutions (1966: 44–5). It always is bound to a specific culture, time, and place.

Nonetheless, American playwrights continue to wrestle with the questions Aristotle set forth. Who is the ideal tragic hero? What constitutes a tragic flaw? How do we understand catharsis? All of the playwrights discussed in this volume can be seen reckoning with this legacy while simultaneously forging a view of tragedy unique to our own era. My contribution on Albee is situated in this liminal place between the classical and the contemporary.

With a playwright as punctilious about language as Edward Albee, one would expect a correlating precision regarding genre categorization for his plays; however, there has been little critical consensus over how to classify his oeuvre. Many of his best-known works are considered dark comedies; others, dramas. The one genre that consistently is ascribed to him is theatre of the absurd, a particular blend of the tragic and the comic that often helps us to understand Albee's worldview and his approach to theatre.

At the heart of Albee's plays one finds characters with a deep yearning for connection—an almost biological imperative to engage meaningfully with other beings. This motif of striving to connect recurs throughout Albee's work. Often, the possibility of connection is foisted upon his characters in the form of an intrusion. No matter the circumstance or attempt to overcome it, Albee's protagonists always are unable to fulfill this fundamental promise of emotional connection; rather than achieving true communion, they are left merely tolerating their intruders. It is this failure to connect that lies at the center of Albee's tragic vision: a perpetual striving to reach others that inevitably leads to loss. Albee's work is a meditation on the essential loneliness at the heart of the human spirit.

Albee's first published play, *The Zoo Story*, premiered in Berlin (1959) and New York (1960) on a double bill alongside Beckett's *Krapp's Last Tape*. *Krapp and Zoo*, as the bill came to be called, was an unprecedented success in the history of off-Broadway, a movement still nascent in the early sixties, establishing a connection between the young Edward Albee and the playwright most associated with theatre of the absurd, Samuel Beckett (Bianchini 2015: 58–9).

This association was cemented further with the publication of Martin Esslin's *Theatre of the Absurd* (1961), one of the most influential books of theatre criticism of the past century. Esslin identified the European writers Beckett, Ionesco, Genet, and Adamov as creators of this new genre, although the writers themselves had no publicly shared philosophical or artistic mission. By grouping them together based on key stylistic and contextual similarities, Esslin single-handedly provided a framework for our understanding of a new kind of theatre.

Esslin's use of "absurd" comes directly from Camus's *The Myth of Sisyphus*, where "absurd" means "out of harmony with reason or propriety, incongruous, unreasonable, illogical" (Esslin 2004: 23). Camus described man's search for clarity amid an insane world as truly absurd, and Esslin saw in these post–Second World War playwrights an affinity with this philosophy: language divorced from meaning, time and place generalized and non-specific, archetypal characters, the abandonment of linear plot structure ... all of these theatrical elements illuminate the Sisyphean futility of trying to make meaning in a meaningless world.

Beyond the four central writers, Esslin included Albee as a proselyte of the form based on several of his early plays, including *The Zoo Story*, *The Sandbox*, *The American Dream*, *The Death of Bessie Smith*, and *Fam and Yam*. Certainly Albee's plots contain elements of the absurd—for example, the archetypal characters Mommy, Daddy, and Grandma in *The American Dream*—but on the whole, his plays are decidedly more realistic than Esslin's absurdist exemplars. Rather than language divorced from reason, such as Lucky's "think" in *Godot* or the final argument that dissolves into nonsense in *The Bald Soprano*, Albee's plays are dense with lexical wizardry. His characters engage in jocund debate over etymology and declension; the situations and locations of his plays tend much more toward realism, even naturalism; and his plots tend to be linear, rather than circular—at least in arc, if not in resolution.

Albee is the only American writer considered in Esslin's original volume, and subsequently many scholars have wrestled with the imprecise fit between absurdist perspectives and American social ideals. Esslin himself suggested that since the American homeland did not experience the devastation of the Second World War, Americans were ill-suited to embrace the bleak existentialism at the heart of European absurdism (2004: 311), a nihilism best expressed by Beckett in *Waiting for Godot*: "They give birth astride of a grave, the light gleams an instant, then it's night once more" (1954: 103). On the contrary, America experienced a period of intense economic growth and prosperity in the postwar years. Coupled with our deeply entrenched, mythic ideals of opportunity, freedom, prosperity, and the American Dream, it is easy to understand the difficulty of tying American writers of the mid-twentieth century, such as Albee, to the existentialist philosophy of postwar Europe.

Indeed, Albee himself was quick to denounce the absurdist label, writing in *The New York Times*, "I don't like labels; they can be facile and can lead to non-think on the part of the public" (1962a: 11). But taxonomies can persist stubbornly, and the absurdist moniker has trailed Albee throughout his half-century career, despite his plays' obvious and clear departures from the genre in both form and substance.

Recently Michael Y. Bennett has reworked Esslin's criteria for absurdism in the 1950s to 1970s, making the idea of tragicomedy more central (2015). This framework is better suited to Albee's canon, allowing us to integrate his incisive wit and biting humor alongside his character's lost and forbidden loves, loneliness, and failure to communicate. For Albee, tragicomedy is the dominant mode for expressing his tragic view. Time and again in his plays, comedy—which may at first arise from absurdist conventions—gives way to the inevitable tragedy that lies beneath. Zinman argues that tragicomedy is a form unique to the twentieth century, with roots in Chekhov, and labels almost all of Albee's plays "tragicomedies" (2008: 5, 148).

Nowhere in Albee's oeuvre are his views on tragedy laid out as explicitly as in his 2002 play *The Goat, or Who Is Sylvia?* Perhaps, after four decades of writing plays mislabeled as comedies or theatre of the absurd, Albee was tired of facile categorizations. Here he modeled his play on the conventions of Greek tragedy as set forth by Aristotle, and subtitled it "Notes toward a Definition of Tragedy."

The Goat, a 100-minute, intermission-less play, focuses on the Gray family. Martin is a fabulously successful architect who has just turned fifty. He is happily married to Stevie, and they share their upper-middle class home with their gay, teenage son, Billy. Soon it is revealed that Martin is having sexual intercourse with a goat he has named Sylvia. What's more, Martin's congress with the animal is not merely a coded attempt to compel audiences to examine their own prejudices about the limits of the morally reprobate in regard to sexual behavior. Martin confesses that he is deeply and spiritually in love with Sylvia, even while insisting that he continues to love Stevie. Emotionally shattered by this revelation, Stevie responds in kind with a literal shattering of vases, plates, and other decorative items carefully placed throughout the couple's immaculate living room. At the end of the play, amid shards of broken glass and pottery, Stevie returns covered in blood, dragging Sylvia's slaughtered carcass behind her.

When setting out to write what would become *The Goat, or Who Is Sylvia?* Albee wanted to explore the theme of tolerance, specifically, "the limits of our tolerance of the behavior of others than ourselves, especially when such behavior ran counter to what we believed to be acceptable social and moral boundaries" (2005:

259). His initial idea concerned a doctor intentionally infecting himself with HIV in order to better understand his patients' suffering. The play was to have focused on the immediate condemnation provoked by the doctor's actions, and asked audiences to reflect on how we discern the boundaries of acceptable behavior. Albee never wrote that play. As is customary in his creative method, he spent a long time incubating the idea, fleshing out characters to the point where they had entire conversations in his head, but before he had the chance to write an initial draft, a play with almost an identical premise appeared in a small off-Broadway production (2005: 260). Albee nonetheless remained committed to exploring tolerance, so he abandoned his initial idea and wrote *The Goat* instead.

The Goat is structured as a classical Greek tragedy and follows all the major characteristics outlined in Aristotle's *Poetics*. It adheres to the unity of time (the events unfold in a twenty-four-hour period over two days), unity of place (the Gray's living room), and unity of action. The tragic hero, Martin, while not literally a king, is modern-day royalty. On the eve of his fiftieth birthday, he has been crowned with the Pritzker prize—the highest honor one can receive in architecture—and also been selected to design The World City, a "two hundred billion dollar dream city of the future ... in the wheatfields of our Middle West" (2008: 553). As introduced by best friend, Ross Tuttle, Martin is an "extraordinary person" (2008: 552), an important requirement for the tragic hero, whose reversal of fortune must be suitably terrifying. Martin is undone not by shame or guilt stemming from an inability to control his bestial desires. His *hamartia* is that he does not comprehend why he should feel ashamed of his relationship with Sylvia.

Albee weaves many allusions to classical Greek tragedy into the text, such as a reference to the Eumenides that foreshadows Stevie's rage (2008: 551). In the play's second scene, where Stevie reacts to Martin's revelation, Albee includes several explicit references to tragedy. Martin warns Stevie to "shut [her] tragic mouth" (597) so that he may finally unburden himself of the entire story, and a short while later, when asked what she is doing, Stevie replies "being tragic" before uttering a series of feral howls (598–9). Stevie's pain and fury over the devastation Martin has brought upon their family erupts in her destruction of their home. As Martin's secrets come spilling out one after another, Stevie encourages him to "go ahead, vomit it all up" (595), a direct reference to catharsis. The Greek prohibition against violence onstage is kept intact; Stevie murders Sylvia offstage, with only the gruesome aftermath presented for the audience's view. Finally, Albee's decision to make Sylvia a goat, as opposed to some other animal, is a classical reference. The word "tragedy" comes from the Greek *tragoidia*, or goat-song. It is believed that perhaps a goat was sacrificed as part of the festival of Dionysius during which the original Greek plays were performed.

The Goat opened on Broadway on March 10, 2002, in a production directed by David Esbjornson, starring Bill Pullman and Mercedes Ruehl. It was Albee's first Broadway premiere in nearly two decades. In the 1960s, Broadway still served as a launching pad for serious new work (Bottoms 2005b: 1). By the time *The Goat* arrived, the American theatrical landscape had shifted substantially, away from the commercial model of Broadway and toward the not-for-profit model of regional theatres. Esbjornson thought it bold to open *The Goat* on Broadway; off-Broadway audiences were more likely to be receptive to the play's provocative moral ambiguity, but Broadway, he felt, gave the play a chance for the excited variety of response the play deserved. At the heart of this challenge was awareness of puzzlement over the play's form. "When was the last time you went to a show on Broadway where everyone was struggling over how or even whether or not you can mix comedy and tragedy?" Esbjornson mused (Solomon 2010: 265).

Capitalizing on the titillation factor, pre-opening publicity teased viewers with a conventional family portrait of Pullman, Ruehl, and Jeffrey Carlson (who played Billy), stiffly posed in formal attire, a docile white-haired goat in their midst. 2002 was an interesting time in the contemporary gay-rights movement. Poised between the landmark legislation allowing civil unions in Vermont (1999) and the soon-to-come Supreme Court decision decriminalizing sodomy in *Lawrence v. Texas*, as well as the Massachusetts Supreme Judicial Court's decision making that state the first to affirm the right to marry for all couples (both 2003), the play seemed ideally situated to reflect the *zeitgeist* surrounding homosexuality in contemporary American culture. What everyone initially mistook as Albee's substitution of bestiality for same-sex love appeared to be no more than a cleverly designed ruse to call out conservative anti-gay rhetoric as prejudiced and hypocritical.

It was this bestiality-as-metaphor lens, packaged within a trademark Albee dark comedy, to which critics initially responded.

Journalists, betraying their discomfort with the material, responded with a "slew of comedic pathologizing and really unforgiveable puns" (Robinson 2011: 62) while carefully avoiding confronting Martin's actual emotional plight. As Albee himself put it, the play is no more about bestiality than it is about flower arranging (2005: 262), yet these initial respondents were unwilling to confront the questions of tolerance and transgressive behavior at the heart of the play. Ben Brantley's first review for *The New York Times* dismissed the play as an interesting but basically unsuccessful comedy: "A Secret Paramour Who Nibbles Tin Cans" quipped the headline (2002a: E1). Despite the fact that an interview with Albee in the production's *Playbill* revealed the play's subtitle, *Notes Toward a Definition of Tragedy*, Brantley was insistent in interpreting it as a monstrous comedy.

Six months later Bill Irwin and Sally Field took over the roles of Martin and Stevie, and Brantley revised his initial review. Despite no changes to text, staging, or design, Brantley discovered a layer of anguish he initially had failed to notice. Writing of Field's performance, he declared, "A sense of overwhelming pain, the kind that screams through Greek tragedies, radiates from *The Goat* these days ... Ms. Field turns Stevie's speeches into Electra-like arias of grief and rage" (2002b: E5). While Brantley attributes this changed response to the actor's interpretation of the role, I suspect that an unconscious bias about style and genre played a part.

Esbjornson divulged that he and scenic designer John Arnone wanted the set to have "a little bit of a classical quality to it, a Greek-tragedy quality" (Solomon 2010: 259). Writing in *Theatre Journal*, one reviewer remarked on the influence of classic Greek architecture in the set design and took care to mention the moment between the second and third scenes in which the entire stage was dimly lit, save for the spotlight on the Greek columns that framed the small, raised platform upstage that appeared almost akin to an altar (Medoff 2003: 165). It was a brief moment, lasting only seconds in the transition from one scene to the next, but it served as a powerful image of the ways the production emphasized the play's roots in Greek tragedy.

Within three years of the Broadway premiere, productions of *The Goat* had opened in several European capitals and various regional theatres in the United States. Scholarly considerations of the play frequently commented on its classical elements. Gainor called it a contribution to the "ongoing theorization of tragedy" (2005: 206) and Falkner an "exercise in applied theory" (2005: 188).

It would be an oversimplification to conclude that Albee's view of tragedy completely accords with that of the ancient Greeks. Contemporary American life contains no suitable corollaries for the polytheistic Greek system of faith, the Greek fear of fate and supernatural retribution, or the Greek understanding of society and the city-state. At best, Albee has grafted his twenty-first-century take on tragedy to an ancient model, not simply adopted the Greeks' views.

Turning now to other Albee plays, I want to shift from thinking about Albee in relation to the classical Greeks to consider other fundamental elements of his tragic vision: the themes of tolerance, loneliness, and the frailty of human connection. In particular, let us consider his five major plays—*The Zoo Story* (1959), *Who's Afraid of Virginia Woolf?* (1962), *A Delicate Balance* (1966), *Seascape* (1975), and *Three Tall Women* (1991)—and examine two universal themes common to these works.

The first unifying theme is that of intrusion. In four of these plays, the major action is precipitated by one or more outsiders intruding upon an orderly stasis. In *The Zoo Story*, drifter Jerry interrupts Peter's quiet Sunday sojourn to a central park bench. In *Virginia Woolf*, Nick and Honey are impromptu middle-of-the-night houseguests for George and Martha. In *A Delicate Balance*, Harry and Edna arrive uninvited and intending to stay for good with Agnes and Tobias, while in *Seascape* the lizards Leslie and Sarah crawl out of the sea and over the dune to disrupt Charlie and Nancy's seaside idyll. In each instance, the intrusion is the inciting incident that propels the narrative forward—it is the problem the protagonist must solve.

Three Tall Women deviates in a number of ways from this pattern. The play's protagonist, the nonagenarian A, is split into three parts, with B and C representing A at earlier points in her life. Here B and C are the intruders, and the invasion comes not from another being but from within the self. The problem facing A is how to unify these three disparate versions of her self—a resolution achieved in the final moments onstage as all three women clasp hands.

No matter how the invasion occurs, the intruders in these plays serve a common function, which illustrates the second unifying theme of Albee's tragic vision: shocking the protagonists out of complacency and forcing them to connect with other beings. Despite the preponderance of married couples in these plays, Albee characters are lonely and isolated. Their tragedies arise from their desire yet inability to connect with others. *The Zoo Story*'s Jerry is emblematic of the Albee protagonist: solitary and lost, desperate to make contact. His main attempts to connect revolve around Peter, but as "The Story of Jerry and the Dog" makes clear, humans are not the only mode through which this desire is manifested. Albee frequently populates his plays with references to non-human creatures, using their animal existence to underscore both our primal need to bond and our sense of loss when that connection cannot be achieved. In his lengthy monologue, Jerry describes his many unsuccessful attempts to reach the dog and then concludes:

> Whenever the dog and I see each other, we both stop where we are. We regard each other with a mixture of sadness and suspicion, and then we feign indifference. We walk past each other safely; we have an understanding. It's very sad, but you'll have to admit that it is an understanding. We had made many attempts at contact, and we had failed ... We neither love nor hurt because we do not try to reach each other. (1999: 21)

Stories of these squandered attempts at connection are echoed throughout Albee's plays. Tobias's parable about his cat in the first act of *A Delicate Balance* is an echo of Jerry and the dog.

Yet the potential to overcome this inability to connect, the potential to break free from isolation represented by the arrival of the plays' intruders, drives these plays to their inexorable conclusions. Tobias, in his final monologue—Albee described it as an aria—pleads for Harry and Edna to stay in his house, to give him the chance to demonstrate that he is capable of the kind of generosity that he has believed is essential to genuine friendship and love: "YOU BRING YOUR TERROR AND YOU COME IN HERE AND YOU LIVE WITH US! YOU BRING YOUR PLAGUE! YOU STAY WITH US! I DON'T WANT YOU HERE! I DON'T LOVE YOU! BUT BY GOD ... YOU STAY!!" (1966: 88). Moments after this desperate plea, Harry and Edna depart, leaving Tobias and his wife, Agnes, alone in their separateness from each other. *Seascape* ends similarly with Leslie and Sarah headed back to the sea, despite Nancy and Charlie's insistence they stay, and the Boy in *Three Tall Women* (A's son) wordlessly fails to connect to his mother as she lies dying. After three hours of savagery toward one another, George and Martha sit together at the end of *Virginia Woolf* amid the proffered, uncertain hope that the killing of their imaginary son will bring them closer. "It will be better," George offers after a long silence. Another long silence, then Martha responds, "I don't ... know" (1962b: 111).

Read through this lens, what is most significant for Albee about Martin's affair with Sylvia is not the physical intimacy, but the emotional connection he forges with the goat. Of all Albee's characters, perhaps only Martin and Sylvia fulfill the promise of communion between self and other that remains so elusive in his other plays. In *Zoo Story, Virginia Woolf, A Delicate Balance, Seascape,* and *Three Tall Women,* the tragedy is that the characters cannot connect to one another; in *The Goat,* the tragedy is that they have. In the end, Sylvia is destroyed, an intruder in the marriage. Despite the bond formed between Martin and Sylvia, Stevie's murder of her leaves Martin in the same sea of isolation and loneliness as Albee's other tragic heroes.

Albee's view of tragedy is situated within a mixed form of tragicomedy, just as American absurdism straddles the divide between comedy and tragedy. We may howl with laughter when Billy scoffs at his father, "You're fucking a fucking goat" (2008: 571), but underneath the humor is Albee's desire to rouse his audiences out of isolation and complacency, challenging us to connect with his characters and with one another. This is Albee's contribution to American tragedy—laughter through tears, tears through laughter, both emotions tinged with regret and loneliness. "I like to catch people like that," Albee remarked, "I like catching people in the middle of a laugh, and them realizing it's not funny— or catching them in the middle of something awful, and realizing that you can laugh at it" (Bottoms 2005a: 239).

References

Albee, Edward (1962a), "Which Theatre Is the Absurd One?" *The New York Times,* February 25. Available online: https://www.nytimes.com/ books/99/08/15/specials/albee-absurd.html (accessed January 7, 2017).

Albee, Edward (1962b), *Who's Afraid of Virginia Woolf?* New York: Dramatists Play Service.

Albee, Edward (1966), *A Delicate Balance*, New York: Samuel French, Inc.

Albee, Edward (1999), *The Zoo Story* [1959] and *The Sandbox* [1960], New York: Dramatists Play Service.

Albee, Edward (2005), *Stretching My Mind*, New York: Carroll & Graf Publishers.

Albee, Edward (2008), *The Collected Plays of Edward Albee*, vol. 3, 1978–2003, New York: Overlook Press.

Beckett, Samuel (1954), *Waiting for Godot*, New York: Grove Press.

Bennett, Michael Y. (2015), *The Cambridge Introduction to Theatre and Literature of the Absurd*, Cambridge: Cambridge University Press.

Bianchini, Natka (2015), *Samuel Beckett's Theatre in America*, New York: Palgrave Macmillan Press.

Bottoms, Stephen (2005a), "Borrowed Time: An Interview with Edward Albee," in Stephen Bottoms (ed.), *The Cambridge Companion to Edward Albee*, 231–50, Cambridge: Cambridge University Press.

Bottoms, Stephen (ed.) (2005b), *The Cambridge Companion to Edward Albee*, Cambridge: Cambridge University Press.

Brantley, Ben (2002a), "A Secret Paramour Who Nibbles Tin Cans," *The New York Times*, March 11: E1. Available online: http://www.nytimes.com/2002/03/11/theater/theater-review-a-secret-paramour-who-nibbles-tin-cans.html?pagewanted=all (accessed January 7, 2017).

Brantley, Ben (2002b), "Surprising Actress as Woman Who Surprises Herself," *The New York Times*, September 30: E5. Available online: http://www.nytimes.com/2002/09/30/theater/theater-review-surprising-actress-as-woman-who-surprises-herself.html (accessed January 7, 2017).

Esslin, Martin ([1961] 2004), *The Theatre of the Absurd*, 3rd edition, New York: Vintage Books.

Falkner, Thomas M. (2005), "Oedipus in New York: Greek Tragedy and Edward Albee's *The Goat, or, Who Is Sylvia?*" in Stratose E. Constantinidis (ed.), *Text & Presentation 2004*, 187–98, Jefferson, NC: McFarland & Company.

Gainor, J. Ellen (2005), "Albee's *The Goat*: Rethinking Tragedy for the 21st Century," in Stephen Bottoms (ed.), *The Cambridge Companion to Edward Albee*, 199–216, Cambridge: Cambridge University Press.

Medoff, Richard B. (2003), "The Goat or Who Is Sylvia," *Theatre Journal* 55 (1): 164–6.

Robinson, Michelle (2011), "Impossible Representation: Edward Albee and the End of Liberal Tragedy," *Modern Drama* 54 (1): 62–77.

Solomon, Rakesh H. (2010), *Albee in Performance*, Bloomington, IN: Indiana University Press.

Williams, Raymond (1966), *Modern Tragedy*, Redwood City, CA: Stanford University Press.

Zinman, Toby (2008), *Edward Albee*, Ann Arbor, MI: University of Michigan Press.

9

Lorraine Hansberry (1930–1965)

Deirdre Osborne
Goldsmiths, University of London

Lorraine Hansberry's legacy as one of America's most significant dramatists and prophetic political and cultural activists is contoured by tragedy. Notwithstanding her premature death, the majority of her work negotiates racism and white supremacy's toll upon black people's lives, from her groundbreaking play *A Raisin in the Sun* (1959) to her journalism, speeches, screenplays, and unfinished adaptations. However, it also brims with the energy of redressing this grim legacy through resisting what Hansberry termed the "vogue of despair" (1963: 181) that white liberal expectations project onto black culture, a theme that Jeremy Glick develops in *The Black Radical Tragic* (2016), arguing that "staging the dialectic of freedom and necessity is configured theoretically from a Black radical position as the interplay between democracy, self-determination and revolution" (2016: 3).

   A Raisin in the Sun and *Les Blancs* (1970)[1] illustrate this direction of Hansberry's dramatic compass. They address the magnitude of two of the most significant systems of violence and displacement in human history that continue to haunt institutional and social relations globally: enslavement and colonization. Translated into more than thirty languages (Bond 1989: 183), *A Raisin in the Sun* has a history of international productions: problematically in countries without African-descent actors (Jakubiak 2011: 541–2), illuminatingly in those facing their previously submerged colonial pasts, such as The Netherlands, South Africa, and Sweden.[2] But the play's direct focus is on America's racism, the roots and consequences of which linger today, as is expressed by the United Nations' Commission on Human Rights (2016):

> The colonial history, the legacy of enslavement, racial subordination and segregation, racial terrorism, and racial inequality in the US remains a serious challenge as there has been no real commitment to reparations and to truth and reconciliation for people of African descent. Despite substantial changes since the end of the enforcement of Jim Crow and the fight for civil rights, ideology ensuring the domination of one group over another continues to negatively impact the civil, political, economic, social and cultural rights of African Americans today. The dangerous ideology of white supremacy inhibits social cohesion amongst the US population.

Hansberry does not simply vilify white hegemonic oppression in its many entrenched forms but articulates the complex effects of the ideological projection of whiteness as neutral, invisible, inevitable, and invariable. Margaret Wilkerson argues that "the tension in her blackness and femaleness" shapes Hansberry's writings through "probing the nature of the individual within the specifics of culture, ethnicity and gender," while not diminishing "the pain, suffering or truths of any one group in order to benefit another" (1994: 7–9). Hansberry centralizes black people's perspectives, but her themes are universal as she engages the variegation and mutuality of socio-historical experiences and multiple traditions.

Although thematically responding to Richard Wright's writings and to Louis Peterson's Broadway-produced *Take a Giant Step* (1953), Hansberry's inspiration for *A Raisin in the Sun* was Irish playwright Sean O'Casey's *Juno and the Paycock* (1924), which she said, "entered my consciousness and stayed there" (1970: 90). Additionally, her use of tragic elements and absurdity connects her generically to the mid-twentieth-century American white male canon of O'Neill, Williams, Miller, and Albee. Hansberry recognized that in relation to the American Dream, the characters Willy Loman and Walter Lee Younger (auguring Maya Angelou's poem "Human Family") are more alike than unalike in sharing "the acute awareness that *something* ... is in the way of his ascendancy" (1963: 180). She resuscitates black characterization from annihilating, racial-performance typology. Harvey Young argues that this typology is "an *idea* of the black body [that] has been and continues to be projected across actual physical bodies" (2010: 4).

The formal and thematic patterns of early-seventeenth-century Jacobean tragedy's pre-realist, social critique are also traceable in Hansberry's politically historicized, creative vision. The genre evolved in English theatre during a period of sociopolitical and religious ferment that culminated in the English Civil War, as profits from trading enslaved African people in the New World consolidated English colonization of the region, engendering the 400-year British Empire. Jacobean tragedy dramatizes a malignant world where individuals strive to survive and flourish amid the dominant social order's corruption, avarice, and self-interest. Its tragic arc offers negligible recourse to justice except through violent revenge. For characters displaying qualities of honor and loyalty, stoicism is the only means of preserving one's dignity. The lack of convincing resolution to disorder points to a meta-context of social injustice that Hansberry's tragedies share. Without necessarily staging bloodshed and death, this possibility is ever-present.

In rejecting pre-set expectations of a disenfranchisement and demise narrative in an oppressive environment, the Younger family's relocation to a white neighborhood—presaging racist-impelled violence—instead celebrates their vibrant exertion of survival, adaptability, and self-fashioning. Hers is a story of "the efforts of the Negro people of the United States to wrest their birthright of full citizenship from a laggard and oppressive nation" (Hansberry 2015: 32). The play's narrative was challenged: see, for example, Harold Cruse's polemic (1967) and George Wolfe's parody (1987), while Amiri Baraka reversed his earlier misgivings and proclaimed it a classic (1987). Hansberry herself seems to have been sensitive to this: Wilkerson salvaged an early draft with the family in their new residence facing an attack (1986: 452)—much as Hansberry recalled her own mother "patrolling our house all night with a loaded German luger, doggedly guarding her four children" (1970: 51). Hansberry's final alteration of the ending illustrates her wresting of her play from under the expectation of violence and adversity as a black family's overarching fate—without denying incontrovertible daily dangers—to testify to the resilience and energy that confirms art's social purpose: imagining alternatives to society's constraints.

The play changed American theatre forever, as James Baldwin recognized: "*Raisin in the Sun* meant so much to black people ... In the theater, a current flowed back and forth between the audience and the actors: flesh and blood corroborating flesh and blood—as we say, testifying" (2011: 63). This "testifying" remains relevant transnationally throughout the African diaspora. In a recent production in Sweden—where Afrophobic hate crime has increased by "24 per cent since 2008" (United Nations 2015: 10)—director Josette Bushell-Mingo used a majority black cast in black roles for the first time in that country and with permission from Hansberry's literary estate restored the bleak and violent ending from Hansberry's early draft. This powerfully underscored the play's tragic trans-historicism in today's international context of displaced families and postcolonial and refugee narratives, amid concurrent attacks on migrant families in Stockholm ("Swedish Tolerance" 2015).

Hansberry inherits a matrilineal politicized aesthetic (Angelina Weld Grimké, Marita Bonner, Mamie Burrill, Georgia Johnson, Eulalie Spence, Zora Neale Hurston) and portends writers such as Angela Davis, Toni Morrison, and bell hooks. Nemiroff suggests that *What Use Are Flowers?: A Fable* is stylistically influenced by Samuel Beckett, but Hansberry described her play as "a bit of a fantasy thing" (1994: 223), which echoes Bonner's *The Purple Flower: A Phantasy That Had Best Be Read* (1927). Both women use allegory as an implicit protest in a context of apocalyptic vision. Parks observes how *A Raisin in the Sun* centralizes "black women's concerns for the continuity of the culture and survival of self and the family" (1995: 200). Hansberry's female characters resist oppressive patriarchal and racial constraints by whatever means they can. Seeking solutions to dilemmas, they refuse stasis, even if it means biding their time. Lena is Hansberry's dramatic vehicle through which collective resolve against a divide-and-rule ideology is articulated. Although critics note Lena's emasculation of Walter (Harris 1995: 116), or her poor financial planning derived from internalized gender bias (Colbert 2011: 46), Lena maintains her family unit's functionality in a hostile society: meta-contextually as a warrior in a racist nation amid the legacy of the Great Migration; micro-contextually as a mother begetting change and renewal.

> We was going backwards 'stead of forwards—talking 'bout killing babies and wishing each other was dead ... When it gets like that in life—you just got to do something different, push on out and do something bigger. (Hansberry 2011: 71)

Such emotional capaciousness will not rest from the struggle even when the character experiences despair: "when do you think is the time to love somebody the most ... It's when he's at his lowest and can't believe in hisself cause the world done whipped him so" (Hansberry 2011: 113). Thus, Lena rallies a potent collective memory of enslavement's survival heritage as a foundation upon which to establish a future. Furthermore, she urges that the fullest landscape of experiences measures a person, rather than generalizations from which stereotyping and injustice grow: "Make sure you done taken into account what hills and valleys he come through before he got to wherever he is" (Hansberry 2011: 114).

From the early twentieth century, African Americans looked toward the African continent as promising a renewal of deep, original ties: culturally, psychologically, spiritually, and geographically. Bush observes that by mid-century "the sweep of national independence movements globally was inextricably linked to the political initiatives of Black Americans engaged in similar, and sometimes overlapping, struggles for freedom, full citizenship and self-determination" (2011: 49). However, as radical black internationalism became ring-fenced by the Cold War impasse, American alliances with anticolonial freedom fighters in postwar decolonizing struggles became more difficult as the fear of communism limited postwar American political freedom.

As with many black American writers of that era, Hansberry's representations are circumscribed by an Africa of the mind. *Les Blancs*, set in a fictional African country ultimately in revolt against the colonial regime, encapsulates the landscape of African independence struggles throughout the 1950s and 1960s. The various standpoints toward African culture in *A Raisin in the Sun* (Walter's spear, Lena's Tarzan, George's "grass huts," Asagai's independence ideals) show the complexities of African Americans' simultaneous affiliations with yet alienation from African heritages. *Les Blancs* was "written by an African *American*," which elicits a double-consciousness as "a condemnation of colonialism in Africa and ... a commentary on race relations in early 1960s America" (Abell 2001: 459). American perspectives in the play are voiced through the debates between Tshembe Matoseh and the white American journalist Charlie Morris—whose name recalls Walter's parodic servility toward "Mistuh Charley" and the colonial plantation source for the original Philip Morris tobacconist merchandise. While it counteracts Jean Genet's *Les Nègres*, Hansberry primarily "considered *The Blacks* 'a conversation between white men about themselves'" (Hansberry 1994: 32).

As Rich has noted, after *A Raisin in the Sun*, Hansberry began removing women from the conversations. Tshembe was originally Candace. This supports Rich's hypothesis that 1950s and 1960s white-majority American audiences would have found implausible a central character who was "a female revolutionary, a confrontational figure, a strong Black woman" (1989: 18)—*all* of which Hansberry was. The omission of black female protagonists in the play, apart from a nonspeaking character, The Woman, is symbolically regressive; however, as Sadler's review of Yaël Farber's 2016 UK production recognizes, "Black men are front and centre here, yet not one black woman utters a word in this play ... There are plenty of black women on stage but they remain mute ... The principal African female is The Woman, a thin, long-limbed woman who stalks the stage as some sort of Mother Africa figure." Farber's production semiotics raise additional problems: "she is barely clothed, with only strips of flesh-colored material covering her breasts and bottom. And her burden is to drag around a huge cauldron to segue between scenes." Moreover, "We see a white man kill a black man, and we see a black man kill another black man. But we never see a black man kill a white man." Sadler's conclusion echoes Rich's: "This was written in the 1960s with an American audience in mind. Maybe Lorraine just thought a black man murdering his oppressor on stage would be a step too far for her audience at that time" (Sadler 2016).

However, Hansberry was a harbinger of decolonization as a topic in American theatre. In the missionary characters Father and Madame Neilsen, she references the less readily known Norwegian colonial presence, "profiting from the white patriarchal rule of South Africa" (Tjelle 2014: 211). Nielsen, a character in diegetic space, is Tshembe's half-brother Eric's father and is murdered in the nationalist uprising. Independence starkly exposes the true dynamic of apparently cordial power relations between settler and indigenous groups. Hansberry's play denounces this as a delusive façade of compliance and submission where colonizers kept African resources away from African resourcefulness. Insightfully, she translated this for the American context, as "a highly concentrated, universal, and deliberate blanket of oppression pulled tightly and securely over 20 million citizens in this country," calling for the groundswell of resistance "to condemn, not only the results of that oppression, but also the true and inescapable cause of it—which of course is the present organization of American society" (Hansberry 2015: 34, 35).

Her prescient words remain a clarion call. The principles of today's Black Lives Matter movement continue Hansberry's activist aesthetics:

Black Lives Matter is an ideological and political intervention in a world where Black lives are systematically and intentionally targeted for demise. It is an affirmation of Black folks' contributions to this society, our humanity, and our resilience in the face of deadly oppression.

Notes

1   Hansberry began *Les Blancs* in 1961. It was completed by her literary executor and ex-husband, Robert Nemiroff, from their conversations and Hansberry's notes. It premiered in New York (November 1970) nearly six years after Hansberry's death and in Europe at the Royal Exchange, Manchester, England, in 2001. See Hansberry ([1972] 1994).

2   In 2016 *Raisin* was produced in the Netherlands in Dutch by Wellmade Productions, in South Africa at the Market Theatre, and in Sweden in Swedish at the Riksteatern.

References

Abell, Joy L. (2001), "African/American: Lorraine Hansberry's *Les Blancs* and the American Civil Rights Movement," *African American Review* 35 (3): 459–70.

Baldwin, James ([1976] 2011), *The Devil Finds Work*, New York: Vintage Books.

Baraka, Amiri (1987), "A Critical Reevaluation: *A Raisin in the Sun*'s Enduring Passion," in Lorraine Hansberry, *A Raisin in the Sun* (unabridged 25th anniversary edition) and *A Sign in Sidney Brustein's Window*, Robert Nemiroff (ed.), 9–20, New York: Plume.

Black Lives Matter, "Guiding Principles." Available online: http://blacklivesmatter.com/guiding-principles/ (accessed January 3, 2017).

Bond, Jean Carey (1989), "Lorraine Hansberry: To Reclaim Her Legacy," *Freedomways* 19 (4): 183–5.

Bush, Roderick (2011), "Black Internationalism and Transnational Africa," in Mojúbàolú Olúfúnké and Olufemi Vaughan (eds.), *Transnational Africa and Globalization*, 39–69, London: Palgrave Macmillan.

Colbert, Soyica Diggs (2011), *The African American Theatrical Body: Reception, Performance, and the Stage*, Cambridge: Cambridge University Press.

Cruse, Harold (1967), *The Crisis of the Negro Intellectual*, New York: William Morrow.

Glick, Jeremy Matthew (2016), *The Black Radical Tragic: Performance, Aesthetics, and the Unfinished Haitian Revolution*, New York: New York University Press.

Hansberry, Lorraine ([1959] 1963), "Willy Loman, Walter Younger and He Who Must Live," *The Village Voice*, August 12, 1959, 7–8. Reprinted in Daniel Wolf and Edwin Fancher (eds.), *The Village Voice Reader*, New York: Grove Press, 176–83.

Hansberry, Lorraine ([1959] 2011), *A Raisin in the Sun*, Deirdre Osborne (ed.), London: Methuen Modern Drama.

Hansberry, Lorraine ([1964, 1965] 2015), "The Scars of the Ghetto" and "Reprise," *Monthly Review: An Independent Socialist Magazine* 67 (1): 32–5.

Hansberry, Lorraine ([1969] 1970), *To Be Young, Gifted and Black: An Informal Autobiography of Lorraine Hansberry*, Robert Nemiroff (ed.), New York: Signet Books.

Hansberry, Lorraine ([1972] 1994), *The Collected Last Plays: Les Blancs, The Drinking Gourd, What Use are Flowers?*, Robert Nemiroff (ed.), New York: Vintage Books.

Harris, Trudier (1995), "This Disease Called Strength: Some Observations on the Compensating Construction of Black Female Character," *Literature and Medicine* 14 (1): 109–26.

Jakubiak, Katarzyna (2011), "The Black Body in Translation: Polish Productions of Lorraine Hansberry's *A Raisin in the Sun* in the 1960s," *Theatre Journal* 63 (4): 541–69.

Parks, Sheri (1995), "In My Mother's House: Black Feminist Aesthetics, Television, and *A Raisin in the Sun*," in Karen Laughlin and Catherine A. Schuler (eds.), *Theatre and Feminist Aesthetics*, 200–28, Madison, NJ: Farleigh Dickinson University Press.

Rich, Adrienne ([1979] 1989), "The Problem of Lorraine Hansberry," in *Blood, Bread and Poetry: Selected Prose 1979–1985*, 11–22, London: Virago.

Sadler, Victoria (2016), "Review: *Les Blancs*, National Theatre 'Powerful but Problematic,'" March 25. Available online: http://www.victoriasadler.com/review-les-blancs-national-theatre-powerful-but-problematic/ (accessed January 3, 2017).

"Swedish Tolerance Questioned as Attacks on Migrants Rise" (2015), *EurActiv.com*, August 24. Available online: http://www.euractiv.com/section/languages-culture/news/swedish-tolerance-questioned-as-attacks-on-migrants-rise/ (accessed January 12, 2017).

Tjelle, Kristin Fjelde (2014), *Missionary Masculinity, 1870–1930: The Norwegian Missionaries in South-East Africa*, London: Palgrave Macmillan.

United Nations, General Assembly, Human Rights Council, 30th Session, Agenda Item 9 (2015), "Report of the Working Group of Experts on People of African Descent on Its Sixteenth Session," August 25. Available online: http://www.un.org/ga/search/view_doc.asp?symbol=A/HRC/30/56/Add.2&Lang=E (accessed January 12, 2017).

United Nations Office of the High Commissioner for Human Rights (2016), "Statement to the media by the United Nations' Working Group of Experts on People of African Descent, on the conclusion of its official visit to USA, January 19–29, 2016." Available online: http://www.ohchr.org/EN/NewsEvents/Pages/DisplayNews.aspx?NewsID=17000&LangID=E#sthash.0cuhsn2x.dpuf (accessed December 31, 2016).

Wilkerson, Margaret (1986), "*A Raisin in the Sun*: Anniversary of an American Classic," *Theatre Journal* 38 (4): 441–52.

Wilkerson, Margaret (1994), "Introduction," in Lorraine Hansberry, *The Collected Last Plays: Les Blancs, The Drinking Gourd, What Use Are Flowers?*, Robert Nemiroff (ed.), New York: Vintage Books.

Wolfe, George C. (1987), *The Colored Museum*, London: Methuen.

Young, Harvey (2010), *Embodying Black Experience: Stillness, Critical Memory, and the Black Body*, Ann Arbor, MI: University of Michigan Press.

10

Amiri Baraka (1934–2014)

Harvey Young
Northwestern University

A lifeless black body is thrown from a subway car. The memory of its recent passing—its murder by a fellow passenger and its removal by a small group of masked fellow riders—lingers. Even the subsequent arrival of an African American male passenger, who sits where the previous one sat, is not enough to dispel the pall of death. In fact, his appearance creates in the audience a foreboding sense of *déjà vu*. A similar fate likely awaits him. We've seen this before. Death, yet again, is on the horizon.

These are the final moments of Amiri Baraka's play *Dutchman*, winner of the 1965 Obie Award for Best New Play. An immediate critical success and described by theatre critic Howard Taubman, writing for *The New York Times*, as "an extended metaphor of bitterness and fury," *Dutchman* appealed both to Greenwich Village esthetes who witnessed the premiere and to a more diverse and popular audience who attended its restaging as street theatre in Harlem. Its continuing appeal stems from Baraka's ability to innovate a new dramatic style influenced by Beat writers and his commitment to portraying the embodied experience of African Americans in a recognizable manner. The result is a tragedy that is existential and undeniably real.

Dutchman features two characters: Clay and Lula. Clay, a *"twenty-two-year-old Negro,"* is a well-dressed, mild-mannered man who travels via subway to visit a friend. When the play opens, he sits quietly in a subway car. The entirety of the action of the play occurs on the subway. Lula, a *"tall, slender, beautiful woman with long red hair"* who is a decade older than Clay, enters wearing *"bright, skimpy summer clothes and sandals"* (3). Although other seats are available, she walks toward Clay, stands next to him, and hovers over him. She awaits his acknowledgment before making a declaration that is thinly disguised as a question, "I'm going to sit down ... O.K.?" They talk and briefly flirt with one another. Sex or, at least, the possibility of sex is in the air. The attraction ends abruptly as their dialogue becomes more pointed and critical. Lula disparages Clay, essentially calling him a *poseur*, a fake or phony. She tells him, "Boy, those narrow-shoulder clothes come from a tradition you ought to feel oppressed by. A three-button suit. What right do you have to be wearing a three-button suit and striped tie? Your grandfather was a slave, he didn't go to Harvard" (1964b: 15). Relentless in her critique of Clay, Lula succeeds in tapping into his reserve of anger at society-at-large for its racism. In response, he freely, publicly expresses his discontent. At one point, Clay proclaims, "Shit, you don't have any sense, Lula, nor feelings either. I could murder you now. Such a tiny ugly throat. I could squeeze it flat, and watch you turn blue" (1964b: 28). The tension escalates until Lula *"brings up a small knife and plunges it into* CLAY's *chest"* (1964b: 30). Fellow passengers aid her by tossing Clay's lifeless body from the train. The scene resets, with the entrance of a new black subway rider.

Written in the early 1960s when Baraka, then LeRoi Jones, was an acolyte and friend of the Beat poet Allen Ginsberg, *Dutchman* merges existentialist perspectives with a recognizable narrative arc steeped in a sociopolitical critique of the recognizably real world. Baraka first encountered the writings of Ginsberg as an enlisted serviceman working as a librarian at the US Air Force Strategic Air Command base in Puerto Rico in the mid-1950s. His voracious appetite for avant-garde writings would lead to a dishonorable discharge following allegations of being a communist sympathizer. Ginsberg's poems helped Baraka to appreciate the power of contemporary poetry to reach a popular audience and to lodge critique. Reflecting on Ginsberg's influence, Baraka recalled, "I liked ... the whole attack on American society, the whole use of language that was unknown or not used in a kind of academic polite society" (quoted in Lee 2004: 127).

After the Air Force, Baraka settled in New York City, wrote to Ginsberg, met the Beat poet, launched his own arts journal, and with his wife Hettie Cohen actively participated in the Beat scene alongside Ginsberg, Jack Kerouac, and Diane Di Prima, among others. Much like the Beat authors, Baraka's early poetry placed a spotlight on subjective experiences of the everyday world that often doubled as a form of political or social critique. However, it differed in that it initially hinted at and later more explicitly focused on an experience of blackness. He opens the poem "An Agony. As Now" (1964a), published shortly before the premiere of *Dutchman*, with the following:

I am inside someone
who hates me. I look
out from his eyes. Smell
what fouled tunes come in
to his breath. Love his
wretched women.

The poem, as *Los Angeles Times* critic Hector Tobar observes, "begins with the writer in an existential crisis." It is this crisis, previously framed by sociologist W. E. B. Du Bois as "double consciousness" ([1903] 1965: 215) and now expanded to more fully consider the internalized conflict of intersecting identities, which defines Baraka's dramaturgy. Such a crisis appears in and, perhaps, may have inspired *Dutchman*. Baraka, referring to the process of composing his most famous play, remembers, "When I wrote the play *Dutchman*, I didn't know what I had written. I stayed up all night and wrote it, went to sleep at the desk and then woke up, and looked at it and said 'what the [f—] is this?'" (quoted in ya Salaam 1998).

In *Dutchman*, Baraka steeps his play in the everyday experience of being black within the United States. The poet-playwright understands that abuse, violence, and even death can target African Americans at any moment, including within seemingly benign settings. Clay, a quiet passenger riding a subway, learns this. In an interview with Kalamu ya Salaam (1998), the playwright credits his grandmother for teaching him about this fact of tragic blackness:

My grandmother would tell me all the time about this Black boy they accused of raping this woman and they cut off his genitals and stuffed them in his mouth and then made all the Black women come there and watch. My grandmother told me that story when I was a little boy. Why would your grandmother tell you that story? Because she wanted you to remember that shit forever.

The story told by Baraka's grandmother is cautionary. She memorably offers a perspective on racial violence within their shared world and essentially advises her grandson to keep his distance from white people, in general, and white women, specifically. This warning also appears in *Dutchman* as Clay's interaction with Lula and the unnamed subway riders (who are reminiscent of the "they" in Baraka's grandmother's story) leads to his murder and disappearance.

Amiri Baraka identifies Clay as a victim. In his article "The Revolutionary Theatre" (1965), he asserts the necessity of establishing a tragic theatre that brings attention to the experiences of the vulnerable. He writes, "Our theatre will show victims so that their brothers in the audience will be better able to understand that they are the brothers of victims, and that they themselves are victims, if they are blood brothers" (2). Baraka's revolutionary impulse is what ultimately sets his dramaturgy apart from the Greenwich Village and Beat authors. Although there is a similar dedication to creating an impressionist theatre, a theatre that represents an individual's perspective on the world, Baraka's early theatrical writings, especially *Dutchman*, underscore the importance of creating art that has the potential to serve as a catalyst for social change and political involvement. There is a commitment to realism in an effort not only to reach audiences and help them connect what they are seeing with their lived realities but also to inspire activism.

Baraka's emphasis on the lived experience of African Americans is evident in his embrace of a blues aesthetic. Influenced by blues artists and their ability to reflect black life through their artistry, the playwright sought to create a blues theatre. In conversation with journalist Michael Limnios, he observed, "The blues is simply a recalling of experience." He added, "The blues is a form of storytelling. It's a kind of narrative song, expressing the past and even what you hope to be the future or you hope not to be the future, one of those two things." This attention to the blues both as an art form and as an existential embrace of the everyday embodied experiences of blackness is what gives Baraka's theatre, especially *Dutchman*, its tragic dimensions.

Tragedy for Baraka exists not in fabricating a story in which a protagonist emerges only to fall as a consequence of poor choices or willful neglect of morality. It is a straightforward depiction of black life as it recognizably is lived. The tragic impresses itself upon black folks. It is exemplified in the experience of Emmett Till, the young boy killed in Money, Mississippi, in 1955 simply for whistling at a white woman, and also that of the boy introduced in Baraka's grandmother's story. Their experiences are neither extraordinary nor rare. In fact, they are quite ordinary and everyday. Baraka's theatre of tragedy exists as a study of quotidian violence targeting black bodies. Clay does not act in a spectacular manner. He simply sits and rides the subway. Nevertheless, he becomes the victim within Baraka's dramatic narrative.

Certainly, the power of Baraka's *Dutchman* anchors itself in the audience's ability to relate to and identify with Clay. This identification operates along multiple registers. There is a general acceptance of the character's experience as being reflective of the larger African American experience and his fate existing as a demonstration of the precariousness of blackness. Indeed, any black person can find himself or herself a target of violence in essentially any scenario or public setting. More generally, the play spotlights a recognizable, real world, societal embrace (and acceptance) of black culture that fails to understand the particularities of black experience. Clay, as his frustration with Lula nears its crescendo, memorably declares,

> They say, "I love Bessie Smith." And don't even understand that Bessie Smith is saying, "Kiss my ass, kiss my black unruly ass" ... Charlie Parker? Charlie Parker. All the hip white boys scream for Bird. And Bird saying, "Up your ass, feebleminded ofay! Up your ass." And they sit there talking about the tortured genius of Charlie Parker. Bird would've played not a note of music if he just walked up to East Sixty-seventh Street and killed the first ten white people he saw. Not a note! (1964b: 29)

In addition, *Dutchman* facilitates audience identification by specifically drawing attention to Clay's experience as a black male. From the entrance of Lula on the subway car, it is evident that he is a potential victim. Even consensual interracial relationships involving black men and white women have resulted in the loss of life. For an audience attending the original production of *Dutchman* in the late 1960s, in the midst of the Civil Rights movement and less than a decade after Emmett Till's murder, the particularly threatened existence of Clay had to have been recognizable.

On yet another level, *Dutchman* facilitated recognition of a middle class anxiety in relationship to blackness. Can you be black and relatively affluent? Lula asserts, "I bet you never once thought you were a black nigger" (1964b: 15). These tensions, uncertainties, and/or anxieties (depending on perspective) have long existed within black communities. For example, Lorraine Hansberry in *A Raisin in the Sun* scripts characters who question the blackness of George Murchison, a comparatively affluent suitor of Beneatha Younger. Literary critic Jiton Sharmayne Davidson contends that class anxiety was something with which Baraka himself wrestled.

> Up until Amiri Baraka, still LeRoi Jones, made his abrupt conversion to Black Nationalism, he was a Beat poet with a nagging angst that did not fit into the bohemian paradigm as expressed in his 1961 satiric poem "Hymn for Lanie Poo," subtitled "Vous êtes de faux Nègres" (roughly translated, "You are the fake Negroes") (2003: 400–1).

This anxiety, an existential crisis of identity, certainly reappears in "An Agony. As Now." *Dutchman* similarly hints at the complexity of intersectional identities and the existence of a black habitus alongside other *habiti*, as I have described it in *Embodying Black Experience*. The authenticity of one's blackness is interrogated in relation to other identity markers. Not only is Clay black *and* male, he is also black *and* male *and* middle class *and* well educated. Each of these additional markers invites a consideration of preconceptions and, perhaps, stereotypes of blackness.

In an article published the same year as the world premiere of *Dutchman*, John Von Szeliski commented on the state of then-contemporary tragedy. He observed that mid-twentieth-century American tragedy diverged from classical tragedy, which centers on misfortune as essentially inescapable despite human freewill and agency. He writes, "Amid all the conjecture about the inferiority of today's tragedy, the truly significant difference between modern and classical tragedians is in philosophical vision—the former's pessimism being no match for the latter's ultimate optimism" (1964: 40). Classical tragedy centers choice and, by extension, agency. A "tragic" end can be averted, if one chooses correctly. Oedipus chooses to kill a stranger, a man whom he later learns was his birth father, and elects to marry a woman whom he later discovers to be his mother. Lessons in morality and ethics appear within the realized consequences of these freely elected choices. Oedipus's recognition of his complicity in the unfolding events motivates him to blind himself in addition to embracing a self-imposed banishment. For the audience, recognition invites pity. It also helps them to understand that tragic consequences can be avoided by acting in a just or moral manner. Szeliski correctly points to a pessimistic streak within modern American drama. This certainly is the case with *Dutchman*. Clay does not make choices that lead to his demise. Although it could be argued that he tempted fate simply by talking with Lula— and countless black men have been cautioned about the dangers of socializing with white women (indeed, Baraka's grandmother's story is an instance of this)—the reality is that the protagonist did not have an option not to interact with Lula. She sought him out. Her movements and speech indicate that she was not going to allow him to ignore her. His fate was sealed at the moment that Lula boarded the train.

The potentiality of black folk being subject to violence is a theme that recurs in the theatre of Amiri Baraka. Reflecting on his plays in "The Revolutionary Theatre," the esteemed playwright observed, "Clay, in *Dutchman*, Ray, in *The Toilet*, Walker in *The Slave*, are all victims" (1964b: 1). The probability, if not the inevitability, of tragedy targeting African Americans interests Baraka. In centering the individual, he not only stages embodied experiences of blackness but also grants audiences insight into the interiority of black thought. He reveals an existential crisis that results from a character's awareness of the futurity of death as well as the tensions resulting from intersecting identities in conflict. Baraka's emphasis on race, character psychology, and the necessity of bringing recognizably real experiences to the stage broadened the parameters of modern American tragedy.

References

Baraka, Amiri (1964a), "An Agony. As Now," in *The Dead Lecturer*, New York: Grove. Available online: https://www.poetryfoundation.org/poems-and-poets/poems/detail/52777 (accessed January 4, 2017).

Baraka, Amiri (1964b), *"Dutchman" and "The Slave"*, New York: William Morrow.

Baraka, Amiri (1965), "The Revolutionary Theatre," *Liberator*, July. Available online: http://nationalhumanitiescenter.org/pds/maai3/protest/text12/barakatheatre.pdf (accessed January 4, 2017).

Davidson, Jiton Sharmayne (2003), "Sometimes Funny, but Most Times Deadly Serious: Amiri Baraka as Political Satirist," *African American Review* 37 (2–3): 399–405.

DuBois, W. E. B. ([1903] 1965), *The Souls of Black Folk*, in *Three Negro Classics*, 207–389, New York: Avon.

Hansberry, Lorraine ([1959] 2004), *A Raisin in the Sun*, New York: Vintage.

Lee, Maurice A. (2004), *The Aesthetics of LeRoi Jones: The Rebel Poet*, València: Universitat de València.

Limnios, Michael (2012), "An Interview with Amiri Baraka," September 30. Available online: http://blues.gr/profiles/blogs/an-interview-with-amiri-baraka-a-leading-figure-who-has (accessed January 4, 2017).

Taubman, Howard (1964), "Dutchman," *The New York Times*, March 25. Available online: http://www.nytimes.com/1964/03/25/the-theater-dutchman.html?_r=0 (accessed January 4, 2017).

Tobar, Hector (2014), "Amiri Baraka captured an outsider's anger, giving it beauty," *Los Angeles Times*, January 9. (Available online: http://articles.latimes.com/2014/jan/09/entertainment/la-et-jc-amiri-baraka-captured-an-outsiders-anger-gave-it-beauty-20140109 (accessed January 4, 2017).

Von Szeliski, John (1964), "Pessimism and Modern Tragedy," *Educational Theatre Journal* 16 (1): 40–6. Available online: https://www.jstor.org/stable/3204376?seq=1#page_scan_tab_contents (accessed January 4, 2017).

ya Salaam, Kalamu (1998), "A Conversation with Amiri Baraka," *Modern American Poetry*. Available online: http://www.english.illinois.edu/maps/poets/a_f/baraka/salaam.htm (accessed January 4, 2017).

Young, Harvey (2010), *Embodying Black Experience*, Ann Arbor, MI: University of Michigan Press.

11

Adrienne Kennedy (1931–)

Werner Sollors
Harvard University

Adrienne Kennedy's drama has affinities to the work of Arthur Miller, Tennessee Williams, Edward Albee, Amiri Baraka, Sam Shepard, and Wole Soyinka. Simultaneously, it echoes the entire dramatic tradition, from Greek tragedy to the theatre of the absurd, from Euripides to Shakespeare, from Chekhov to Maurice Maeterlinck, and from Strindberg to Eugène Ionesco. Inspired by the themes of Hollywood movies and by cinematic techniques, Kennedy's highly acclaimed and frequently staged works have been praised as surrealistic dream plays, hauntingly fragmentary and nonlinear lyrical dramas, high points in the development of the American one-act play, and dramatic harbingers of feminist themes in African American women's writing, inspiring artists from Ntozake Shange to Anna Deavere Smith. Kennedy's dramatic work has an unmistakable style, characterized by fragmentation, ritualistic repetition and variation, and radical experimentation with character and plot. While it comes to life most fully in theatrical production, it also is indebted to the literary form of lyrical drama that invites reading and rereading.

Adapted by Werner Sollors from his introduction to *The Adrienne Kennedy Reader* (University of Minnesota Press, 2001).

Kennedy's works confront social and psychological terrors, past and present. Her drama is autobiographically inspired, shaped by her experience and generational vantage point, and packed with allusions to American popular culture. Her most important works explore the tragic condition of daughter, mother, father, sibling, and lover in the painful web of American race and kin relations in which violence can erupt at any point.

In a recent statement that gives expression to her vision of tragedy, Kennedy fuses a specific, telling detail of her family story with a general aesthetic principle and the theatrical tradition:

> Tragedy. is my mother standing at the stove singing Sometimes I Feel Like A Motherless Child she would say to me my mother died when I was a child and I lived with my grandmother in a house overlooking the cemetery. Sometimes I sat on the steps looking at the graves. Suddenly loudly my grandmother cried out didn't you hear me call you. I called you. Bring me a switch. Bring me a switch. From the peach tree. And suddenly she would beat me until I had whelps all over my body. I never knew why.
>
> Tragedy is innocence visited by dark cruelties.
>
> And in the Theatre as in Seagull Hamlet Streetcar these cruelties must lead to death or madness.
>
> Ghostly visitations are in all tragedy ... on my mother's deathbed she relived the grandmother beatings. (Personal email to the author, August 7, 2016.)

Born Adrienne Hawkins in Pittsburgh in 1931, the playwright spent her childhood and youth in Cleveland, with frequent visits to Montezuma, Georgia, where most of her relatives were living. It was there, she remembers, at a place she could reach only by Jim Crow train cars from Ohio, that her neighbor Sarah Clara gave Kennedy the inspiration for the names of two of her dramatic protagonists. There, too, a procession of black churchgoers gave her a feeling of aesthetic intensity that resurfaced later when she viewed Giotto's frescoes. Fairy tales, complicated stories about racial ancestry, and the lore of a mythical England as the ultimate country of origin and the home of Jane Eyre further intensified her sense of the South. In response to reading William Faulkner she later wrote, "He reinforced what I, as a child, had felt in my visits to Georgia to see my grandparents: that the South was a strange mesh of dark kinship between the races" (Kennedy 1987: 98)—and Montezuma was also the place where her great-grandmother had whipped her mother.

In Cleveland at age sixteen Kennedy saw a production of Tennessee Williams's *The Glass Menagerie* at the Karamu Theater and immersed herself deeply into the world of Hollywood, admiring the stars Bette Davis, Lena Horne, Paul Robeson, and Orson Welles. She remembers traveling in a Jim Crow car, clutching an issue of *Modern Screen* with Clark Gable on the cover (Kennedy 1987: 33). After graduating from Ohio State University and marrying Joseph Kennedy, she moved to New York, began writing, and was drawn to modern art and theatre, especially the plays of Arthur Miller, Tennessee Williams, Chekhov, and Lorca. She broke into print with the experimental short story "Because of the King of France" in 1960, during a prolonged stay in Europe and Africa, publishing it under the pen name Adrienne Cornell in the African journal *Black Orpheus*.

After reading works by African writers Chinua Achebe and Wole Soyinka and studying masks in Ghana, Kennedy "started the lines of two plays, *Funnyhouse of a Negro* and *The Owl Answers*, and the lines had a new power, a fierce new cadence," as she remembers (Kennedy 1987: 119). "Not until I bought a great African mask from a vendor on the streets of Accra, of a woman with a bird flying through her forehead, did I totally break from realistic-looking characters" (Kennedy 1987: 121).

In the 1960s and 1970s, Kennedy created an impressive group of experimental plays. *Funnyhouse of a Negro* (1964), coproduced by Edward Albee, won Kennedy her first Obie award. The drama presents four aspects of a self (the character Sarah): Patrice Lumumba, the first president of the Congo after its independence from Belgium, who was assassinated in 1961 (when Kennedy was staying in Ghana), is associated with an African patrimony and the figure of a father; Christ is both the childhood savior and a sinister entity who also is linked with the image of marriage, especially Mary's in Giotto's fresco; Queen Victoria was inspired by Sir Thomas Brock's Carrara marble statue in front of Buckingham Palace, which threateningly comes to life as a white figure of domination and terror; and finally, the Duchess of Hapsburg, Charlotte Maria Amelia, the sister of Belgian

King Leopold II who is better known as the beautiful, romantic wife of Maximilian, the ill-fated Hapsburg Emperor of Mexico. Charlotte went insane when the Mexican enterprise failed and her husband was executed upon Benito Juarez's victory. Her part was played by Bette Davis in William Dieterle's lavish film *Juarez* (1939), a movie that impressed Kennedy deeply, perhaps all the more because of Charlotte's comment to Maximilian that they are at the site "of the very halls of Montezuma," a remark that must have carried special meaning for Kennedy as if it were a reference to her family's Southern home.

These four selves embody tragic collisions of black and white, male and female, and colonialism and independence. Yet as Sarah's selves, these figures also are strangely identical. They speak and repeat the same lines, at times in unison, Greek-chorus fashion. The masks, with their "great dark eyes that seem gouged out of the head," furthermore evoke Oedipus, and the dominant issue is the "recognition of myself," or, paradoxically, the "recognition against myself" (Kennedy 1970: 257, 263). In such a context, the queen's famous question from *Snow White*, "who is the fairest of them all," reveals troubling cultural connotations.

Though the title evokes the image of an amusement park, the play has serious overtones: it explores a split heritage and the central self's suicidal refusal to accept part of that heritage—or to recognize herself in that part. One could find echoes in Kennedy's own family memories. Her father, whom she later associates with Patrice Lumumba, took her to a performance by Paul Robeson, read her poetry by Paul Laurence Dunbar, and told her stories of race heroes and heroines like W. E. B. Du Bois or Mary Bethune. Her mother, the daughter of a rich white peach grower and his black employee, looked to her like "a combination of Lena Horne and Ingrid Bergman" (Kennedy 1987: 50). She had chosen her daughter's first name after the actress Adrienne Ames (Kennedy 1987: 10). The family story was embedded in an American story of racial antagonism despite actual kinship, for, as Kennedy knew well, like most "Negroes" in Montezuma, she had both black and white relatives. Kennedy sometimes uses the term "Negroes" or "White People" in quotation marks and sees a political antagonism that kinship does not bridge: "'White People': They tried to hold you back ... 'Negroes': We were underdogs, and underdogs must fight in life" (Kennedy 1987: 14, 11).

Repetitions and variations of long passages create a rhythm of twelve "movements" in *Funnyhouse* that extends beyond characters, plot, or any sense of a stable setting. In the repetitions, strong images, such as those of a dreamlike Africa or the mother's loss of hair, become haunting. Kennedy also develops an elaborate bird imagery with religious, racial, mythical, familial, and existential associations, without settling on any one meaning. Inspired by verse 6 in Psalm 55, the Holy Ghost in Giotto's fresco, an African bird mask, Poe's "The Raven," and the spiritual "Sometimes I Feel Like a Motherless Child," the bird image also alludes to the tradition of the "Flying African," explored later in Toni Morrison's novel *Song of Solomon* (1977). The owl in particular, as a bird of wisdom associated with the motherless Greek goddess Pallas Athena, keeps a fairly constant presence in Kennedy's work.

In Kennedy's next play, *The Owl Answers* (1965), the presentation of changing sets and divided characters continues and intensifies. Clara Passmore appears to be a figure indebted to the myth of the mother. Her last name may allude to racial "passing"—and in her the themes of illegitimacy, racially mixed identity, conflicts between mother and father, and cultural tensions between England and America converge. Characteristically, the set is a collage of Old and New World places, all of which strangely coexist: "*The scene is a New York subway car is the Tower of London is a Harlem hotel room is St. Peter's*". The characters have alternating identities, and the figures of Shakespeare, Chaucer, and William the Conqueror form the Greek chorus of an English literary tradition that challenges Clara's claim to an English ancestry. The first word of the play, which this English chorus addresses to Clara, is "Bastard." The complex family relations, reminiscent of Langston Hughes's play *Mulatto* (1935), are represented through Clara's changing identities as white man's "blood" daughter, black cook's daughter, black reverend's foster daughter, Virgin Mary, and owl.

Clara refers to England as the place of "our ancestors," yet this ancestry denies her a place as descendant. A female equivalent of "everyman," she does not bear the name of her white father (Mattheson) that would establish an ancestral entitlement. It is as if half her parentage did not count in the strange racial genealogy that Clara confronts. Now that her father "died today or was it yesterday" (an allusion, perhaps, to the beginning of Albert Camus's novel *The Stranger* (1942), a classic existentialist statement of confrontation with the absurd), she is not even permitted to attend his funeral. St. Paul's universalist promise of a Christianity without ethnic boundaries seems forgotten in St. Paul's Chapel, where the funeral is held. England, the home of the Brontës, does not welcome the avid *Jane Eyre* reader, Clara, who repeatedly speaks the loaded sentence, "I was the only Negro there." Refused acceptance in the white father's world that is so clearly a part of her, Clara denies her relationship to her father and tries to create, and then to fend off with a knife, new alternative father- and God-figures for herself on the New York City subway. The mother's way to St. Paul's Chapel is through suicide, a path Clara does not follow. Instead, she turns into an owl—a move toward animal imagery as part of magical transformations and as a counter-statement on racism that Kennedy continues in later plays.

In *A Rat's Mass* (1966), the siblings who are the main characters are surrealistically and literally represented as half animal and half human, reminiscent of a Max Ernst collage. Two *"pale Negro children"* are also half rats: *"BROTHER RAT has a rat's head, a human body, a tail. SISTER RAT has a rat's belly, a human head, a tail"*. A mass, complete with transubstantiation and a religious procession, provides the setting for Kennedy's strategy of ritualistic repetition, subtly revealed as the children play hide-and-seek in an attic. Rosemary, the ostentatious Christian, has worms in her hair, Medusa-fashion, and represents the lure of evil, perhaps as a perverted Pied Piper of Hamlin for Brother Rat and Sister Rat. The non-rat Rosemary is arrogant about her background and, though loved by the siblings, turns out to be an accomplice of fascist killers who act out a nightmarish Anne Frank scenario for the half-rat brother and sister in hiding.

A Lesson in Dead Language (1966) presents another character who is both human and animal by identifying the Teacher also as a White Dog. The setting is a Latin class which turns into an absurd ritual of instruction, vaguely reminiscent of Eugène Ionesco's play *The Lesson*. The play obviously alludes to Shakespeare's *Julius Caesar*, in particular Joseph Mankiewicz's cinematic adaptation.

Sun (1968) was written in memory of Malcolm X and is dedicated to Kennedy's father. This doubling of father and black political martyr-hero continues the pattern of the identification of the black father and the world of Patrice Lumumba and Paul Robeson. The theme of the play, the violent death of black leaders who struggle for the liberation of their people, is presented in an unusual lyrical form. Man is the only character and speaker in the circular pageant, whose pace is marked by cosmic and human orbits. One sequence sets the stages of embryo, birth, and early youth against the background of an orange sun spinning, slowly being replaced by a yellow sun and a black sun, a sequence reminiscent of images of light in Langston Hughes's poem "As I Grew Older" (1925).

Kennedy's plays are the condensed expression of a theatrical mind that has integrated diverse autobiographical, political, and aesthetic elements into an effective modern form. Read together, these plays constitute a full-fledged modern attempt at rewriting Greek family tragedy, complicated by the American difficulties with interracial kinship. Hegel saw the tragedy of *Antigone* in the dramatic collision between obligations to the state and to the family that brings down Antigone as well as Creon, the ruler but also her uncle. Kennedy's drama, in the tradition of Countée Cullen's *Medea* (1934) and Langston Hughes's *Mulatto* (1935), explores the tension between race and family as a modern tragic collision that brings along its own "dark cruelties." It is no coincidence that Kennedy, like Wole Soyinka in his *Bacchae* (1973), has also published a contemporary adaptation of Euripides, her *Electra and Orestes* (1980).

Kennedy's literary career has been long and productive. In 1967, while in London, she collaborated on the dramatization of John Lennon's book *In His Own Write*. In 1987 she published *People Who Led to My Plays*, which the novelist Ishmael Reed calls a "new form of black autobiography" (quoted in Colleary 2016). That memoir in the experimental form of quick glimpses also sheds much light on Kennedy's personal approach to drama; she drew on it for her play *June and Jean in Concert* (1995). Her later dramatic works, such as her cycle *The Alexander Plays* (1992), extends the more overtly political side of her work while continuing to present her familiar division of a lyrical persona into antithetical selves. During the last two decades, she has collaborated on plays with her son Adam. Adrienne Kennedy's work—Suzan-Lori Parks called it "totally cool" (1996)—constitutes a truly significant contribution to the formal possibilities of tragedy in the modern world.

References

Colleary, Eric (2016), "Celebrating the Reissue of Adrienne Kennedy's Memoir," *Cultural Compass*, March 25, Harry Ransom Center, University of Texas at Austin. Available online: http://blog.hrc.utexas. edu/2016/03/25/celebrating-the-reissue-of-adrienne-kennedys-memoir/ (accessed January 12, 2017).

Kennedy, Adrienne ([1964] 1970), *Funnyhouse of a Negro*, in William Brasmer and Dominick Consolo (eds.), *Black Drama: An Anthology*, 251–72, Columbus, OH: Charles E. Merrill.

Kennedy, Adrienne (1987), *People Who Led to My Plays*, New York: Knopf.

Parks, Suzan-Lori (1996), "Adrienne Kennedy," *BOMB* 54. Available online: http://bombmagazine.org/article/1929/adrienne-kennedy (accessed January 12, 2017).

12

August Wilson (1945–2005)

Sandra G. Shannon
Howard University

In the summer of 1990—shortly after *The Piano Lesson* had won him his second Pulitzer Prize—August Wilson asserted to interviewer Vera Sheppard, "Tragedy is the greatest form of dramatic literature," and then went on to explain:

> suffering is only a part of black history ... I am going to show that this culture exists and that it is capable of offering sustenance. Now, if in the process of doing that, you have to explore the sufferings of black America, then that is also part of who we are. And I don't think you can ignore that because our culture was fired in the kiln of slavery and survival. (2006: 103–5)

Throughout his career Wilson wrote in this vein, fashioning a series of towering dramas reflecting the gamut from despair to ebullience for life that African Americans experienced from the post-slavery era to the twenty-first century. Working within the tradition that runs from the ancient Greek dramatists through Shakespeare, Ibsen, Chekov, and Shaw, and on to the Americans O'Neill, Williams, and Miller, Wilson in his American Century Cycle develops the conventional tragic form in ways that more accurately reflect fundamental cultural differences of the people he calls "Africans in America."

I wanted to present the particulars of black American culture as the transformation of impulse and sensibility into codes of conduct and response, into cultural rituals that defined and celebrated ourselves as men and women of high purpose. I wanted to place this culture onstage in all of its richness and fullness and to demonstrate its ability to sustain us in all areas of human life and endeavor and through profound moments in our history in which the larger society has thought less of us than we have thought of ourselves. (1999: viii–ix)

Continuing his 1990 interview with Vera Sheppard, Wilson admitted, "My sense of what a tragedy is includes the fall of the flawed character; that is certainly a part of what is in my head when I write" (2006: 104). But in a separate interview in 1991 he added, "I try not to portray any of my characters as victims" (Shannon 2006: 140). It is in the spaces between his characters' personal flaws and their valiant struggle to avoid victimization where Wilson fashions his signature tragedies, such as *Fences* (1986), *Seven Guitars* (1995), and *King Hedley II* (1999).

In their Introduction to *PMLA*'s special 2014 issue on tragedy, Helene Foley and Jean Howard lament our modern loss of a tragic sensibility amid the brutal chaos of the contemporary world and its constant news coverage:

Daily the news media lay tragedies at our doorsteps: school shootings, imploding states, global warming, the slow death of democratic structures. What, we must ask, does tragedy as a literary phenomenon have to do with any of these things? In everyday parlance, the term often seems emptied of meaning. If the word simply suggests something sad, banality is the consequence. Is the loss of a pet, even a beloved pet, tragedy? ... To some people, certainly, tragedy as a literary genre is old and boring, loved by Greeks but of little relevance now. (2014: 617)

Foley and Howard's comment is understandable, but by focusing on world affairs, it distances us from our more private experiences of our own lives. While thoroughly grounded in the unique, racially charged experience of African Americans, Wilson is working broadly in the tradition espoused by Arthur Miller in his now-classic 1949 essay "Tragedy and the Common Man." Like Miller, Wilson writes

of people whose lives are far from grand but who nonetheless have
cherished aspirations that are fundamental to their sense of self,
who struggle against powerful social forces engulfing them, and
who strive to have their dignity recognized. These themes are not
limited by ethnicity or nationality nor silenced by the devastation
of world affairs. They are at the heart of human experience, and as
such they give Wilson's work its universal significance and appeal.

The ten plays in Wilson's American Century Cycle reveal a fluid
approach to tragedy, reflecting both a debt to the Greeks and a precise
sensitivity to the multifaceted experience of African Americans
and the roots of that experience in slavery. But like novelist and
folklorist Zora Neale Hurston, Wilson believes that although the
slave past needs to be acknowledged, it need not be defining. In her
1928 essay "How It Feels to Be Colored Me," Hurston quipped:

> I am not tragically colored ... Someone is always at my elbow
> reminding me that I am the granddaughter of slaves. It fails to
> register depression with me. Slavery is sixty years in the past.
> The operation was successful and the patient is doing well, thank
> you. The terrible struggle that made me an American out of a
> potential slave said "On the line!" The Reconstruction said "Get
> set!"; and the generation before said "Go!" I am off to a flying
> start and I must not halt in the stretch to look behind and weep.
> Slavery is the price I paid for civilization, and the choice was not
> with me. It is a bully adventure and worth all that I have paid
> through my ancestors for it. (1928: 153)

Like Hurston, Wilson pushed back against the stereotype of the
tragic, helpless, victimized, emasculated Negro so often depicted in
early African American fiction and drama, such as Eugene O'Neill's
Emperor Jones (1920), Paul Green's play *In Abraham's Bosom*
(1926), and DuBose Heyward's musical *Porgy and Bess* (1935) as
well as in Richard Wright's collection of short fiction *Uncle Tom's
Children* (1938). But Wilson's pushback against "tragic" to describe
the entire black experience also is tempered by his advocacy for
today's African Americans to acknowledge more fully that "peculiar
institution" of slavery as part of their past. This revisionist thrust
that informs each of his American Century Cycle plays does not
ignore the tragic circumstances of slavery; rather, as the playwright
notes, "I sought then to ... [give] the facts of history a different

perspective, creating, in essence, a world in which the black American was the spiritual center" (1992: H5). Wilson's mission is to "rewrite history," a mission shared by African American neo-slave narrative writers, such as Toni Morrison, Edward P. Jones, Margaret Walker, and Octavia Butler, who engaged in the process of re-memory and recovery and who maintain control over the historical narrative while doing so.

Hurston's absolute refusal to play the victim and her resolve to reject the "tragically colored" label anticipates Wilson's insistence on avoiding victimized character portrayals. However, the two writers diverge on the place that tragedy holds in their writing. Of course, Hurston's comments must be regarded within the context of a time when, as William Braithwaite observed in Locke's groundbreaking anthology *The New Negro*, "Negro life was a shuttlecock between the two extremes of humor and pathos" (1925: 31). Preoccupation with the tragic "Negro" stereotype, especially during the Reconstruction era, kept him more of a myth than a man. Conversely, Wilson seemed to feel that fingering the jagged grain of tragedy is a first step toward personal and collective spiritual release for both himself and for fellow African Americans. He opened up to Bill Moyers during a 1988 interview:

> You discover that you're walking down this landscape of the self, and you have to be willing to confront whatever it is that you discover there. The idea is to emerge at the end of the landscape with something larger than what you had when you went in— something that is part of the illumination of the truth. If you're willing to wrestle with your demons, you will find that your spirit gets larger. And when your spirit gets larger, your demons get smaller. For me, this is the process of art. The process of writing the plays is a very liberating thing. (Moyers 1989: 178)

The origins of August Wilson's unconventional ideas about tragedy and African Americans are grounded in the slave experience, an enduring legacy that later morphed into Jim Crow laws, vigilante violence, white supremacy, and continued marginalization and oppression. One certainly can make the case that the source of angst among Wilson's largely male cast members is the lingering impact of slavery, whether it be Citizen Barlow in *Gem of the Ocean*, set in 1904, or Harmond Wilks in *Radio Golf*, set in 1995.

Wilson's art consistently dramatizes the long-term effects of the suppressed psychological trauma caused by the many horrors of slavery.

Wilson's insistence on foregrounding the slave experience in his American Century Cycle plays is reminiscent of symbolism attached to the Ghanaian Sankofa bird, which holds that one cannot proceed into the future without first acknowledging what has brought it about. His adaptation of this principle calls for tragic endings to await any of his lead male characters who dare to forget or deny their pasts. Those guilty of this denial fall tragically from grace into epic chaos and calamity on a scale similar to the cosmic retribution levied against Greek or Shakespearean tragic heroes. As I have noted elsewhere, "self-mutilation, convulsions, arrested speech, unexplained scars, incarceration, domestic turmoil, splintering of the nuclear family structure, and mental trauma that manifests itself in either neurosis, schizophrenia, or dementia" are regularly visited upon the descendants of slaves who opt to distance themselves emotionally or physically from the South—and, by extension, from Africa (Shannon 1997). African Americans, according to Wilson, committed a cardinal sin by giving up land ownership, by exiting the south, and by "transplanting" themselves in the north.

Wilson's own words provide a useful introduction to the tragic design of his plays. An abundance of interviews published between 1984 and 2004 outline the defining features of his vision (see Bryer 2006). In Wilson's tragic design, character portrayals are more important than plot design: that is, each play coalesces around a single tortured soul whose symptoms, as the play suggests, can be traced as far back as the legacy of slavery. Wilson explained to Bonnie Lyons, "For me plot grows out of characterization, so there are no plot points. The play doesn't flow from plot point to plot point" (Lyons [1997] 2006: 213). Wilson's privileging of character has resulted in recurring stories of angry, dispossessed African American males whose stories grab and keep our attention, whether they triumph in reunions and reconciliations or self-destruct under the weight of cosmic retribution for mistakes of their own making. Taken together, Wilson's string of troubled and combative African American lead characters is as fitting a subject for tragedy as were members of the elites portrayed by the Greeks and Shakespeare.

A look at Wilson's American Century Cycle reveals an additional central element in the character types that become exemplars of

Wilson's approach to tragedy. Long before his plays' beginnings, Wilson's strong, male, lead characters have confronted conflict—emotionally and psychologically crippling conditions in which his plays show they continue to be mired. When Troy Maxson, King Hedley II, or Floyd Barton make their first entrances, it is indeed *in medias res*: they already are embroiled in simmering controversy, the full spectrum of which is slowly revealed. Troy, who has killed a man, harbors smoldering resentment for being shut out of the Major Leagues. He enters with talk of having filed a complaint against his employer for unfair treatment on the job. King Hedley II loathes his biological mother, Ruby, for leaving him as an infant and placing him in the care of a surrogate. Floyd "Schoolboy" Barton has squandered the trust of his girlfriend, Vera, by cheating on her with another woman. All three bring to the scene a healthy supply of psychological baggage, still bearing scars from previous losses, emotional or physical trauma, alienation, or abandonment. Some are able to muster sufficient energy and self-respect to continue to wage war rather than acquiescing to a rigged system. Others find a semblance of agency in their abilities to speak to power, to hunt down a foe, or to lie in wait to settle a score, even if physical harm or death awaits them. These characters maintain a sense of personal pride and compensate for their deprived possibilities as American citizens in often misunderstood ways that qualify them as Wilson's ultimate examples of tragic figures.

Wilson referred to such characters as "warriors"—those who have been essentially shut out of the system but who remain too stealthy for the label "victim." Wilson used the word "warrior" to describe a string of uncompromising, bad-ass characters who frequently butted their heads against the established order. Defined literally, a "warrior" is one who engages aggressively in a cause or conflict. However, for Wilson, the term also suggests abiding by a code of ethics or a system of belief out of which character is built. In the place of the physical armor and weaponry that one might associate with great African warriors, such as Hannibal or Shaka Zulu, Wilson's characters possess a noble stature and spirit of righteous resistance that links them to these African exemplars: both share an absolute rejection of victimhood, despite the fact, as Wilson says of his characters, that they "because of that spirit, find themselves on the opposite side of society that is constantly trying to crush their spirit" (Moyers 1989: 179).

August Wilson was adamant not to create tragic figures who are victims of fate or to cast them at the end his plays as hopeless pariahs or abject failures. Instead, his warriors, rebels, and spectacle characters such as Herald Loomis, Levee, King Hedley II, Troy Maxson, Ma Rainey, Boy Willie, and Hambone—like poet Claude McKay's men—do not concede defeat; rather, they stand their ground while "pressed to the wall, dying, but fighting back!" (McKay 1919: 290). They rail against injustice and demand their due from a system that essentially has shut them out. Though death looms large among them, end of life for Wilson's reconstructed tragedians often signals new beginnings and cause for celebration along with reconciliation and reunion. Wilson's tragic figures go beyond the very basic pleas for the acceptance of one's humanity that is so reminiscent in the current Black Lives Matter international movement against violence. His tragedies elevate the focus upon black life to increase self-awareness and accountability as well as to embrace the cultural traditions that have sustained them.

For Wilson, tragedy exists in the confrontation of this warrior spirit with the experience director Lloyd Richards has called "deprivation of possibility": a combined feeling of "pride, frustration, exploitation, and internecine aggression."[1] Both Richards and Wilson found characters impacted by this condition emblematic of a pervasive form of tragedy experienced by Africans in America who historically have been cut off from the nation's promise—characters for whom the elusive American Dream is at best fraudulence. At first, these characters naively play by the rules, but eventually they discover that these rules invariably change just as a pathway to achieve their goals comes into view. The situation is described poignantly by restaurateur Memphis Lee in *Two Trains Running* (1990b):

I'm going back to Jackson and get my land one of these days. I still got the deed. They ran me out of there but I'm going back. I got me a piece of farm down there. Everybody said I was crazy to buy it cause it didn't have no water on it. They didn't know my granddaddy knew how to find water. If there was water anywhere under the ground he'd find it. He told me where to dig and I dug a well. Dug sixty feet down. You ain't got no idea how far that is. Took me six months hauling dirt out this little hole. Found me some water and made me a nice little crop ... Jim Stovall, who I bought the land from, told me my deed say if I found any water the sale was null and void. (72)

For Wilson, tragedy results when portals are closed, leaving individuals with absolutely no hope of improving the circumstances of their lives. When asked his thoughts on the amount of unabashed praise heaped upon him whenever he returns to his native Pittsburgh Hill District, he explained:

It says that it could have been any one of them, that there is a tremendous amount of talent that is wasted; that for every Louis Armstrong there are a hundred people whose talent gets wasted; that there are no avenues open for them to participate in society, where they might prove whatever is inside them. Those same people have vital contributions to make to society. They could solve some of the problems—transportation, housing, whatever. But no one is asking them. They're not allowed to participate in the society. (Moyers 1989: 172)

Joan Herrington captures this social background to Wilson's vision of tragedy in her observations on *King Hedley II*: "King is told he does not count, and he quickly comes to recognize the basic injustice of his world. 'They got everything stacked up against you as it is. Every time I try to do something they get in the way. It's been that way my whole life. Every time I try to do something they get in the way'" (Herrington 2007: 171; Wilson 1999: 54). King's repeated references to the nameless "they" indicate his awareness that every avenue of the African American's advancement or success in America is guarded and often outright blocked by white power brokers. Conflict occurs and a tragic fall ensues for Wilson's tragic hero prototypes when they confront rather than retreat from barriers constructed by self-appointed guardians of the American Dream.

Nonetheless, Wilson's characters are not simply victims of circumstance; they also have personal flaws that drive their ruin. For King the conflict is fueled and sustained by his street gang mentality that can best be described as "An eye for an eye; a tooth for a tooth": No bad deed can be left unanswered. The challenge for Wilson, as Herrington has noted, is Aristotelian: to shape a tragic hero "so that his nobility is clearly apparent despite his failings" (Herrington 2007: 176).

The death of the hero is fundamental to both Greek and Shakespearean tragedy. Accordingly, the demise of aristocrats Oedipus and Julius Caesar, for example, is linked directly to cosmic retribution for succumbing to one or more human frailties. Death is also often the fate of the tragic common man throughout Wilson's American Century Cycle. While not aristocrats—but nonetheless noble—blues musician Floyd Barton (*Seven Guitars*), garbage man Troy Maxson (*Fences*), and handyman King (*King Hedley II*) meet tragic ends in ways not entirely unlike Arthur Miller's Willie Loman (*Death of a Salesman*) and Joe Keller (*All My Sons*). That they are Africans in America, however, negates a one-size-fits-all approach in assessing the tragedy of the common man of another race and culture.

Assessing the tragic deaths of common men of noble stature in Wilson's canon takes on more culturally authentic meaning when analyzed through the lens of Yoruban belief systems. According to Wilson critic Harry Elam, "Soyinka's 'The Fourth Stage' has much in common with Wilson's mission in his theatrical cycle" (2004: 170–1). The playwright's often-repeated refrain that "these are Africans in America," privileges such reading. For Wilson, then, as it is for Nigerian theorist Wole Soyinka, the relationship between tragedy and death is symbiotic—what Soyinka regards in "The Fourth Stage"[2] as an ongoing "mutual correspondence" among spirits of the deceased and the living. He anchors this view within Yoruban ritual:

> Yoruba metaphysics holds the view of there being three major areas of existence. What you might call the traditional Yoruba sensibility is constantly in touch with and aware of these three. It's the world of the unborn, the world of the dead, and the world of the living. There is a mutual correspondence between these three areas. But I believe there is also a fourth which is not often articulated but which I recognize as implicit. It is not made obviously concrete by rituals, by the rituals, by the philosophy that is articulated by the Ifa priests. This is the fourth area—the area of transition. It is the chthonic realm, the area of the really dark forces, the really dark spirits, and it also is the area of stress of the human will. (1973: 22)

Read through the lens of Yoruban cosmology, then, one can regard the tragic deaths of characters such as Eli in *Gem of the*

Ocean, Floyd Barton in *Seven Guitars*, Troy Maxson in *Fence*s, and King in *King Hedley II* as portals to the realm of the ancestors. As in the final scene in *The Piano Lesson*, when summoned by the living in times of peril and angst, they intercede.

Wilson is among the most self-aware of our dramatists: his vision of tragedy is not just implicit in his plays but expressed explicitly in his many interviews. He noted to David Savran in 1987: "I try to present positive images, strong black male characters who take a political stand ... I try to position my characters so they're pointed toward the future. I try to demonstrate the spirit of the character" (Savran 2006: 30). The "spirit of the character" for Wilson often is expressed in struggles, both publicly social and privately psychological. As he said to Kim Powers in 1984 in reference to the ambitious but thwarted trumpeter Levee in *Ma Rainey's Black Bottom* (1982), he is "trying to wrestle with the process of life the same as all of us. His question is, 'How can I live this life in a society that refuses to recognize my worth, that refuses to allow me to contribute to its welfare—how can I live this life and remain a whole and complete person?'" (Powers 2006: 7).

While keenly aware and insightful about the uniqueness of the struggle of Africans in America against what Lloyd Richards called the "deprivation of possibility" because of our nation's racism (see note 1), Wilson also understands the universally human elements of this struggle: Wilson's heroes, as he says above, "wrestle with the process of life same as all of us ... how can I live this life and remain a whole and complete person." That willingness to wrestle with life is fundamental not just to Wilson's vision of human experience but also to his vision of the role of art. Responding to Vera Sheppard a quarter century ago when asked explicitly if his plays were tragedies, Wilson replied with realism about the struggles his characters face, sensitivity to the nuances of human experience, and hope for the role of drama in transforming the future:

> I would certainly hope so—My sense of what a tragedy is includes the fall of the flawed character; that is certainly a part of what is in my head when I write ... there is a great deal of humor in human life, and I think I find the humor, but the overall intent of the plays I write is very serious ... I think it is important that we understand who we are and what our history has been, and what our relationship to society is, so that we can find ways to

alter that relationship and, more importantly, to alter the shared expectations of ourselves as a people. (Sheppard 2006: 103–4)

One has to wonder what kind of plays a Wilson in his seventies would be writing about the America of today.

Notes

1   Director Lloyd Richards used the phrase "deprivation of possibility" in direct reference to Wilson's *Ma Rainey's Black Bottom* (1982). See Reed (1987: 93)
2   In his essay "The Fourth Stage" (1973), regarded by many as one of the most important theoretical works not only on Yoruba theatre but on Yoruban philosophy, Soyinka argues that "no matter how strongly African authors call for an indigenous tragic art form, they smuggle into their dramas, through the back door of formalistic and ideological predilections, typically conventional Western notions and practices of rendering historical events into tragedy." He develops an aesthetic of Yoruban tragedy based, in part, on the Yoruban religious pantheon (including Ogun and Obatala) (120).

References

Braithwaite, William Stanley (1925), "The Negro in American Literature," in Alain Locke (ed.), *The New Negro*, 29–44, New York: Atheneum.
Bryer, Jackson R. and Mary C. Hartig (eds.) (2006), *Conversations with August Wilson*, Jackson, MS: University Press of Mississippi.
Elam, Harry (2004), *The Past as Present in the Drama of August Wilson*, Ann Arbor, MI: University of Michigan Press.
Foley, Helene P. and Jean E. Howard (2014), "Introduction—The Urgency of Tragedy Now," *PMLA* 129 (4): 617–33.
Herrington, Joan (2007), "King Hedley II: In the Midst of All This Death," in Christopher Bigsby (ed.), *Cambridge Companion to August Wilson*, 169–82, Cambridge: Cambridge University Press.
Hurston, Zora Neal ([1928] 1979), "How It Feels to Be Colored Me," in Alice Walker (ed.), *I Love Myself When I'm Laughing … And Then Again When I'm Feeling Mean and Impressive*, 152–5, New York: The Feminist Press at the City University of New York.
Lyons, Bonnie ([1997] 2006), "An Interview with August Wilson," in Jackson R. Bryer and Mary C. Hartig (eds.), *Conversations with August Wilson*, 204–22, Jackson, MS: University Press of Mississippi.

McKay, Claude (1919), "If We Must Die," in David Levering Lewis (ed.), *The Portable Harlem Renaissance Reader*, 290, New York: Penguin.

Miller, Arthur ([1949] 1996), "Tragedy and the Common Man" reprinted in Robert A. Martin and Steven R. Centola (eds.), *The Theatre Essays of Arthur Miller*, 3–7, New York: Da Capo Press.

Moyers, Bill (1989), *A World of Ideas: Conversations with Thoughtful Men and Women about American Life Today and the Ideas Shaping our Future*, New York: Doubleday.

Powers, Kim ([1984] 2006), "An Interview with August Wilson," in Jackson R. Bryer and Mary C. Hartig (eds.), *Conversations with August Wilson*, 3–11, Jackson, MS: University Press of Mississippi.

Reed, Ishmael (1987), "In Search of August Wilson," *Connoisseur*, March.

Shannon, Sandra ([1991] 2006), "August Wilson Explains His Dramatic Vision," in Jackson R. Bryer and Mary C. Hartig (eds.), *Conversations with August Wilson*, 118–54, Jackson, MS: University Press of Mississippi.

Shannon, Sandra (1997), "The Transplant that Did Not Take: August Wilson's Views on the Great Migration," *African American Review* 31 (4): 659–66.

Sheppard, Vera ([1990] 2006), "August Wilson: An Interview," in Jackson R. Bryer and Mary C. Hartig (eds.), *Conversations with August Wilson*, 101–17, Jackson, MS: University Press of Mississippi.

Savran, David ([1987] 2006), "August Wilson," in Jackson R. Bryer and Mary C. Hartig (eds.), *Conversations with August Wilson*, 118–54, Jackson, MS: University Press of Mississippi.

Soyinka, Wole (1973), "The Fourth Stage: Through the Mysteries of Ogun to the Origin of Yoruba Tragedy," in Douglas William Jefferson (ed.), *The Morality of Art: Essays Presented to G. Wilson Knight by His Colleagues and Friends*, 119–34, London: Routledge and Kegan Paul.

Wilson, August (1982), *Ma Rainey's Black Bottom*, New York: Plume.

Wilson, August (1986), *Fences*, New York: Plume.

Wilson, August (1990a), *The Piano Lesson*, New York: Plume.

Wilson, August (1990b), *Two Trains Running*, New York: Plume.

Wilson, August (1992), "Characters behind History Teach Wilson about Plays," *The New York Times*, April 12: H5. Available online: http://www.nytimes.com/1992/04/12/theater/theaterspecial/03teach.html (accessed January 7, 2017)

Wilson, August (1995), *Seven Guitars*, New York: Penguin.

Wilson, August (1999), *King Hedley II*, New York: Theatre Communications Group.

Wilson, August (2006), *Gem of the Ocean*, New York: Theatre Communications Group.

13

Sam Shepard (1943–2017)

Shannon Blake Skelton
Kansas State University

In a 2016 interview with Alexis Soloski in *The New York Times*, playwright Sam Shepard revealed an affinity for the works of Eugene O'Neill, noting that *A Long Day's Journey Into Night* is "the greatest play ever written in America." Shepard follows this adulatory proclamation by emphatically adding that "what I wanted to do was to destroy the idea of the American family drama." In these comments, featured in a piece coinciding with a revival of Shepard's Pulitzer Prize–winning masterwork *Buried Child* (1978), Shepard is seemingly realigning his own artistic vision. Since the early 1990s, Shepard consistently has cited two titans of European theatre—Brecht and Beckett—as his greatest influences, yet here he consciously recognizes the influence of one of America's greatest tragedians. Shepard's explicit acknowledgment of O'Neill is not surprising. Like O'Neill, Shepard has explored a wide variety of modes, genres, and aesthetics. Though O'Neill experimented with a multitude of approaches to theatre, it is primarily his tragedies featuring characterizations of the American family that have remained artistically resilient. Similarly, despite years of experimentation in subject and form, it is Shepard's Family Cycle, namely *Curse of the Starving Class* (1977), *Buried Child* (1978), and *A Lie of the Mind* (1985) that has cemented his legacy as a canonical dramatist. Also like O'Neill, Shepard has merged mythic, universal human concerns with more personal obsessions. For Shepard, the tragedy of the American family is specifically located in the violent and destructive legacies inherited by sons. This concern, combined with a depiction of ritual acts serving as responses to these legacies and codes of masculinity, characterizes Shepard's particular expression of American tragedy.

Neither O'Neill nor Shepard can be viewed as a strictly autobiographical writer, yet both depict in their major plays families destroyed through reckless parental figures who have an insatiable taste for intoxicating substances. Alcoholism, despondent fathers, sibling rivalry, and nightmarish visions of the American Dream are to be found in both writers' bodies of work. Shepard's father, a former military pilot, was an abusive alcoholic who abandoned his family and exiled himself to the desert only to die in a fashion not too dissimilar to that of the father struck down by an automobile in *A Lie of the Mind* (1985). Shepard's witnessing of his father's decay through alcohol and violence forever altered his view of masculinity. Shepard admits that he "grew up in a condition where the male influences around me were primarily alcoholics and extremely violent" (Roudané 2002: 71). As a result, Shepard's drama serves as an interrogation of the destruction wrought by alcohol and masculine codes.

Initially emerging in the Off-Off Broadway scene of the 1960s, Shepard was hailed as a visionary talent whose esoteric works mixed popular culture, violence, rock music, and American mythology into a vital concoction that redefined American theatre. For Shepard, the traditions of drama existed on a continuum with other cultural products. Indeed, Shepard's primary influences were not theatrical. The young Shepard looked toward "jazz, rock and roll music, abstract and pop art, television serials and comic books, beat poetry, Jung and Freud ... Laurel and Hardy, California kitsch, film noir, sentimental romance" for inspiration (Bottoms 1998: 269). His early works, impenetrable to most commercial theatre patrons, were slowly replaced in the late 1970s with a new aesthetic that welcomed a variation on realism or "modified realism" as Shepard scholar Leslie Wade terms it (1997: 94). This aesthetic allowed for Shepard's plays to be accessible and appreciated by wider audiences.

As his work gained acclaim, Shepard cautioned, "If they're expecting me to be Eugene O'Neill, they may be disappointed"

(Wade 1997: 98). Unlike O'Neill, Shepard tends to embrace dark humor, absurdity, and chaos, while placing primacy on the dynamics of performance rather than on the text as a static work of literature. Elucidating the difference between the staging of his own work and O'Neill's plays, Shepard warned, "You can't possibly do [a play of mine] as a Eugene O'Neill play. I've seen [my plays] done over and over again in a macabre, stone-faced, methodical quasi-tragic form, and it's deadly" (Bigsby 2002: 14). As a result, Shepard himself is a theatre practitioner, often directing his own works in close collaboration with his performers.

Although he has written more than forty plays in a career that has spanned five decades, Shepard's reputation rests primarily on his works during a relatively brief number of years, 1977–1985, when he unleashed a potent and visceral vision of American tragedy: *Curse of the Starving Class* (1977), *Buried Child* (1978), and *A Lie of the Mind* (1985). These three plays, components of his Family Cycle, plunge further than any of his previous work into the destructive psyche of the American male and the tragedy of the American family. This also is the period when Shepard was becoming popularly recognized as an actor, screenwriter, and tabloid celebrity because of his romance with actress Jessica Lange. As a result, he became "lionized as a writer of the American soil, the playwright who most ably captures the country's collective dreams, fears, and desires" (Wade 1997: 7). Like O'Neill, Tennessee Williams, and Arthur Miller before him, Shepard began serving as America's reigning celebrity-playwright, perhaps the last iteration of that fading hyphenate from the twentieth century.

At the center of each play in the Family Cycle is a past traumatic event committed by the patriarch. Essentially, in some action prior to the events of the play, the father has traumatized the family through an event motivated by his allegiance to outdated codes and modes of masculinity. As a result, the family members who have survived the trauma must endure the legacy of the patriarch's actions and suffer under their inability to repair the damage inflicted. Yet, through ritualism, characters within the plays attempt to confront, exorcise, or sometimes even embrace these codes and modes that were the root of the past trauma. For Shepard, the American family brought to destruction through the violence of the patriarch serves as the Great American Tragedy. The failure of the American family—and perhaps of America itself—is rooted in the recklessness and violence of the father, which often is connected to corrupted notions of masculinity.

According to Leslie Wade, "Writing domestic drama has emerged as a requisite exercise for our country's playwrights," yet Shepard's visions of the family veer away from the staid expectations of the genre. Shepard utilizes elements of the domestic drama and infuses it with tragedy, while also radically "imprinting the form with his signature avant-garde devices: the trance monologue, arbitrary character transformations, and surrealistic stage images" as well as epiphanic moments, esoteric rites, and unclosed conclusions. His vision of tragedy borrows the established traditions of the form while imbuing them with devices and approaches developed in 1960s and 1970s avant-garde and alternative performance practices (Wade 1997: 94).

Though Shepard had previously veered into the territory of family dynamics with plays such as *The Rock Garden* (1964), *Holy Ghostly* (1969), and *Action* (1974), his first full-throated interrogation of the American domestic sphere occurred with 1977's *Curse of the Starving Class*. Weston is a violent drunk, whose estranged wife, Ella, is attempting to sell their dilapidated house and farm. Their son Wesley is unpredictable and prone to disturbing actions, while their sensible and artistic daughter Emma dreams of escaping to Mexico to flee the chaos of her family. The play opens amid the wreckage of the family home. The previous night, the father had returned, once again drunk, and the alcohol had unleashed his violence. It is revealed that he has destroyed the front door. Throughout the play, we discover that the father's alcoholism and destructive tendencies have driven away his wife and daughter and are irreparably altering his son Wesley. As a result, the son is psychologically—and later, physically—transforming into his father. Despite Wesley's attempts to repair the destructive actions of Weston, the young man remains, like his father, withdrawn and unpredictable.

At the conclusion of the play, the father Weston and the son Wesley have reversed roles. Weston has transformed into a dutiful husband folding laundry while Wesley has decayed into a destructive force, wearing his father's clothes and assuming the vicious role of patriarch. Although Wesley laments his devolution, he accepts that "every time I put one thing on it seemed like a part of him was growing on me. I could feel him taking over me" (196), and in the end, Wesley—like Vince in *Buried Child*—submits to his legacy.

As Wade has noted, "*Curse of the Starving Class* is in chief concerned with inherited ills passed through the generations; the play consequently evokes a strong sense of blood determinism" (1997: 98). The transformative and destructive forces of Shepard's characters are biologically determined and doom subsequent generations to repeat the mistakes of the patriarch. This notion is introduced early in *Curse of the Starving Class*. Emma notes that her brother Wesley is much like their father Weston, both sharing, "A short fuse ... Runs in the family. His father was just like him. And his father before him. Wesley is just like Pop, too. Like liquid dynamite" (152).

As with many of Shepard's destructive male forces, the biologically determined inclination toward violence is often unleashed through a bottle of cheap liquor. Emma subsequently reveals that her father almost killed a man who he believed to be having an affair with Ella. Emma explains that "It's chemical. It's the same thing that makes him drink. Something in the blood. Hereditary. Highly explosive" (152).

This genetic curse inevitably becomes manifest in Wesley. Almost in a trance, Wesley takes up his father's clothes and the physical indicators of his transformation reflect the internal processes taking place on a hereditary and biological level. The mother Ella recognizes this, explaining, "It's a curse. I can feel it. It's invisible but it's there ... It goes back and back to tiny little cells and genes ... We inherit it and pass it down, and then pass it down again" (174–5). The mistakes of the father have impacted not only a single individual but the family as a whole. Because of this shared trauma, the family members often find themselves linked by their experience. It is as if the "bloodline itself becomes a curse: the past catches up with one, the child paying for the sins of the father. The family curse extends both backward to the past and forward into the future" (Adler 2002: 113).

The hauntings of the father—transgressions previously committed that have immediate impact upon the characters at the center of the play—also are viewed as a type of poison or rot arising from this patriarchal inheritance. Wesley admits, "I saw myself infected with it. That's how. I saw me carrying it around. His poison in my body" (167). Wesley, bemoaning the incursion of outside forces into their farmland, complains, "They've moved in on us like a creeping disease. We didn't even notice" (193), but in actuality he is speaking about the infection of his biological predisposition to transform into his father. With this transformation, Wesley inherits the past's outdated modes and codes of masculinity.

Yet, not all family members are inheritors of such traits. Weston explains to Emma, "You're the only one who doesn't have it. Only us," for Emma is "gentle" and an "artist" (175). As a daughter, it seems that Emma is immune to the curse of the father. For sons such as Wesley, it is impossible to outrun the male's tragic destiny; it is determined from birth. This unwanted inheritance is what creates the tragic circumstances for characters in the present, yet these are placed into motion by actions that predate the concerns of the play.

In *Curse of the Starving Class*, Shepard also incorporates ritualistic actions, as if to prompt the audience to identify elements of the play with larger, mythic concerns and traditions. A lamb, a symbol of innocence in Abrahamic traditions and Christianity, is slaughtered off-stage by Wesley. When its skinned corpse is brought on-stage, visitors to the family farm believe it to be a dead goat, an explicit reference to the "goat song" of early Greek tragedy and a ritualized reference to the tragedy of the father's slaughter of innocence within the play. More than any other writer of his generation, Shepard consciously utilizes ritualistic actions on stage to convey a sense of the mythic, at times aligning his characters with archetypes from both European and Native American traditions. For Shepard, the rituals of the individual—often mysterious and arcane—connect the personal stress of existence with larger concerns of culture. Indeed, the ritualistic actions of characters and Shepard's use of visceral and primordial imagery seemingly link the private struggles of American families with the mythic stresses of Greek tragic figures.

Buried Child (1978), with its revelations of incest and infanticide, thematically echoes the plots and dynamics of *Oedipus Rex* and *Medea*. Patriarch Dodge wastes his days on the couch of his decaying Illinois farm. His wife, Halie, entertains men from the community, ignoring her estranged husband's drunken madness. Dodge and Halie have two sons: the eldest, emotionally distant Tilden, who has recently returned from isolation in the desert, and Bradley, an amputee who gains great delight in inflicting violence on the rare visitor. Tilden's son Vince arrives at the farm with his girlfriend, Shelly, in tow. Strangely, no one recognizes Vince and no family member will even acknowledge Vince's relation to the family. When

Vince travels to the liquor store in town, Shelly is victimized by the family and learns the awful truth that shattered them: years ago, Tilden and Halie, mother and son, produced a child. Ashamed of the child, Dodge drowned the baby and buried it in the backfield. The incestuous relationship was not at the core of the family's tragic fall, but rather the infanticide. The killing was committed in an effort to retain the family's position within the community. Successful in the clandestine murder and burial, the family nonetheless has fallen in standing and further decayed into madness and brutality.

After Vince returns from visiting the liquor shop, he is transformed by alcohol into a violent monster, and is then recognized and embraced by the family as one of their own. Casting off Shelly, Vince assumes his birthright, remains with the traumatized family, and embraces his role as the next generation in the family's lineage. Through alcohol, Vince accepts his destiny screaming, "I've got to carry on the line. I've gotta see to it that things keep rolling" (130). As Vince revels in his transformation, Shelly realizes that her vision of the family "was no hallucination! It was more like a prophecy" (122)—indeed, a phantasmagoric prophecy.

Buried Child deploys perhaps the darkest and most powerful example of ritualism in Shepard's dramaturgy. The damaged Tilden—whose son born of incest was murdered by Dodge and buried on the farm—returns mutely from the farm's fields, which have been barren for decades, with corn. He then buries Dodge, who is lying on the couch, with the husks, completely covering him except for his head (81). The exact meaning of this esoteric burial rite is undetermined beyond an action of silent retribution, yet the power of such haunting imagery reaches toward the unknowable traditions of ritualism, which is later continued with Tilden's depositing an armful of carrots into Shelly's arms. The significance of these ritualized actions are seemingly bound up with issues of heredity, generational transitions, biological determinism, and legacy.

Shepard's final entry in the Family Cycle is 1985's *A Lie of the Mind*. Chronicling the conflict between two families, the center of the play is the destructive and abusive relationship between the married Jake and Beth. When Jake nearly beats Beth to death, they both retreat to their families, resulting in a conflict between their clans.

Though the play features the results of spousal abuse and the impact of mental decay, the dreadful occurrences that set the tragedy into motion began long before the action depicted on stage. Jake, the abusive and at times deranged husband at the center of the tragedy, suffers as a result of his own dead father. Years prior, Jake had sought out his father, who, like many of Shepard's other fathers, had abandoned the family. Disgusted with him, Jake treated the alcoholic to a night at the bars and intentionally neglected him, allowing him to wander drunkenly down a road to be killed by a car. Broken by his father's abandonment, Jake has traumatized himself further through arranging his father's death. Though Jake is suspicious of his wife and her acting teacher, it is these traumas that have forever damaged him and have, paradoxically, transformed him into the rightful son of his father. Though the father is not present in the play, when Jake retreats to his family's home, he is embraced by his mother and immediately infantilized. Curled in bed in his childhood room, surrounded by model airplanes and clutching an American flag, Jake assumes the role of son once again, seemingly seeking answers to his inheritance of madness and violence from a father who is represented only through ephemera, such as dusty military medals. As the final play of the Family Cycle, *A Lie of the Mind* viscerally presents the effects of domestic violence while also interrogating the legacy of masculinity and madness willed to sons from their fathers.

Shepard's Family Cycle performs an autopsy of sorts on the American family, determining the cause of its demise to be patriarchal sins, often rooted in outdated masculine codes of behavior, which linger and haunt subsequent offspring. This inheritance from the father is unavoidable and predetermined, as much through fate and prophecy as through biological and genealogical dynamics.

Shepard reached his cultural moment—and perhaps artistic apogee—with the Family Cycle plays from the late 1970s to the mid-1980s. In this unique contribution to American drama, the one-time rock-and-roll playwright turned to that "most traditional of American dramatic forms, the family play" (Wade 1997: 94) and by giving it a dark but distinctive twist achieved membership amid the hallowed pantheon of America's greatest playwrights, such as O'Neill, Hellman, Williams, Miller, Inge, Hansberry, and Wilson.

Nonetheless, at the conclusion of the Family Cycle, Shepard was not finished pursuing the tragic dynamics of the American family. His plays *The Late Henry Moss* (2001) and *Heartless* (2012) plunge deeper into the core of fractured families, with mixed results. *The*

Late Henry Moss, Shepard's most autobiographical play, concerns two brothers who visit the home of their recently deceased father. Through flashbacks, the siblings argue, drink, fight, and transform as they reckon with the legacy of their father's domestic violence.

Heartless has Shepard lighting out into new territories, specifically that of a matriarchal family. Once again, the sins of the men haunt the surviving family members, but those who provide testimonials are women. Shepard's investigations of the dynamics of men and the damage they inflict upon women and families here utilize elements of the supernatural and transformationalism, tying the work to elements of classical tragedy.

Shepard's recent *A Particle of Dread (Oedipus Variations)* (2013) embraces elements of Sophoclean tragedy turning them into a pulpy vision—in both gore and genre—that borrows from police procedurals as well as Shepard's own well-trodden obsessions. With nightmarish visions of abuse and murder, Shepard attempts to locate resonances between his own dramatic subjects and Greek tragedy, yet the resulting work, inarguably visceral, reveals fewer connective points than one would hope.

The efficacy of Shepard's tragic vision of the American family has more or less waned since his cultural moment of the 1980s. That said, Shepard's tragic vision of the family—perhaps even more than those of such luminaries as O'Neill, Williams, and Miller— has wielded a staggering amount of influence on subsequent writers working in a similar mode. Infusing his cruel and brutal tragedies with dark humor as well as the grotesque and the fantastic, Shepard's Family Cycle has helped shape the tragic visions of contemporary dramatists such as Tracy Letts, Neil LaBute, and Martin McDonagh. Letts, with his rural, Midwestern settings populated by dysfunctional families of addicts and alcoholics, embraces Shepard's tone of humorous desperation. LaBute's interrogation of masculine codes and revelations of the cruelty of men infuses Shepard's tragic vision with characters even more despicable than Shepard's creations. McDonagh, with his shocking violence and tales of familial contention—most obvious in the Shepardian *Lonesome West* (1997)—imports Shepard's sensibilities to non-American settings. Because of the wide variety of modes and genres explored through his body of work, Shepard is not often considered a tragedian; nonetheless, his tragic vision remains the most brutal interrogation of the family within the American canon.

References

Adler, Thomas P. (2002), "Repetition and Regression in *Curse of the Starving Class* and *Buried Child*," in Matthew Roudané (ed.), *The Cambridge Companion to Sam Shepard*, 111–22, Cambridge: Cambridge University Press.

Bigsby, Christopher (2002), "Born Injured: The Theatre of Sam Shepard," in Matthew Roudané (ed.), *The Cambridge Companion to Sam Shepard*, 7–33, Cambridge: Cambridge University Press.

Bottoms, Stephen J. (1998), *The Theatre of Sam Shepard: States of Crisis*, Cambridge Studies in American Theatre and Drama (9), Cambridge: Cambridge University Press.

Roudané, Matthew (2002), "Shepard on Shepard: An Interview," in Matthew Roudané (ed.), *The Cambridge Companion to Sam Shepard*, 64–80, Cambridge: Cambridge University Press.

Shepard, Sam ([1977] 1986a), *Curse of the Starving Class*, in *Sam Shepard: Seven Plays*, New York: Bantam.

Shepard, Sam ([1978] 1986b), *Buried Child*, in *Sam Shepard: Seven Plays*, New York: Bantam.

Shepard, Sam ([1985] 1986c), *A Lie of the Mind*, New York: Dramatists Play Service.

Soloski, Alexis (2016), "Sam Shepard Takes Stock of 'Buried Child' and the Writer's Life," *The New York Times*, January 28. Available online: http://www.nytimes.com/2016/01/31/theater/sam-shepard-takes-stock-of-buried-child-and-the-writers-life.html (accessed January 22, 2017).

Wade, Leslie A. (1997), *Sam Shepard and the American Theatre*, Contributions in Drama and Theatre Studies, Lives of the Theatre 76, Westport, CT: Greenwood Press.

14

David Mamet (1947–)

Brenda Murphy
University of Connecticut

Classical tragedy is not the first thing that comes to mind when David Mamet is mentioned. He is better known for minimalist plays that feature scenes of gritty realism and the expletive-strewn street argot that has come to be known as "Mametspeak." The self-described "gang comedy" (Kane 2001: 64) of *Glengarry Glen Ross* has come to be seen as Mamet's characteristic aesthetic. But he has had a long-standing interest in tragedy, particularly as defined by Aristotle. He has written that the "purpose of theater, like magic, like religion—those three harness mates—is to inspire cleansing awe" (Mamet 1998a: 69). He believes that "tragedy is cleansing because it confronts us with our humanity, with our capacity for evil" (Kane 2001: 181), but that fundamentally, it is based on human choice. In an interview, Mamet said that when a character is presented with what appear to be good and evil alternatives, tragedy says, "'choose which one you want to be. Whichever one you choose, you're going to be wrong, and, P. S., you never had a choice to begin with. You're just human.' And we leave shaken and perhaps better for the experience" (Kane 2001: 181). Time and again, Mamet has reiterated that tragedy is fundamentally about revealing truth. "Tragedy is about horrific things," he said in an interview. "It's about bringing the hidden to light so that one can grieve. And that's why tragedy, in the perfect form, is cleansing, because it enables us to deal with repression ... And as Freud would have said, instead of living a happy life, be more capable to live a life of ordinary misery" (Kane 2001: 209).

Perhaps because he sees revelation as central to tragedy, Mamet sees Aristotle's description of recognition and reversal at the heart of tragic structure. He has described his play *The Shawl* as

> a twentieth century version of the idea that what the hero is following and what he ends up with may be two very different things, but they are nonetheless related in the subconscious ... what happens at the crucial moment, as Aristotle says, is that the protagonist undergoes both recognition of the situation and a reversal of the situation. (Kane 2001: 66)

On the other hand, he has said that "although it has aspects of tragedy in it" (Roudané 1986: 48), *Glengarry Glen Ross* cannot be called a tragedy because of its unresolved ending, lacking the classical tragic elements of recognition, reversal, and catharsis.

Mamet has identified four of his plays as classical tragedies on the Aristotelian model: *American Buffalo* (1975), *The Woods* (1977), *Oleanna* (1992), and *The Cryptogram* (1994). In broad terms, *American Buffalo* and *The Cryptogram* are family tragedies that are specifically about the failure of parent figures to protect the young people in their charge.[1] *The Woods* and *Oleanna* are about the failure of human communication due to the inability of the characters to negotiate the complex relationships among language, power, and human emotions.

In *American Buffalo*, the protagonist and parent figure is Don Dubrow, the owner of a junk shop who operates in a marginal urban economy that blurs the lines between business and criminality. At the beginning of the play, Don is teaching Bobby, a young drug addict he has taken under his wing, about business, which he says is, "people taking *care* of themselves" (Mamet 1976: 7, Mamet's italics). What is important to Don is that Bobby understand "there's business and there's friendship," and he tells Bobby, "what you got to do is keep clear who your friends are, and who treated you like what" (Mamet 1976: 7). He warns him, "there's lotsa people on this street, Bob, they want this and they want that. Do anything to get it. You don't have *friends* this life ..." (Mamet 1976: 8, Mamet's italics and ellipsis). As Mamet has described it, Don, at the beginning of the play, is "trying to teach a lesson in how to behave like the excellent man to his young ward" (Kane 2001: 67). Don's moral position is "that one must conduct himself like a man, and there are no extenuating circumstances for supporting the betrayal of a friend" (Kane 2001: 48).

In the course of the play, Mamet said, Don is "tempted by the devil into betraying all his principles" (Kane 2001: 67). Don, who feels he has been cheated on the price of a Buffalo nickel by a customer, has a plan to steal the man's coin collection and sell it to a shady dealer. He has planned the burglary with Bobby, but his friend Teach, a more professional thief, convinces him that Bobby probably will bungle it. Teach champions capitalism, or as he puts it, "free enterprise"—"The freedom ... of the *Individual* ... To Embark on Any Fucking Course that he sees fit ... In order to secure his honest chance to make a profit" (Mamet 1976: 72–3, Mamet's italics and ellipsis). He succeeds in shaming Don for putting his loyalty to Bobby ahead of "business":

> All I mean, a guy can be too loyal, Don. Don't be dense on this. What are we saying here? Business ... We both know we're talking about some job needs more than the kid's gonna skin-pop go in there with a *crowbar.* (Mamet 1976: 34, Mamet's italics)

In the end, Teach convinces Don that he "cannot afford (and simply as a *business* proposition) you cannot afford to take the chance" (Mamet 1976: 35, Mamet's italics), and he should let Teach do the burglary. Don betrays Bobby by cutting him out of the deal, succumbing to Teach's values by placing "business," or self-interest, above "loyalty."

Later, when Teach convinces Don that Bobby has pulled off the burglary with someone else despite Bobby's denials, Don betrays him again by allowing Teach to beat him and telling him, "you brought it on yourself" (Mamet 1976: 94). When they find out that Teach was wrong, Mamet has said, Don

> undergoes ... recognition in reversal—realizing that all this comes out of his vanity, that because he abdicated a moral position for one moment in favor of some momentary gain, he has let anarchy into his life and has come close to killing the thing

he loves. And he realizes at the end of the play that he has made a huge mistake, that, rather than his young ward needing lessons in being an excellent man, it is he himself who needs those lessons. That is what *American Buffalo* is about. (Kane 2001: 67)

As a result of his realization, Don not only asks and receives forgiveness from Bobby, but forgives Teach as well. Although the damage has been done, both to Don's relationship with Bobby and physically to Bobby and to Don's shop, which Teach has smashed up in a fit of rage, Don tries to salvage what he can and go on. As the play ends and Don and Teach finally work together to take Bobby to the hospital, there is a sense that what Mamet calls their "family constellation" (Kane 2001: 161) has been reconstituted. This play is perhaps the clearest demonstration in Mamet's work of his sense of the importance of recognition and reversal to tragedy.

The Cryptogram embodies Mamet's belief that "every tragedy's based on deception; that's the meaning of the, the tragic form ... something has been hidden and can only be uncovered, uncovered at great expense. And when it is uncovered we say, 'Oh, my gosh, it was in front of me the whole time'" (Kane 2001: 153, ellipsis in original). The audience's experience of the play is centered in the point of view of John, a ten-year-old boy whose world and sense of identity are shaken in the course of the play. Like *American Buffalo*, the play is rife with betrayals, beginning with John's father Robert's failure to show up to take him on a much-anticipated camping trip. Instead, in a deliberately melodramatic revelation at the end of Act 1, John finds a letter from his father to his mother, Donny, saying that he is leaving her. In Act 2, it is revealed that Del, a gay family friend who professes to love Donny, has allowed Robert to use his room for his meetings with a woman, and has lied to Donny about it. While Del insists, "this is the only bad thing I have ever done to you," Donny tells him to get out of her house and breaks down in grief. She in turn fails her maternal duty to John, sending him off to bed rather than giving him any comfort when he comes downstairs and tells her he heard voices calling him and went outside to look through the window into his room, where he saw a candle burning, which led him to the realization, "I'm perfectly alone" (Mamet 1998b: 43–4).

In Act 3, the consequences of these realizations play out. Del attempts propitiation for his betrayal of Donny, saying that "it is not the sins we commit that destroy us, but how we act after we've committed them" (Mamet 1998b: 48). But Donny refuses to forgive him, instead exacting some revenge by telling Del that the pilot's knife Robert gave him as a kind of compensation for his cooperation in deceiving her was not the precious wartime trophy he thought it was but just a souvenir bought on the street in London. When Donny later claims that in telling him, "I didn't mean to hurt you," Del responds, "Oh, if we could speak the truth, do you see, for one instant. Then we would be free" (Mamet 1998b: 50).

In Act 3, John twice asks Donny, "do you ever wish that you could die? ... It's not such a bad feeling (*Pause*) Is it?" (Mamet 1998b: 45). John comes downstairs after he's been sent to bed, complaining that his mind is racing and he's cold. Preoccupied with her own problems, Donny sends him upstairs again, telling him he has to go to sleep: "If you do *not* sleep, *lay* there. Lay in bed. What you think about there is your concern. No one can help you. Do you understand? *Finally each* of us ... Is alone" (Mamet 1998b: 51, Mamet's italics and ellipsis). John keeps asking for a special blanket, but Donny tells him she's put it away in the attic. The blanket is a highly freighted symbolic object in the play. After Donny and Robert bought it in London, they made love under it, used it as a coverlet to keep them warm, and wrapped John in it when he was a baby. For John, and for Donny as well, the blanket represents the warm and comforting fabric of their family. Donny knows it was torn and packed away long ago, but John continues to cling to it in the face of an alarming loss of emotional stability. In Act 1, John is very upset because he thinks he is the one who tore the blanket, but Donny, partly to reassure him and partly to get him to go upstairs to bed, tells him, "it was torn long ago. You can absolve yourself" (Mamet 1998b: 21).

In Act 3, in exchange for his promise not to come back downstairs, Donny says John can have the blanket. When John comes back anyway, Donny's anger at her betrayal by Del and Robert erupts in her screaming at John for having broken his word. "Go away. You lied," she says. "I love you, but I can't like you." Blind to her child's need for her care, Donny instead demands of him, "Can't you see that I need comfort? Are you blind? For the love of God." When John says he can't get the blanket because the box it is in is tied with string, Del gives him the pilot's knife to cut it. John keeps repeating that he hears voices calling him, but Del tells him to "take the knife and go." As he mounts the stairs, John says, "They're calling my name. (*Pause*). Mother. They're calling my name" (Mamet 1998b: 55–7).

As John Lahr so aptly put it, *The Cryptogram* delineates "the dynamics of a soul murder" (Lahr 1994: 73). In the tradition of classic tragedy, Mamet leaves the final consequence of the play's betrayals offstage, leaving the audience to imagine what John does with the knife. Michael Feingold wrote that, in the New York production that Mamet directed, the staircase that is the dominant element of the set seemed "to stretch up to a dark infinity; the son's last slow ascent of it ... makes the audience gasp ... intensely" (Feingold 1995: 97).

Mamet has called *The Woods* "a play about heterosexuality" (Kane 2001: 68). A highly literary work, it was his earliest attempt to write seriously about the relationships between men and women after his successful comedy about the 1970s singles scene, *Sexual Perversity in Chicago* (1974), and it perhaps represents the tragedy that is latent in this dark comedy. Its plot is simple. A young couple, Nick and Ruth, are spending the weekend together for the first time, at a cabin on a lake that is owned by Nick's family. Ruth sees his invitation as a sign that Nick wants to bring their relationship to a higher level of commitment and has brought a gift for him, a bracelet that she has had engraved, "Nicholas. I will always love you. Ruth" (82). Observing the neoclassical unities of time, place, and action, Mamet sets the play on the porch of the cabin, and its three scenes take place within a 24-hour period, at dusk, at night, and in the morning. In the first scene, Ruth does most of the talking. She spends a good deal of time acknowledging Nick's apparent fear of intimacy and preparing him for her suggestion that they make a long-term commitment to each other. Mamet has said that *The Woods* is "a dreamy play, full of the symbology of dream and the symbology of myth, which are basically the same thing" (Kane 2001: 68). Its meaning is conveyed through the imagery of stories the characters tell and dreams they relate, as well as through their own rather overt use of symbolism and allegory. In the play's opening speech, Ruth sets up the central problem of their relationship and the central theme of the play by describing Nick's existential isolation in the guise of a story about some seagulls she had observed on the lake:

These seagulls they were up there, one of them was up there by himself.
He didn't want the other ones.

They came, he'd flap and get them off.
He let this one guy stay up there a minute. (Mamet 1987: 13)

Ruth is hoping to get Nick to let her stay up there with him for a long time, but she doesn't realize the depth of his fear of intimacy. This comes out in the third scene, the next morning, when he tells her a dream he has had. He dreams that the family's cottage is burning and (like *The Cryptogram*'s John), he hears someone calling his name. What is calling him is a bear that has come "to crawl beneath my house. This house is *mine* now. In its hole it calls me." The bear is standing upright and has a huge erection. Nick feels that he is "singed." The bear speaks a human language. "He has these thoughts and they are trapped inside his mouth. His jaw cannot move. He has thoughts and feelings, BUT HE CANNOT SPEAK." When Ruth asks what the bear wants, Nick replies, "I DO NOT KNOW!" (Mamet 1987: 112, Mamet's italics).

Nick's obvious fear of his own sexuality is connected with his inability to communicate intimately with another human being on any terms. Like a child, he hopes this will be done for him, without emotional risk to himself. In the second scene, he tells Ruth that he dreams of "homes and things ... Living in them. Being warm." He daydreams about someone he would share his home with: "we would meet and we would just be happy." Ruth tries to create a path to a realistic relationship for them by suggesting, "sometimes things are different than the way you thought they'd be when you set out on them ... Things can be unexpected and be beautiful if we will let them. (*Pause.*) And not be frightened by them, Nick." But she is unsuccessful, and their offstage attempt to make love alters their relationship for the worse. When Ruth gives Nick the bracelet, he refuses to wear it, and Ruth decides to go home (Mamet 1987: 66–8).

In the third scene, Nick tries to get Ruth to stay, while she insists that their relationship is over. Nick tells Ruth of his belief that he would meet a person and she would say:

"Let us be lovers." (*Pause.*)
She'd ask me.
"I know who you are. (*Pause.*)
I know you.
I know what you need.
I want to have your children. (*Pause.*)

I understand you.
I know what you are." (Mamet 1987: 109)

When Nick insists that he would "fall down and thank God" and
kiss the Earth if such a woman appeared, Ruth responds, "You
read too many books" (Mamet 1987: 109–10). She now sees
the impossibility of fulfilling her own romantic notion of their
relationship at this point, and when Nick tells her the dream about
the bear, and asks her whether he is insane, she first tries to comfort
him as she would a child and ends up slapping him in the face
to break his hysteria. The outcome of their exchange is that Nick
finally is able to tell Ruth that he loves her, but it is too late, and she
can respond only, "Thank you" (Mamet 1987: 116). Mamet offers
a germ of hope within the Aristotelian scene of pathos that ends
the play, however. As Ruth cradles Nick in her arms, she repeats
the story of the "Babes in the Woods" that her grandmother had
told her, ending with the words, "the next day" (Mamet 1987:
119). It is clear that, much as they might love each other, Nick and
Ruth cannot possibly come together in a mature and committed
relationship. But Mamet has suggested that there is "salvation" in
the play, in that Nick, who is "trying to live in a rational world,
is dragged kicking and screaming into some kind of emotional
maturity" (Bigsby 1985: 58). This recognition comes too late to
forestall the inevitable reversal in the trajectory of his relationship
with Ruth, but it does suggest the compensatory knowledge that
comes with it.

At the center of *Oleanna* is a failure of human communication. Its
two characters, Carol and John, are well-meaning but deeply flawed
people who become engaged in a power struggle that emerges from
each character's inability to understand, or even listen to, what
the other character is saying. John is a forty-something Assistant
Professor of Education with a wife and son; he is undergoing his
review for tenure and promotion. Although the committee has
announced that tenure is forthcoming, it is not yet official. On the
surface, John exudes a confident and rather arrogant intellectual
demeanor, but this masks a profound insecurity, which is gradually
revealed in the course of the play. He confesses that he always has
felt stupid, that he hated his teachers and the educational system
growing up, and that, when he recently met with the tenure
committee who held his future employment in their hands, he felt

an urge to "*vomit*, to, to, to puke my *badness* on the table, to show them: 'I'm no good. Why would you pick *me*?'" (Mamet 1992: 23, Mamet's italics).

During the course of Act 1, a series of telephone calls makes John increasingly anxious that he and his wife are going to lose the house they are buying on the strength of the future employment that will come with his tenure award. These calls interrupt the increasingly intense conversation with his student Carol, who has come to his office, ostensibly to get his help in understanding the "concepts" and "precepts" he uses in class, although she really is there to try to get him to give her a better grade so that she can get her degree and, as she says, "get on in the world" (Mamet 1992: 12). She is terrified of failing, and tells John, "I don't understand what anything means ... and I walk around. From morning 'til night: with this one thought in my head. I'm *stupid*" (Mamet 1992: 12, Mamet's italics and ellipsis).

These two people, who lack sensitivity and the ability to empathize with others to begin with, are in no fit state to carry on the conversation that takes place in Act 1. John, who sees only a projection of his younger self in Carol, assumes she is as angry at the system as he always has been and offers to throw out the rules and begin the course over for her. He promises her an A if she will continue meeting with him in his office to discuss the ideas in the course. While accepting this "deal," Carol, who only wants entré into the system, not to overturn it, either misunderstands or deliberately misconstrues his intention, and acts two and three play out as an escalating series of attempts and failures to communicate with each other after Carol reports John's actions to the tenure committee as sexual harassment: "He said he 'liked' me. That he 'liked being with me.' He'd let me write my examination paper over, if I could come back oftener to see him in his office" (Mamet 1992: 48). At the end of Act 2, John, acting out his frustration, physically restrains Carol to try to get her to listen to his appeal to retract her testimony. At the end of Act 3, it emerges that she has pressed legal charges against him: "I was leaving this office, you 'pressed' yourself into me. You 'pressed' your body into me ... under the statute. I am told. It was battery ... and attempted rape" (Mamet 1992: 78).

Mamet describes *Oleanna* as "a tragedy about power" (Kane 2001: 125). He says that Carol and John are "two people with a lot to say to each other, with legitimate affection for each other. But protecting their positions becomes more important than pursuing their own best interests. And that leads them down the slippery slope to a point where, at the end of the play, they tear each other's throat out" (Kane 2001: 125). In 1992, when the play premiered, it stirred a good deal of controversy over the issue of sexual harassment. In the immediate wake of the Clarence Thomas confirmation hearings, Mamet was accused of casting Carol in a negative light and directing the audience's sympathy toward John, making him into a victim of the extremes of political correctness. Mamet consistently has maintained that he doesn't "take, personally take the side of one rather than the other. I think they're absolutely both wrong, and they're absolutely both, both right. And that's to the extent that the play aspires to—or achieves—the status of … a tragedy" (Kane 2001: 144, ellipsis in original). At the end of Act 3, in response to Carol's order, "don't call your wife 'baby'" (79), John grabs and beats her, spewing misogynistic invective. His claim to be a civilized man and an enlightened educator has now been reduced to the use of brute force and hate speech against a student. Finally, as Carol cowers on the floor below him, he looks at her. Then he lowers the chair he has been holding over his head, goes to his desk, and starts arranging the papers on it. He looks over at her, and says "well." She looks at him and says, twice, "Yes. That's right" (Mamet 1992: 80).

The meaning of the ending has been debated, and it is of course completely dependent on the way the director stages the scene in a given production. Mamet has directed the play twice, in its original stage production and in the film adaptation that was made in 1994. John was played by Mamet's longtime friend and collaborator William H. Macy in both versions. Mamet's interpretation of the scene is evident in the film, as a look of bewilderment, followed by utter grief, crosses Macy's face while he observes the cowering figure of Carol (Debra Eisenstadt) on the floor. Mamet has described John as the play's protagonist, saying that "he undergoes absolute reversal of situation, absolute recognition at the last moment of the play. He realizes that perhaps he is the cause of the plague upon Thebes" (Kane 2001: 119). In the context of *Oleanna*, he also said in an interview that tragedy is the most difficult form to write,

> where the hero or heroine is going to his … Aristotle tells us, come to the end of the play and realize that he or she is the cause of their own problems and undergo[es] a change of the situation

at the last moment of the play ... such that the audience will say, "Oh my God, now I understand. I've seen something that is both shocking and inevitable." (Kane 2001: 145, ellipses in original)

There is no doubt in the play that John's character and actions carry the seeds of his destruction. As Carol tells him, "what has *led* you to this place? Not your sex. Not your race. Not your class. YOUR OWN ACTIONS" (Mamet 1992: 64, Mamet's italics).

As committed as he is to Aristotle's description of tragedy, Mamet is aware of the dissonance that happens when applying it to modern life. This emerges in parodic form in *Boston Marriage* (2002), a comedy of manners written in the style of Oscar Wilde. The play is framed by a far-fetched comic plot. In the first act, Anna, a seemingly well-to-do single woman, receives a visit from her former lover Claire. Anna is hopeful that they can rekindle their relationship, telling Claire that she has acquired a "protector" who has cleared her debts, has given her the ostentatiously large emerald necklace she is wearing, and is paying her a monthly stipend, and that she and Claire can now afford to live comfortably together. But Claire has come to ask if she can use Anna's house for an assignation with a very young woman she is interested in. Though angry and jealous, Anna agrees, but when the girl arrives, she asks Claire what Anna is doing wearing her mother's necklace.

This "discovery" ends the first act, and the rest of the play is spent hatching a scheme to explain the necklace, a far-fetched plan in which Anna and Claire will pose as clairvoyants, claiming that the protector had given them the necklace to divine the source of his wife's illness. They invite the whole family to a seance, but Anna receives a letter from the protector's attorney informing her that the family has "decamped," and her "consultation fees" have been discontinued. It demands the immediate return of the necklace, "absent which ... legal remedies, criminal proceedings, bailiff, theft ... jail" (Mamet 2002: 92–3, Mamet's ellipsis).

In another twist, Anna tells Claire that she can't find the necklace and believes that the maid has stolen it and gone off. Anna prepares for jail. When Claire sees that a picture of her has a prominent place among the belongings Anna packs, her feelings for her come out, and she tells her she is prepared to join her.

In quick final twists, the maid returns and tells Claire where the necklace is, but Claire doesn't tell Anna, and she also gives up one final chance for a tryst with the young lady. Then, in the final lines of the play, Anna reveals to the maid that she has known where the necklace was all the time, and tells her to give it to the lawyer as she goes off to meet Claire.

Other than its witty Wildean dialogue, uncharacteristic for Mamet, this play is noteworthy for the elements of classic Greek tragedy that pervade the comic plot. Early in the play, Mamet introduces the concept of fate or destiny, which Anna has the arrogance to violate. Of her scheme to live with Claire while receiving the benefits of her protector, Claire warns her:

Claire   Do not tempt fate.

Anna   He worships me. What could go awry?

Claire   Has he, for example, a wife? (Mamet 2002: 6)

After the necklace is revealed to the Protector's daughter, Anna says, "Fell circumstance. Oh, how you chastise my presumption. I am undone" (Mamet 2002: 44). Later, in a parodic soliloquy, she cries, "Oh, fate inexorable. Oh, fate misthought at first to be but circumstance, revealed at last as the minute operations of the gods. Oh fate but our own character congealed into a burning glass. Focus your cleansing light upon me, and I shall be cleansed" (Mamet 2002: 51). She appeals to Claire, "Have I not undergone ... 'a reversal'" (Mamet 2002: 56).

After the letter from the lawyer reveals that the life she had planned has been destroyed, Anna shows some enlightenment along classical Greek lines, as she suggests that "*true* happiness" (Mamet 2002: 93) might lie, not in obtaining the object of one's lust, but "in being *free* of it" (Mamet 2002: 95, Mamet's italics). As the play's denouement proceeds, she urges Claire to "Make that Leap. That, that Act of Renunciation," that "State of Grace," "of *acceptance*" and pursue a quiet life in which they could be happy, "as long as one has not 'done evil'" or "caused *pain*" (Mamet 2002: 97–8, Mamet's italics). Finally, Claire confesses, "I am the cause of your misfortune" (Mamet 2002: 106), and Anna forgives her. When Anna asks Claire if she is "resigned to accompany [her] into Exile," Claire responds that she is "not resigned but honored" (Mamet 2002: 112).

Applying tragic discourse to Anna's pursuits at first seems to emphasize their triviality, as when, preparing to leave for jail, she says that the "most profoundly difficult of human tasks" is not to forgive one who has wronged you, but "to pack when rushed" (Mamet 2002: 106), but it also inspires a second look that suggests the tragic element embedded in this trivial comedy. *Boston Marriage* is Mamet's unique take on Wilde's notion of a trivial comedy for serious people, a tragicomedy in which the comic not only embraces but overwhelms the tragic as Anna and Claire finally do manage to cheat fate with their machinations and the devotion that they, at bottom, feel for each other, and to embark on a future life together.

Neatly embedded within *Boston Marriage*'s tragicomedy are not only the concepts of fate and resignation that are endemic to classical Greek tragedy, but also the Aristotelian structural model that is familiar from the plays Mamet has written and described as straightforward tragedies. When thinking of tragedy, he seems to have been preoccupied since the 1970s with Aristotle's conception, particularly the recognition and reversal that are crucial elements of *American Buffalo* and *Oleanna*, the many-layered revelation of truth that is at the heart of *The Cryptogram*, the catharsis and pathos that end *The Woods*, and the all-pervasive conviction of the human necessity to make choices, even under the condition that "whichever one you choose, you're going to be wrong, and P.S., you never had a choice to begin with" (Kane 2001: 181). Perhaps all of Mamet's explorations into the possibilities of classical tragedy for the contemporary stage share one ultimate goal: that the audience, having experienced the play, leave "shaken and perhaps better for the experience" (Kane 2001: 181).

Note

1   In Mamet's *Faustus* (2004), a modern version of the Faust legend, Faust's tragic downfall is also caused by his betrayal of his family.

References

Bigsby C. W. E. (1985), *David Mamet*, London: Methuen.
Feingold, Michael (1995), "Codehearted," *Village Voice*, April 25: 97.
Kane, Leslie (ed.) (2001), *David Mamet in Conversation*, Ann Arbor, MI: University of Michigan Press.

Lahr, John (1994), "Betrayals," *New Yorker*, August 1: 73.

Mamet, David (1976), *American Buffalo*, New York: Grove.

Mamet, David (1987), *The Woods. Lake Boat. Edmond*, New York: Grove.

Mamet, David (1992), *Oleanna*, New York: Grove.

Mamet, David (1998a), *Three Uses of the Knife: On the Nature and Purpose of Drama*, New York: Columbia University Press.

Mamet, David (1998b), *The Cryptogram*, New York: Dramatists Play Service.

Mamet, David (2002), *Boston Marriage*, New York: Vintage.

Mamet, David (2004), *Faustus*, New York: Vintage.

Roudané, Matthew C. (1986), "Public Issues, Private Tensions: David Mamet's *Glengarry Glen Ross*," *South Carolina Review* 19: 35–47.

15

Marsha Norman (1947–)

David Palmer
Massachusetts Maritime Academy

To understand the tragedy in Marsha Norman's most famous play *'night, Mother* (Pulitzer Prize 1983), think of Agamemnon and his daughter Iphigenia on the beach at Aulis.[1] The focus and meaning of that story changes from Aeschylus' *Agamemnon* to Euripides' *Iphigenia in Aulis*, but the basic situation is clear. The god Artemis is angry at Agamemnon because he has killed one of her sacred deer. She becalms the wind at Aulis so that Agamemnon cannot launch his fleet to attack Troy, and she vows the wind will not change until Agamemnon slays his daughter as a sacrifice. Agamemnon must decide where his true identity lies: is he the indomitable public general or the devoted private father? He cannot be both. There are at least two tragedies here, even ignoring the grief and fury of Clytemnestra, Agamemnon's wife and Iphigenia's mother, which will lead to the cascading agony in the *Oresteia*. There is the terror of Iphigenia and the anguish of Agamemnon as he struggles to decide which of two dearly held values he will abandon. Iphigenia's tragedy is her death despite her innocence; Agamemnon's is the painful acknowledgment of betrayal he must carry no matter which path he chooses.

This may seem like an exceptionally distant and highbrow story to relate to a Marsha Norman play. Norman began gaining recognition in the late 1970s for her gritty dramas of sad and angry, socially marginalized Americans, such as *Getting Out* (1977) and *Third and Oak* (1978), works that were grounded in some way in her experiences in her hometown of Louisville, Kentucky, just after graduate school, working as a teacher of emotionally disturbed children at the Kentucky Central State Hospital (Brown 1996: xv; Norman 1998: 2). Along with the writer of absurdist comedies Christopher Durang, she is codirector of the Playwrights Program at Julliard; has written extensively for movies and television, including a year as co-executive producer of *Law & Order: Criminal Intent*; won a Tony Award in 1991 for her book for the musical *The Secret Garden*; and gone on to do books or librettos for four other Broadway musicals, including 2016's award-winning *The Color Purple*, a revival of the 2006 musical for which Norman earned a second Tony nomination. An inductee into the Theatre Hall of Fame, Norman has had a long, productive, lauded, and varied career without specifically focusing on tragedy (Norman, *marshanorman. com*). Nonetheless, there are strong parallels between the classic Greek tragic tale of Agamemnon and Iphigenia and Norman's story in *'night, Mother* about Jessie Cates and her mother, Thelma, in rural middle America. Consider the following quotation from Leslie Kane's article (1989) and the comment it contains by Norman on her own work in general:

> Marsha Norman dramatizes the personal crises of ordinary people struggling to have a self and be a self. "What interests me is survival," says Norman, "what it takes to survive. I find people very compelling who are at the moment of choice. Will they die or go on? If they go on, in what direction or for what purpose?" (255)

Exploring these parallels between an evening at Thelma and Jessie's home and a father and daughter on the beach at Aulis provides insights not just into tragedy but into the way a peculiarly American kind of tragedy arises in our culture.

'night, Mother opens on the living area of a modest but relatively new home "*built way out a country road.*" A bedroom door dominates the back of the set. The date is the early 1980s, basically the year in which Norman wrote the play. The play runs in real time; clocks are placed throughout the set on which the

audience can see time pass, "*the action beginning about 8:15.*" The house is comfortable if cluttered. Norman states explicitly that nothing about the set should "*make a judgement about the intelligence or taste of Jessie and Thelma.*" Nor should anything about their accents or appearance distance them from the audience. The entire scene "*should simply indicate that they are very specific real people,*" the American everywoman. It is clear that they have lived together a long time and have developed a "*sense of routine comfort*" (Norman 1983: 4–7).

Jessie is around 40 and a bit physically unsteady because she has epilepsy, which she believes prevents her from holding a job. She moved back home with her mother after she and her husband separated and acts in many ways as her mother's housekeeper. Her adolescent son, Ricky, is estranged from his parents and grandmother and has become a petty criminal. Jessie was close to her father, much closer than her mother was. He died when Jessie was an adult but before she moved back home years earlier. Jessie almost never steps outside the house.

Thelma is some twenty years older than Jessie: roughly sixty. She also is not employed and occupies her time with simple indulgences: Hershey bars and peanut brittle, television, meandering conversations and local trips with her friend Agnes, who, unlike Jessie and Thelma, drives. Thelma has a son, Dawson, Jessie's older brother, who lives nearby, is married, and has children. They come to visit, but Jessie likes neither Dawson nor his wife. As Norman says in her opening stage directions, Thelma and Jessie live a life of relaxed routine and modest comfort, a leisurely, often uninspiring passing of time.

Tonight, however, Jessie seems unusually energetic and focused, which Thelma at first finds slightly confusing but unimportant until Jessie starts asking about where her father's gun is and announces she plans to kill herself in a couple of hours (13–14). The rest of the play swings back and forth between frantic and quiet conversations as Jessie tries to explain her reasons for wanting to die and Thelma tries both to understand Jessie and to prevent her from acting.

As the scenes unfold, it becomes clear that Jessie has lost her sense of agency: her sense that she is capable of action with significant purpose that can give meaning and direction—and thus some kind of genuine joy—to her life. She no longer can tolerate her life's passivity and aimlessness. She tells her mother, "I'm just not having a very good time and I don't have any reason to think it'll get anything but worse" (22). She feels lonely, disconnected, and confined, like a rider on an uncomfortable bus who has no real destination and thus no reason not simply to get off now (24). She has lost any sense of authenticity, any sense that she fully exists:

> That's what this is about. It's somebody I lost, all right, it's my own self. Who I never was. Or who I tried to be and never got there. Somebody I waited for who never came. And never will. (50)

Killing herself is at least one thing Jessie believes she actually can do. It will end her life—in the future of which she does not have much faith anyway—but it will recover her sense of agency and thus of pride. When her mother tells Jessie she doesn't have to kill herself, Jessie replies: "No, I don't. That's what I like about it" (21). For Jessie, part of the appeal of killing herself is that it is one of the few things she feels she can do by choice: it is something she believes she can accomplish and nothing is compelling her other than her own free decision. As she'll say later, "This is how I have my say. This is how I say what I thought about it *all* and I say NO" (49). (See Roudané 1996: 131.)

Thelma replies to Jessie's ideas harshly:

> You're acting like some little brat, Jessie. You're mad and everybody's boring and you don't have anything to do and you don't like me ... and you're miserable and it's your own sweet fault. (25)

But, of course, Thelma's complaint is exactly Jessie's point. Jessie does indeed feel she has been acting like a brat and waiting for something magically to change her life as she drifts through incapable of significant action. She replies to her mother: "And it's about time I did something about it" (25). Suicide for Jessie is an expression of autonomy (see Paige 2005: 394, and Norman's comments on the play in Betsko and Koenig 1987: 327–30, 339–40). Killing herself is the only thing left she feels she actually can control and accomplish.

In a 1983 interview—coincidentally but perhaps not accidentally, given the *zeitgeist*, one year after Norman wrote *'night, Mother* and one year before President Ronald Reagan would run for re-election with the slogan of optimism "It's morning again in America"— Arthur Miller suggested that the American Dream is "the largely unacknowledged screen in front of which all American writing plays itself out—the screen of the perfectibility of man" (Miller and Roudané [1983] 1987: 361). American national mythology envisions the country as a land of freedom and opportunity, where having a thriving life is not just a possibility but practically a promised political right.

Here, Miller may have captured the source of Jessie's despair: she has been unable to feel connected to that Dream.[2] This connection is not a matter of will, something a person just does, like deciding to reach for a pencil, as Thelma suggests when she urges Jessie just to get interested in something (23–5); rather, it is what William James in his writings on the self calls "a live hypothesis": a belief that arises in a person providing sufficient faith in the possibility of an outcome for the person to be motivated to act (James [1896] 1992: 457–9). The liveness of a hypothesis is not an act of will; it is a feeling that arises, and feelings, unlike mere behavior, cannot be willed. For example, you can will yourself to behave as if you respect or even love someone, but you cannot merely will the feeling into actual existence; the feeling must arise on its own. Jessie's problem is that she cannot find her way to the feeling that her life is worthwhile. She suffers under not the promise but the demand of the American Dream, its inherent idea that for lives to be worthy and livable they must contain some sense of purpose and thriving; they cannot be merely the mindless, essentially empty passage of time, even if that is a life of comfort. By the standard of the American Dream, Jessie experiences herself as a failure. She no longer believes there is anything she can do to capture a sense of meaning, joy, and flourishing in her life. There is, however, one "hypothesis," as James calls it, that is "live" for Jessie: she does believe she can kill herself, a purposeful act that will achieve an end to her painful despair. In planning to kill herself, Jessie recovers her sense of agency and an accompanying joyful pride in who she is: a kind of self-respect. That is why she has spent the past weeks so carefully and enthusiastically organizing her own death.

However, as Jessie knows well, Thelma will be devastated by her suicide. Her self-imposed death does not come without a high price to other people, especially to this person whom Jessie perhaps loves most deeply of all (see Brustein [1983] 1996: 160–2). This realization makes Jessie like Agamemnon at Aulis: for ten years (22) she has struggled with the question of whether to try continuing to live or to die, fully aware that the path that ends her own pain inflicts pain on others. What obligations does she have? What rights? Whose needs should she most honor: her own or her mother's?

Jessie's suggestion of suicide brings on three crises for Thelma. First, Thelma is worried about how she will manage the day-to-day functioning of her life without Jessie's help (48). Jessie understands this, and for weeks leading up to the play's action she has been working hard to organize the household so that Thelma can manage it.

Secondly, Thelma is afraid that somehow her own inadequacies are the cause of Jessie's despair and her motive to kill herself, especially her handling of Jessie's epilepsy in her youth (18, 37, 45, 47). Thelma does not want to have to take on this guilt. Jessie also works throughout the play to establish her own autonomy and separation from Thelma, reassuring her, sometimes angrily, that the suicide "doesn't have anything to do with you" (47).

The third crisis, however, is the most devastating for Thelma and is the source of Thelma's own tragedy. Just as Agamemnon's decision to sail required Iphigenia's death, Jessie's plan for suicide destroys Thelma's comfortable sense of self. Jessie and Thelma have shared a life of letting time drift by and trying to deny disappointments, such as the lack of fulfillment in Thelma's marriage to Jessie's father (34). Thelma does not want to take on the self-examination that Jessie has been enduring. As Thelma says, "I don't like things to think about. I like things to go on!" (36). Using denial to control her disappointment, Thelma has been able to move through her life with a kind of mindless comfort (23, 25). But Jessie now rejects that life as insufficient to keep her engaged with living, which means Thelma now must confront her own life and consider whether her satisfaction is misplaced. That confrontation drives Thelma into an anxious rage:

> (*Really startled.*) Jessie! (*Quiet horror.*) How dare you! (*Furious*) How dare you! ... You make me feel like a fool for being alive, child, and you are so wrong! I like it here, and I will stay here until they make me go, until they drag me screaming and I mean screeching into my grave. (51)

Jessie understands her mother's terror, but Jessie also is coming to see her own sometimes-too-deep concern for other people as one of the sources of the crippling stasis and pain she experiences. Beginning to feel torn as she considers whether she actually can go forward with the suicide, she says, "Everything I do winds up like this. How could I think [Thelma] would understand?" (49).

The problem for Thelma is that she realizes how intertwined her life is with Jessie's. If Jessie rejects her own life, she must be rejecting Thelma's as well. Jessie understands this, but she also feels she herself has needs and rights (47). After a violent exchange, both Thelma and Jessie are overwhelmed, but their loving connection begins to re-emerge. Norman describes it as follows:

> *Mama is nearly unconscious from the emotional devastation of these last few moments. She sits down at the kitchen table, hurt and angry and so desperately afraid. But she looks almost numb. She is so far beyond what is known as pain that she is virtually unreachable and Jessie knows this, and talks quietly, watching for signs of recovery.* (52)

Clearly, Jessie loves her mother and is concerned for her. Nonetheless—and I'm suggesting still struggling with ambivalence—Jessie is determined to at least confront the moment of actual personal choice: will she meet her own need to regain a sense of agency—of purposeful action—by killing herself, or will she meet her beloved mother's needs by continuing to drift through life?[3] Despite Thelma's efforts, Jessie slips by her mother into the bedroom at the back of the stage and locks the door.

Although Jessie has exited, it is important to understand that actually two characters are still on stage for the audience. A half page of monologue remains for Thelma, her tortured pleas with Jessie not to kill herself, before we hear the shot, which Norman's stage directions say, *"sounds like an answer, it sounds like NO"* (58). As an audience, we imagine Jessie behind the door for these seconds, hearing Thelma's sorrow, questioning herself, wondering what to do. Whose needs will be primary? Can she actually commit an action she knows full well is so cruel, especially to someone she loves? Can her need for a moment of self-respect, a sense that she actually is capable of purposeful action, justify the pain she will cause? Can she turn toward authenticity or is the price too high in leaving a life of mindless, meaningless drift? Like Agamemnon at Aulis, Jessie must decide who she is. The shot gives a cataclysmic answer.

Thelma "*collapses against the door, tears streaming down her face, but not screaming anymore*: Jessie, Jessie, child ... forgive me. (*A pause.*) I thought you were mine" (58). To understand Thelma's tragedy, we must understand what she means by that last line and why she asks for forgiveness.[4] In saying "mine," Thelma is not saying she thought of Jessie as her mere possession, a kind of object, someone who was there only to serve with no life of her own; rather, Thelma is talking about lost trust, just as Iphigenia in stunned terror confronted her father at Aulis. "I thought you were mine" means "I thought I could depend on you. I thought you were a part of the world I could count on to remain true and constant and comforting, not something that could be challenging to my sense of who I am, undermining of my self-worth, a source of impeding terror rather than of solace. I thought we were in agreement about how to go at the world and that I could count on you for comforting companionship as we took that sometimes frightening journey together."

Thelma's tragedy is that her trust has been broken, not just trust in Jessie, but because Jessie's suicide is a rejection of Thelma's own way of living, trust in her own life.[5] If Jessie, whom she thought she knew so well, is someone she did not understand and cannot trust, what is there she can trust? How can she go on? Thelma asks forgiveness for the emptiness and denial with which she has lived her life, which she now tragically must face in some fashion, and for having allowed Jessie to be drawn into it, a life of little authentic joy or meaning, little more than an absurd passing of time filled with Hershey bars and peanut brittle. Thelma calmly but brokenly goes to the phone and calls her son, Dawson. We do not hear her conversation, but her deepest question has to be this: Jessie just has rejected our lives as meaningless and absurd; how do we go on?

Confronting emptiness and the absurd in this particular way is the peculiarly American kind of tragedy, one set against the backdrop of the optimism of the American Dream, as Arthur Miller pointed out (Miller and Roudané [1983] 1987: 361–2). It is the tragedy that Blanche DuBois faces or Willy Loman, a tragedy faced by Tobias in Albee's *A Delicate Balance* and with greater rage by Walter Lee Younger in Hansberry's *A Raisin in the Sun* and by Troy Maxson in

August Wilson's *Fences*. The Dream promises that all of us through simple daily activities will find a path to success and fulfillment, a sense of thriving. This achievement will take some diligence but not heroic effort. That is America's claim to being a special place: America claims to have removed the impediments to opportunity for the everyman, and therefore we all should thrive—it's been promised, and in a darker more threatening way, also demanded. But some of us cannot arrive at that sense of thriving—it is not, after all, as William James made clear, an act of will; it arises as a feeling about ourselves as we engage in the world. When we cannot find that feeling, all our efforts seem purposeless and absurd. Our self-respect and our ability to take joy in life fall apart—and that is an experience of tragedy, especially for someone imbued with the American Dream.

Notes

1   Parallels also have been drawn between Thelma and Jessie and Vladimir and Estragon in Beckett's *Waiting for Godot*. See Kane (1989: 255, 265, 267).

2   For what may seem a different interpretation of the role of the American Dream in Jessie's decision, see Bigsby 1999: 232, where he holds that a sense of having failed to fulfill the American Dream has no role in Jessie's despair, which is based on a more general sense that her life is "pointless existence." I think the difference between my view of Jessie and Bigsby's may rest on differences between us on the role of materialism in the American Dream rather than on different interpretations of Norman's play.

3   For different interpretations, where Jessie is less ambivalent and motivated by a loss of a sense of community or even revenge, see Brugnoli (2014: 234) and Whited (1997: 65–74).

4   For a different interpretation of what Thelma means by "I thought you were mine," see Browder (1989: 109–13).

5   Other commentators suggest that Thelma does not suffer such a crisis. See, for example, Drew (1996: 92–3), who suggests that Thelma has been happy with her limited life and psychologically will be able to continue in essentially the same way. See also Norman's remarks on Thelma in Betsko and Koenig (1987).

References

Betsko, Kathleen and Rachel Koenig (1987), "Marsha Norman," in *Interviews with Contemporary Women Playwrights*, 324–42, New York: William Morrow.

Bigsby, C. W. E. (1999), *Contemporary American Playwrights*, Cambridge: Cambridge University Press.

Browder, Sally (1989), "'I Thought You Were Mine': Marsha Norman's *'night, Mother*," in Mickey Pearlman (ed.), *Mother Puzzles: Daughters and Mothers in Contemporary American Literature*, 109–13, Westport, CT: Greenwood Press.

Brown, Linda Ginter (ed.) (1996), *Marsha Norman: A Case Book*, New York: Routledge.

Brugnoli, Annalisa (2014), "Marsha Norman," in Martin Middeke, Peter Paul Schnierer, Christopher Innes, and Matthew C. Roudané (eds.), *The Methuen Drama Guide to Contemporary American Playwrights*, 224–42, London: Bloomsbury.

Brustein, Robert ([1983] 1996), "Don't Read This Review! *'night, Mother* by Marsha Norman," *The New Republic*, May 2. Reprinted in Linda Ginter Brown (ed.), *Marsha Norman: A Case Book*, 159–62, New York: Routledge.

Drew, Anne Marie (1996), "'And the Time for It Was Gone': Jessie's Triumph in *'night, Mother*," in Linda Ginter Brown (ed.), *Marsha Norman: A Casebook*, 87–94, New York: Routledge.

James, William ([1896] 1992), "The Will to Believe," in Gerald E. Myers (ed.) *William James, Writings 1878–1899*, 457–79, New York: The Library of America.

Kane, Leslie (1989), "The Way Out, the Way In: Paths to Self in the Plays of Marsha Norman," in Enoch Brater (ed.), *Feminine Focus: The New Women Playwrights*, 255–74, New York: Oxford University Press.

Miller, Arthur and Matthew C. Roudané ([1983] 1987), "An Interview with Arthur Miller," in Matthew C. Roudané (ed.), *Conversations with Arthur Miller*, 360–75, Jackson, MS: University Press of Mississippi. Originally published in *Michigan Quarterly Review* (24), 1985, 373–89.

Norman, Marsha (n.d.), marshanorman.com (Norman's personal website) (accessed January 25, 2017).

Norman, Marsha (1983), *'night, Mother*, New York: Dramatists Play Service.

Norman, Marsha (1998), *Collected Works: Volume 1*, Lyme, NH: Smith and Kraus.

Paige, Linda Rohrer (2005), "'Off the Porch and into the Scene': Southern Women Playwrights …" in David Krasner (ed.), *A Companion* to *Twentieth-Century American Drama*, 388–405, Malden, MA: Blackwell Publishing.

Roudané, Matthew C. (1996), *American Drama Since 1960: A Critical History*, New York: Twayne Publishers.

Whited, Lana A. (1997), "Suicide in Beth Henley's *Crimes of the Heart* and Marsha Norman's *'night, Mother*," *Southern Quarterly* 36 (1): 65–74.

16

Tony Kushner (1956–)

Claire Gleitman
Ithaca College

It should come as no surprise that an author who wrote the following about his relationship to queerness—as an identity, a politics, and a literary style, which he terms "fabulousness"— is known for writing plays that resist straightforward genre classification:

> What are the salient features of fabulousness? Irony. Tragic history. Defiance. Gender-fuck. Glitter. Drama ... For style to be truly fabulous, one must completely triumph over tragedy, age, physical insufficiencies, and just as important, one's audiences must be made aware of the degree of transcendence, of triumph; must see both the triumph and that over which triumph has been made. In this the magic of the fabulous is precisely the magic of the theater. (Kushner 1997: 31)

Of course, a great deal of modern drama, and modern literature generally, is stylistically fluid. But Kushner arguably goes further in transgressing generic boundaries: his magisterial *Angels in America* has been described as both tragedy (Wallace 2007: 85–7) and Shakespearean romance (Clum 2000: 249). Throughout his career, he has melded seemingly disparate forms, weaving together the real and the surreal, the tragic and the farcical, the here-and-now and the supernatural, so that the resulting plays are rather like (to adopt Kushner's own charming image) lasagnas, in which all "the yummy nutritious ingredients you've thrown [in] have almost-but-not-quite succeeded in overwhelming the basic design" (Kushner 1995: 61). Through his embrace of "the pleasurably polymorphous" (Solomon 1997: 118), Kushner has widened the horizons of tragic form to imbue it with a vehemently historicized faith in the possibility of what lies beyond tragedy, that place where "The Great Work Begins" (Kushner 2013: 290).

Angels in America—an epic two-part play written in the early 1990s—provides a perfect example of what we might call Kushner's "genre-fuck," because it features conventions of tragic form while subverting tragic expectations. *Angels* also exhibits a tragic view of human life, which it portrays as fraught with devastation and loss, and yet it "consistently attests," as David Savran has argued, "to the possibility not only of progress but also of radical—almost unimaginable—transfiguration" (Savran 1995: 131). In other words, *Angels* contains tragic elements but refuses to be contained by tragedy, either formally or thematically.

Angels in America takes place between 1985 and 1990, at the height of the Reagan era and in the early years of the AIDS epidemic. The audacity of Kushner's intentions is signaled by his subtitle: "A Gay Fantasia on National Themes." In his portrait of America at a particular historical moment, when "Millennium Approaches" (the title of Part One), Kushner invokes a broad array of seminal "national themes" in such a way as to gesture backward to the nation's origins and forward to the future consequences of that past. *Angels*'s perspective on those themes—such as America's alleged status as the city on the hill, its idealization of self-reliance, and its faith in the possibility of endless journeying—is skeptical and exuberantly queer, both in the sense of "fabulousness" and because of the fact that all of its primary male characters are either out or closeted homosexuals. The play also calls for cross-gender casting for its minor roles and two of its females (Hannah and the Angel) have fluid sexual identities. Yet the historical moment that *Angels* dramatizes is rife with rigidity and disease: both the literal disease, AIDS, which ravages human bodies, and an equally corrosive social and spiritual disease that takes the form of a rapacious individualism plaguing the American body politic.

The chief spokesman for a political philosophy that disregards the many in favor of the supreme self is Roy Cohn, a character closely based on the infamous New York City lawyer best known for illegally tampering in the Ethel Rosenberg case and serving as Senator Joseph McCarthy's zealous anti-communist henchman in the early 1950s. Slightly less widely known is the fact that Cohn was a closeted homosexual, though he worked avidly to deny it; Cohn died of AIDS in 1986 but insisted to the end that he had liver cancer. As incarnated in *Angels*, Roy's credo of fervent self-interest is encapsulated by the unsolicited advice he offers to a young (also closeted) gay man, Joe Pitt, whom he hopes to groom as his protégé and flunky:

> Joe. You must do this ... Love: that's a trap. Responsibility: that's a trap too. Like a father to a son I tell you this: Life is full of horror; nobody escapes, nobody; save yourself. Whatever pulls on you, whatever needs from you, threatens you ... Let nothing stand in your way. (61)

This is the American ideal of Emersonian self-reliance gone nightmarishly wrong.

As the play's central embodiment of the notion that responsibility to others is a trap and identity is entirely contingent upon where one fits "in the food chain, in the pecking order" (51), Roy has shades of Milton's Satan—he tries to tempt Joe to help him, like the prince of darkness, to "turn off the sun" (70)—as well as of Shakespeare's Iago; his bewitching magnetism is matched only by his megalomania. If tragedy necessarily involves evil, it is Roy who appears to personify it. The first and last word Roy utters is "Hold" and indeed he is a prophet of stasis, of a reactionary conservatism that demands that we stand precisely where we are, looking neither forward nor back and grasping for power and profit. Barely human, he longs to become less so: "I wish I was an octopus," he tells Joe, "a fucking octopus. Eight loving arms and all those suckers" (11). He continues, "I see the universe, Joe, as a kind of sandstorm in outer space with winds of mega-hurricane velocity, but instead of grains of sand it's shards and splinters of glass" (13). As this remark suggests, the circumstances of *Angels*'s characters have "cosmic implications," a hallmark of tragedy in the classical sense (Exum 1996: 6).[1] Seismic shifts in the divine and national realms reverberate outward to impact personal acts, fueling the storm of glass shards that Cohn describes.

If Cohn is the play's satanic prophet, envisioning meaningless chaos in the midst of which one can do no more than strive to save oneself, *Angels* features two other visionaries whose insight is more humane. Like Cohn, both are sick and try to avoid grappling with that sickness. One, Harper Pitt, Joe's wife, is a valium-addicted, agoraphobic Mormon who at first denies what she dimly perceives: that her husband is gay. Yet intuitively she sees in her condition larger ecological, physiological, and geopolitical dimensions: "People who are lonely, people left alone, sit talking nonsense to the air, imagining ... old fixed orders spiraling apart." She imagines the ozone layer as

a kind of gift, from God ... guardian angels, hands linked, make a spherical net, a blue-green nesting orb, a shell of safety for life itself. But everywhere, things are collapsing, lies surfacing, systems of defense giving way. (16)

The "old fixed orders spiraling apart" allude not just to Harper's disintegrating marriage and her fraying religious faith but to the radical social and political changes of the last decades of the twentieth century. The "systems of defense giving way" refer explicitly to the hole in the ozone layer but also are suggestive of AIDS—a disease that attacks the immune system so that it no longer can defend against disease—as well as the Strategic Defense Initiative, which Reagan first announced in 1983 and which was meant to act as a barrier against nuclear weapons, though many critics regarded it as both ineffective and geopolitically combustible.

Harper's fluid metaphor for the ozone layer stands at the poetic and political heart of *Angels*. The angels' clasped hands create a "spherical net" protectively encasing "life itself," but when they loosen, humans become vulnerable. The image, albeit supernatural, suggests the dissolution of the human community, to which Kushner also refers in his Afterword: "The smallest indivisible human unit is two people, not one; one is a fiction. From such nets of souls societies, the social world, human life springs" (333). The source of the play's tragedy is the unraveling of that net of souls, which has occurred because of a collective abandonment of the collective, aided and abetted by Reagan's domestic agenda, which enshrined into policy the individualist impulse to be "Selfish and greedy and loveless and blind" to others' needs. A character named Louis utters those lines as he indicts himself for his "irresponsible" abandonment of his sick lover, while recognizing his behavior as part of a broader pattern characteristic of "Reagan's children" (77).

Louis's lover is Prior Walter, the play's other chief visionary. Stricken with AIDS, Prior finds himself the unhappy recipient of divine attention; he is deemed a prophet by an angel who bursts theatrically through his bedroom ceiling in the closing moments of *Millennium*. Long before that astonishing—or, as he describes it, "*Very* Stephen Spielberg" (125)—visitation, Prior has premonitions that indicate his status as reluctant seer, deeply in touch, as is Harper, with the contemporary *zeitgeist*. In an early conversation with Louis, Prior tells a story about one of his ancestors, a captain of a ship that sank off the coast of Nova Scotia. The seventy survivors were packed on a leaky longboat; eventually, most were cast overboard so that nine could live. Prior remarks:

> I think about that story a lot now. People in a boat, waiting, terrified, while implacable, unsmiling men, irresistibly strong, seize ... maybe the person next to you, maybe you, and with no warning at all ... you are pitched into freezing, turbulent water and salt and darkness to drown. (42)

Prior's image of people gathered together—literally in the same boat—who are nevertheless terrifyingly alone and at the mercy of something random and pitiless, captures his own plight as an AIDS sufferer as well as the larger existential condition of humans in a godless universe whose only constant is abandonment.

Despite the fact that *Angels* pronounces itself a "Gay Fantasia" and thus a play that will move freely between forms, there is much about Part One that might prompt us "to falsely code" it as a tragedy (Chaudhuri 1995: 256), both formally and in its portrait of human experience. The perverse amorality advocated by Roy gradually beguiles others—mainly Louis and Joe—who are decent but flawed, and worms its way into the nation's collective psyche: "There are no angels in America," Louis says grimly, picking up on Harper's metaphor, "no spiritual past, no racial past, there's only the political" (96). There is, it seems, only the inescapable, barren now within which Prior grows sicker, Harper retreats into madness, and *Millennium* moves toward a climax in which "human freedom comes into conflict with the demands of the cosmic order"—a crucial feature of "fully developed" tragedy (Exum 1996: 6). Prior finally confronts that cosmos in the form of a magnificent angel who seems on the verge of demanding an act of messianic self-sacrifice.

But *Angels in America* does not end here. Part Two, *Perestroika*, reveals its flip side, which constitutes, to borrow a phrase Raymond Williams applied to Brecht, a "rejection of tragedy" (Williams 1966: 190). *Perestroika* quickly deflates our expectations regarding the Angel, who turns out to be a crushing, even comical, disappointment: she has a persistent cough, she can't carry off her miracles terribly well, and while wrestling with Prior she tears a muscle in her thigh. The message she brings is not revelatory but desperate, even pernicious: God has become infected by humanity's lust for motion, prompting Him to light out for some unknown territory. Hence, the Angel demands that Prior, and the rest of us, "STOP MOVING!" (172). This advice links her with Cohn, whose gospel, we will recall, is "Hold." Prior's personal sense of abandonment, by Louis and by his country, leads him briefly to consider the Angel's counsel. But in the end he rejects it: "We can't just stop. We're not rocks. Progress, migration, motion is ... modernity" (275).

Meanwhile, Roy is felled by the disease he denied having but is not cast out of the community of humankind—the usual fate for tragic villains. Rather, he is forgiven by a trio of characters (two alive, one dead) who deliver a Kaddish over his corpse, implicitly acknowledging him as human, not evil incarnate. Yet forgiveness is not accompanied by amnesia; after completing the Kaddish, Louis and Ethel Rosenberg pronounce Roy a "sonofabitch" (267).

As for Harper, she finds the will to detach herself from Joe and embarks on a journey to San Francisco on an airplane—no small step for an agoraphobic. While doing so, she has a vision in which she imagines "souls of the dead, of people who had perished, from famine, from the plague," rising from their graves:

And the souls of these departed joined hands, clasped ankles, and formed a web, a great net of souls ... and the outer rim absorbed them, and was repaired. Nothing's lost forever. In this world there is a kind of painful progress. Longing for what we've left behind, and dreaming ahead. (285)

Harper's conception of "painful progress," which requires looking backward with longing and forward with hope, is crucial to *Angels*'s success in moving beyond tragedy while retaining a "new tragic consciousness," one that is "firmly committed to a different future: to the struggle against suffering learned in suffering" (Williams 1966: 203). Harper envisions the restoration of a "net of souls" not by angels, but by humans engaged in a collective act of forgiveness, as their deaths were caused by famines and plagues likely exacerbated by human neglect, as AIDS for so long was.

Angels concludes with an Epilogue that takes place at the Bethesda Fountain in New York's Central Park in 1990. Contrary to the usual trajectory for a protagonist in tragedy, Prior remains alive. We see on stage not a pile of bodies but rather a group of characters who have found their way toward a fragile fellowship. Following the forgive-but-do-not-forget logic that allowed Roy to receive Kaddish but also to be proclaimed a sonofabitch, Louis is part of this community, forgiven for his selfish acts but not reembraced as Prior's lover. Still, he is present: flawed but not beyond hope, like the America the characters recognize themselves as inhabiting. Prior's last words, addressed to the audience, are full of anticipatory promise:

> This disease will be the end of many of us, but not nearly all, and the dead will be commemorated and will struggle on with the living ... We won't die secret deaths anymore. The world only spins forward. We will be citizens ... You are fabulous creatures, each and every one. And I bless you: *More life.* The Great Work Begins. (290)

But Prior's optimism is tempered by an acknowledgment that the "Great Work" remains to be performed; to accomplish it, we must reckon with the horrors of the past as a way to advance beyond them. Historical contingency—the subtle ways the present emerges from the past—has not come to an end. Some sources of instability have found redress (Louis notes that the Berlin Wall has fallen), but others continue to loom, many of which cannot be known or sufficiently anticipated: Hannah wonders aloud "what'll happen in places like Yugoslavia" (288). By placing us in a precisely historicized moment while calling attention to the radical uncertainty of what lies ahead, Kushner urges his audience to recognize their ability, indeed their obligation, to intervene in constructing the shape of that beckoning future.

In like fashion, the stylistic fluidity, or fabulousness, of *Angels in America* underscores its philosophical as well as its political implications. Repeatedly and insistently, in his treatment of genre, character, gender, and theme, Kushner counterpoints rigidity with fluidity, stasis with motion, the grim present with a possible, altered future. "You can't live in the world without an idea of the world," Hannah posits, "but it's living that makes the ideas" (289). Ideas exist but they are not immutable, and they need not determine the shape of the ideas that succeed them, any more than preexisting genres must determine the shape of plays yet to be written. Similarly, though Kushner suggests that human experience may be irredeemably tragic, he also insists that it is not the case that it *must* be so. *Angels in America* employs elements of tragic form but triumphs over tragedy, queering genre to challenge us to imagine other futures yet to be conceived.

Note

1   Exum (1996: 6) cites Joseph Wood Krutch, who attributed the death of tragedy in the modern era to the fact that "we no longer believe in the grandeur of the human spirit or in the cosmic implications of human deeds." *Angels in America*, however, clearly does.

References

Chaudhuri, Una (1995), *Staging Place: The Geography of Modern Drama*, Ann Arbor, MI: University of Michigan Press.

Clum, John M. ([1992] 2000), *Still Acting Gay: Male Homosexuality in Modern Drama*, New York: St. Martin's Press.

Exum, J. Cheryl (1996), *Tragedy and Biblical Narrative*, Cambridge: Cambridge University Press.

Krutch, Joseph Wood (1981), "The Tragic Fallacy," in Robert Willoughby Corrigan (ed.), *Tragedy: Vision and Form*, second edition, New York: Harper and Row.

Kushner, Tony ([1992] 2013), *Angels in America: A Gay Fantasia on American Themes*, revised and complete edition, New York: Theatre Communications Group.

Kushner, Tony (1995), *Thinking about the Longstanding Problems of Virtue and Happiness*, New York: Theatre Communications Group.

Kushner, Tony (1997), "Notes about Political Theatre," *Kenyon Review* 19: 19–34.

Savran, David (1995), "The Theatre of the Fabulous: An Interview with Tony Kushner," in Per Brask (ed.), *Essays on Kushner's "Angels,"* 127–54, Winnipeg: Blizzard Publishing.

Solomon, Alisa (1997), "Wrestling With *Angels*: a Jewish Fantasia," in Deborah R. Geis and Steven F. Kruger (eds.), *Approaching the Millennium: Essays on "Angels in America,"* 134–50, Ann Arbor, MI: University of Michigan Press.

Wallace, Jennifer (2007), *The Cambridge Introduction to Tragedy*, Cambridge: Cambridge University Press.

Williams, Raymond (1966), *Modern Tragedy*, London: Chatto and Windus.

17

Suzan-Lori Parks (1963–)

Soyica Diggs Colbert
Georgetown University

Suzan-Lori Parks's drama focuses on the roles everyday people play in history, accentuating the distinction between recognizable and unrecognizable historical figures. Calling attention to the similarities and differences between her characters and their namesakes, *The Death of the Last Black Man in the Whole Entire World* (1990) features "Before Columbus" rather than Christopher Columbus, *The America Play* (1994) depicts "the foundling father, as Abraham Lincoln" rather than a founding father, *Fucking A* (2000) portrays "Hester Smith" rather than Hester Prynne, and *Topdog/Underdog* (2001) presents "Lincoln" rather than Abraham Lincoln (Parks 1995: 100; 1995: 158; 2001: 115; 2002: 2). The names of the figures that people Parks's plays appear simultaneously familiar and unfamiliar in order to invite the audience into an identifiable world with a new twist. Parks's drama makes history, recalling well-known individuals, stories, and scenarios while shifting important elements of the narrative, including the figure's race or the dynamics of key historical relationships. These subtle and important changes reconfigure the shape of history through drama; Parks's plays retell historical narratives to not only redeem the present but also to place purchase on the past.

Parks's drama does not fit neatly into literary definitions of tragedy because it focuses on the sometimes unfortunate and more often terrible circumstances of everyday people. In addition, many of her protagonists are black. The way race shapes the present and past circumstances of her characters draws attention to the operation and necessity of counter-histories. *The Death of the Last Black Man in the Whole Entire World* depicts the repeated and violent execution of a character named "Black Man with Watermelon" (1995: 101). In the play, the central character experiences the collective history of violence against black men, including lynching and electrocution. The play questions the type of historical circumstances that would enable an end to such violence. What context would make his death the last death? The violence that Black Man with Watermelon experiences presents him as a figure bound by historical and contemporary circumstances outside his control. The characterization shows how Parks's work does not align with Hegel's definition of tragedy, which posits, "*truly* tragic action necessarily presupposes either a live conception of *individual* freedom and independence or at least an individual's determination and willingness to accept freely and on his own account the responsibility for his own act and its consequences" (1975: 1205). Parks's drama questions black people's access to freedom and independence, given the violent circumstances that often circumscribe expressions of their will.

Hegel's definition establishes the power of the individual to participate in rectifying tragic circumstances. Parks's drama aligns with and exceeds Arthur Miller's articulation of tragedy, which accounts for the ability of everyday people and not just "great" men and women to participate in the course of history. Miller argues for the quotidian nature of tragedy, saying, "The tragic right is a condition of life, a condition in which the human personality is able to flower and realize itself. The wrong is the condition which suppresses man, perverts the flowing out of his love and creative instinct" ([1949] 1996: 5). The everydayness of tragedy also informs its impact. Miller states, "Tragedy enlightens—and it must, in that it points the heroic finger at the enemy of man's freedom. The thrust for freedom is the quality in tragedy which exalts. The revolutionary questioning of the stable environment is what terrifies. In no way is the common man debarred from such thoughts or such actions" ([1949] 1996: 5). In Miller's formulation, the suffering of the tragic hero helps to transform the audience by enlightening and terrifying. The emotional catharsis hopes to arrest the forces that circumscribe man's freedom. Parks's drama not only seeks to arrest those forces in the present but to demonstrate how those forces cohere as a result of historical relationships.

Parks's essay "from Elements of Style" explains how she conceptualizes history as "time that won't quit," which offers insight into her ideas about how tragic events in the world relate to dramatic tragedy (1995: 15). The recurring ghostly quality of time aligns with the haunting that often emerges in dramatic tragedy (for example, in *Hamlet*), but in Parks's drama the constitutive nature of recurrence functions as a method to revise and reinterpret, moving history forward rather than indulging the compulsion to rid history of its ghosts.[1] Parks describes her signature style as "Rep and Rev," which she borrows from jazz music. She explains that in jazz the composer or musician "will write or play a musical phrase once and again and again; etc.—with each revisit the phrase is slightly revised. 'Rep & Rev'... is a central element in my work; through its use I'm working to create a dramatic text that departs from the traditional linear style to look and sound more like a musical score" (1995: 15). The act of return also constitutes a form of departure that transforms repetition from a cycle of pain to a necessary training ground for remaking history. Parks concludes, "a text based on the concept of repetition and revision is one which breaks from the text ... which cleanly ARCS" (1995: 9). Parks presents history disrupted and reconfigured through repetition and revision. Her style reconfigures familiar histories to shift the trajectory of the narrative from a continuous line to one with disruptions and returns.

Nonetheless, Parks's drama also often presents colloquial forms of tragedy—terrible calamities—that call attention to the literary genre of tragedy's ability to account for the lives and losses of black people. Her drama contains traditional tragic elements: haunting, suffering and living with death and despair, and some formal attributes, most notably her use of choruses. This chapter will explore how Parks combines her new vision of tragedy and its social role with these traditional roots, how her engagement with the thematic and formal attributes of dramatic tragedy comments on the possibility of individual and collective freedom in futures still tethered to unrecognizable pasts. Parks's drama rethinks historical narratives to loosen the hold of calamities, such as slavery and racialized violence, as determining factors for black subjects in the twentieth and twenty-first centuries while acknowledging how those pasts continue to impact national narratives.

Parks's drama deliberately depicts history as a narrative practice that includes and forgets certain people. Telling history requires casting leading men and women and supporting actors. The shape the narrative arc of history takes implicitly establishes possibilities for the present and the future. Parks's engagement with the past frees black people in the present from histories of exclusion, degradation, inferiority, and perpetual loss. In two of her plays, *The America Play* (1995) and *Topdog/Underdog* (2001), the protagonist, a black man, impersonates Abraham Lincoln.

Topdog/Underdog addresses the seeming incongruity of a black man playing Honest Abe to reveal the presidential as a racialized category sustained through violence. The play depicts two brothers named Lincoln and Booth who devise various schemes to survive. Lincoln struggles throughout the play to keep his job as an Abraham Lincoln impersonator at a local arcade, and Booth sustains himself by stealing. Although adept at theft, Booth aspires to become a Three-card Monte dealer as skilled as Lincoln was before his retirement from the street card game. Three-card Monte, a shell game, features a dealer and a player, called a "mark." The game begins with the dealer and the player each placing a bet. The dealer then places three cards face down on a board: two cards of one color, say red, and one of the other color, black. The dealer shows the player the black card and then quickly moves the cards around. Once the reorganization of the cards is complete, the dealer instructs the player to choose the black card. If the player is correct, he or she wins the pot; if not, the dealer wins.

Booth explains that he wants to learn how to become a dealer because he sees it as a legitimate job in which the outcomes will be based on his own skill and fair chance. By the end of the play, however, Lincoln teaches Booth the con at the heart of the game and their relationship. Lincoln induces Booth to play a game of Three-card Monte with him in which Booth bets his inheritance. Lincoln wins that game and explains, "That was yr mistake. Cause its thuh first move that separates thuh Player from thuh Played. And thuh first move is to know that there aint no winning" (2002: 106). In order to get Booth to play the game, Lincoln convinces Booth that he has a chance of winning by appealing to him as his brother. The betrayal not only shows the false hope of the game but also of their familial relationship. Lincoln allows Booth to believe that he will learn to throw the cards well enough to win the game. Parks also uses the phrase "there aint no winning" from *Topdog/Underdog* in *Fucking A* (2001: 117). In both plays it draws attention to the limits of the American ideal of meritocracy as faith in individual freedom, genuine opportunity, and the power of hard work. No matter how hard they try, Park's protagonists are prevented from playing central roles in historical narratives.

During the play, Lincoln asks Booth to help him rehearse his routine for the arcade because he fears termination. Lincoln asks Booth for feedback and he replies, "I dunno, man. Something about it. I dunno. It was looking too real or something" (2002: 50). Lincoln explains that patrons prefer the artifice of performance rather than the specificity within historical accuracy, even though they see his performance as a part of a historical narrative. Lincoln laments, "People are funny about they Lincoln shit. Its historical. People like they historical shit in a certain way. They like it to unfold the way they folded it up. Neatly like a book. Not raggedy and bloody and screaming. You trying to get me fired" (2002: 50). Lincoln's caution against the veracity of his performance, its "looking too real," reveals the necessity to sanitize national history, the bloody circumstances of both the president's death and of the black men who also died in events that led to Abraham Lincoln's gaining the moniker the "Great Emancipator." In addition, Lincoln's comment about the order of history, saying, "People like they historical shit in a certain way. They like it to unfold the way they folded it up. Neatly like a book," speaks directly to the conventions of tragedy as a narrative driven by an inevitable outcome. The order and conventions associated with tragedy also require the sacrifice of certain figures. Quoting Raymond Williams, Jeremy Matthew Glick argues:

> By the time we get to a post-*Crucible* Arthur Miller, the Ibsenian tragic martyr fails to console ... "This sense of personal verification by death is the last stage of liberal tragedy." *The Crucible's* heroic martyr cynically morphs into the disconnected individuals depicted by Arthur Miller in *Death of a Salesman* and *A View from the Bridge* ... This rings the death bell for liberal tragedy. (2016: 32)

The function of liberal tragedy to produce catharsis through the individual redemption of a common man falls into distress when Miller and others begin to question the possibility of redeeming a world intent on Cold War destruction. Miller's *After the Fall* (1964) interrogates the possibility for a world threatened by catastrophic destruction. Given the possibility of nuclear war, the idea of the loss of a singular redemptive hero becomes less compelling. Parks's drama does not invest in the idea of redemption through the loss of an individual, but it does recalibrate what is understood as redemptive versus negligible loss.

In order for Parks's Lincoln to produce a compelling reenactment of the president's death, he must mask himself. Parks's drama disrupts conventions about the sacrifice of the hero as depicted in ancient and modern tragedy by depicting the historical and personal sacrifices that underpin the heroic figure as a force that continues to impact the shape of history after the hero's death. Lincoln, the character in Parks's play, "makes it look easy but [its] hard," meaning the impact of Abraham Lincoln as a tragic figure continues to inform perceptions of him and the shape of American history after his death. Parks's character must contend not only with the actual Abraham Lincoln but also with his historical legacy.

By play's end, Booth kills Lincoln not because of historical inevitability but because the rules of the social game are stacked against them. Although seemingly nihilistic, the commentary *Topdog/Underdog* makes on history serves to empower the audience in two distinct ways: by revealing how American history forgets black suffering and by offering strategies to reimagine history in order to provide different opportunities for and interpretations of black subjects in the present.

Through the names of characters, Parks's dramas often comment on how recognizability produces compassion and, in alignment with ancient and modern drama, allows for catharsis in response to the death of a purportedly great man. As Adrian Poole argues, "Tragedy is interested in the verbs that philosophers want to turn into nouns ... we are connected, even interconnected, by complex systems of cause and consequence, in which questions of innocence and guilt are all caught up and embroiled, and from which no one should expect to be exempted" (2005: 54–5). The idea of connection and our interconnection organizes Parks's drama and informs her deployment of figures who draw the audience into relationships with certain histories as well as the world of the play. For example, she names her protagonist "Ulysses" in her civil war drama *Father Comes Home from the Wars* (2015) in order to give the story of a black confederate soldier an epic dynamic. The use of recognizable names enables the spectator to feel an initial familiarity and comfort in Parks's world so that a black man playing Lincoln becomes less of a stretch for the audience's imagination and, as a consequence, mourning his death becomes less improbable. Her plays craft worlds that dismantle the limitations race places on people's social roles. In order to do this, Parks must rethink national narratives and their heroes and villains in her dramas.

Similar to her expansion of who qualifies as a tragic figure in *Topdog/Underdog*, in *Venus* (1996) Parks depicts a main character who has the same name and physical attributes of an historical figure, and in *The America Play* (1994), the central character named "the Foundling Father, as Abraham Lincoln" describes himself as follows: "There was once a man who was told he bore a strong resemblance to Abraham Lincoln. He was tall and thinly built just like the Great Man. His legs were the longer part just like the Great Mans legs." Nevertheless, there were distinguishing characteristics between the two men. "The Lesser Known had several beards which he carried around in a box. The beards were his although he himself had not grown them on his face" (1995: 159). Like Parks's character Lincoln in *Topdog/Underdog*, the artifice of the Foundling Father's beards calls attention to the lengths he must take to approximate the president. The costume draws attention to the cultivation of the historic figure and in so doing aligns the work of historical narrative with the work of the playwright. In "Possession," an essay in *The America Play and Other Works*, Parks asserts,

> a play is a blueprint of an event: a way of creating and rewriting history through the medium of literature. Since history is a recorded or remembered event, theatre, for me, is the perfect place to "make" history—that is, because so much of African-American history has been unrecorded, dismembered, washed out, one of my tasks as a playwright is to—through literature and the special strange relationship between theatre and real-life—locate the ancestral burial ground, dig for bones, find bones, hear the bones sing, write it down. (1995: 4)

The impulse at the heart of dramatic tragedy to right history emerges in Parks's repurposing of historical figures to tell the stories of individuals whom history has forgotten, for example, in *Topdog/Underdog* two brothers who have been abandoned by everyone they know, including their parents, lovers, and friends. Parks is rejecting Raymond Williams's compelling argument that "tragedy is derived from a particular complicated yet arguably continuous history" (2006: 33). Parks's dramas seek to disrupt the continuity of history and reconfigure its elaboration.

Playing a literary version of the shell game depicted in *Topdog/Underdog*, in *Fucking A* (2000) Parks references the name of Nathaniel Hawthorne's protagonist in *The Scarlet Letter* (1850) and recalls one of the novel's central themes: the scapegoating of women. As in the novel, Hester here serves as an embodied representation of the debts of her fellow citizens. Through Hester, *Fucking A* explores how race, class, and gender contribute to the tragic circumstances of familial estrangement and personal tragedy.

Fucking A tells the story of an abortionist, Hester, who works tirelessly to earn enough money to pay a fine that will enable her son's release from prison. Hester's occupation as an abortionist produces the scorn of the community and so she is branded with an "A" and wears a bloody apron throughout the play. A cruel twist of the drama, however, proves Hester's efforts futile. In the time she amasses the money to free her son, he escapes from jail setting a mass of bounty hunters in pursuit. In the final scene of the play, Hester executes her son to save him from the brutal murder that the lynch mob will inflict. The play ritualizes the death of Hester's son and links it to lynching practices. In so doing, *Fucking A* situates the racialized and gendered violence in the play within a long history of violence in the United States, dating back to the nineteenth century. The play ends with Hester singing the "Working Woman's Song" and going back to work:

I dig my ditch with no complaining
Work in the hot sun, or even when its raining
And when the bitter day finally comes to an end
Theyll say— (2001: 221)

The play seeks to reconfigure a national narrative, *The Scarlet Letter*, to account for the experience of working-class women of color. It presents its tragic elements in various ways, from linking Hester's story to an iconic national tragic narrative to focusing on a society that requires personal advancement to depend on the suffering of others.

Early in the play Hester establishes the way her occupation as an abortionist creates a hopeless world:

> Midnight. Everyone should be in bed. But theyre not. Itd be nice if they was all in bed and not on their way to me. Cept the more they stay in bed the more they get in trouble. Then they gotta come to Hester for *die Abah-nazip* [the abortion] ... Their troubles yr livelihood, Hester. Hhh. There aint no winning. (2001: 117)

Hester's complaint "The more they stay in bed the more they get in trouble" establishes the cultural ideology that organizes action in the play. The sexual pleasure produces pain that enables Hester to make a living but also results in her clients' loss. The world of the play denies women access to unmitigated pleasure and places them in a position similar to that of the protagonists of *Topdog/Underdog*: constantly looking for how to make a deal.

Fucking A places sex at the center of the economy, depicting how it informs social and political relationships. Similar to Hawthorne's protagonist, Hester here is punished by the community, which brands her left breast with an "A" that stinks and weeps (2001: 125). The brand marks Hester as ostracized and abortion as socially unacceptable even though she serves a vital purpose for her community and her job provides one of the few ways she can raise the funds to pay for her son's release from prison, to pay his/their/the debt. Her brand and bloody apron visually signify her community's inherent violence, yet she alone must bear the weight of the communal transgressions.

Parks also applies her dramatic practice of digging up forgotten historical dynamics to both unfamiliar and well-known black people. In her play *Venus* (1996), Parks references the historical person Saartjie Baartman, a South African woman who was displayed as a sideshow freak in Europe during the nineteenth century. Baartman's story is a classic tale of colonial domination, but Parks's play, as I argue elsewhere, does not focus on the historical Baartman but instead on how the legacy of Baartman informs realities for black women in the twentieth century.[2] Similar to Parks's Lincoln plays, *Venus* depicts key distinctions between Parks's character and the historical figure to demonstrate differences as well as similarities. The distinctions specify the historical project, which does not aim to discover the truth of Baartman's life and captivity but rather to question the fascination with the objectification of the black female body; the play positions Baartman as an historical victim. Once again, Parks's drama seeks to trouble the historical narrative to reveal what possibilities for redemption emerge through the process of making—remaking, reinterpreting—history. In Parks's work, making history serves as one remedy for tragic suffering.

Dramatic tragedy focuses on the shape of history as a remedy to suffering and the ways in which individuals emerge as historical actors. Raymond Williams's critique of Arthur Miller's liberal tragedy questioned the distinguished American playwright's focus on the individual hero. Parks's alignment of her characters with historical figures complicates the dialectical relationship between hero and mass culture that underpins Glick's compelling description of the black radical tragic tradition as an aesthetic that reshapes mass history. While acknowledging Williams's views on the end of liberal tragedy, Parks also endorses Gloria T. Hull's assertion of the abiding power of the individual. Hull writes, "black writers still believe in human possibilities and thus have not abandoned the concept of 'the hero'" (1978: 151). Parks depicts her characters not only as individuals who may indeed be heroic in their own ways but also in reference to historical roles; her plays comment not merely on the individual characters but on our accepted understanding of the historical roles themselves, revealing how the roles become containers that interact with their content to shape our understanding. Through characterization, Parks implicitly explores the relationship between content and form:

> as I write along the container dictates what sort of substance will fill it and, at the same time, the substance is dictating the size and shape of the container. Also, "form" is not a strictly "outside" thing while "content" stays "inside." It's like this: I am an African-American woman—this is the form I take, my content predicates this form, and this form is inseparable from my content. No way could I be me otherwise. (1995: 8–9)

Discussions of form usually correspond to artistic mediums. Parks's example of an identity category as a form creates a bridge between her artistic practices and the constitution of the social sphere. In Parks's formulations of roles, both in drama and in life, she seeks to reshape content and form, putting pressure on the idea of individual character in isolation from the vicissitudes of the person's situation.

Similarly, Parks's presentations of collectives through choruses in *The Death of the Last Black Man in the Whole Entire World*, *Venus*, and *Father Comes Home from the Wars* often function to communicate the multiple historical arcs or commonsense histories that the plays rethink. Harvey Young argues that Parks's use of choruses follows the model set by ancient Greek dramatic productions in which "the Greek chorus represented the citizenry." Young explains,

> Although historical studies of the form of Greek dramatic production disagree on the exact composition of the chorus—they generally agree that they were not comprised of professional actors, dancers and/or singers. To attend a play and to witness the actions of the chorus was to watch your neighbors play the role of members of the community on stage. (2007: 30)[3]

In Parks's drama, collectives are composed of figures who may repeat a single story but nevertheless have distinctive versions to tell. *The Death of the Last Black Man in the Whole Entire World* is composed of panels that function similarly to scenes. The three panels in the play that feature choruses are called "Panel II: First Chorus," "Panel IV: Second Chorus," and "Final Chorus." Each one presents "figures" repeating phrases that correspond to their viewpoint and tell a distinctive version of a similar history. Similar to the role of a chorus's song in a Greek tragedy, the three panels serve to stich the play together, creating a more cohesive whole, but they also demonstrate the multiplicity and lack of uniformity in a collective. There is a narrative hybridity in the collective—its multiple contents transform the form. In Parks's drama the commonsense knowledge that frames the audience's relationship to the play and establishes a connection between the audience and the chorus multiplies with the varied perspectives of the members of the chorus. Rather than a singular shared commonsense perspective, Parks's chorus allows for a diversity of popular understandings.

Through the presentation of the chorus, Parks shifts historical trajectories and reconfigures historical assumptions, expanding the histories that can be told and the tragedies that may be redressed.

Familiar and yet surprising, Parks's drama remembers the past, populating it with new figures, shifting and disrupting narrative archives, and multiplying points of view to reconfigure what counts as tragic and worthy of mourning. Parks's return to the past through repetition and revision, which often takes a ritualized form in the drama, transforms the shape and disrupts the continuity of history. Through the drama's engagement with history, Parks also reshapes dramatic tragedy, making room not only for Arthur Miller's common man but also for the specificity of experience among communities of people.

Notes

1   Several writers have considered how Parks rethinks the shape of history through her drama, but the focus of the commentary often does not take up how her practice of writing history participates in a tradition of dramatic tragedy. One notable exception is chapter 5 of Carpio (2008). For consideration of Parks's drama and its engagement with history, see Elam and Rayner (2001), Colbert (2011), and Schneider (2011).
2   See chapter 2 of Colbert (2017).
3   For additional analysis of the role of the chorus in Parks's work, see Geis (2008).

References

Carpio, Glenda (2008), *Laughing Fit to Kill*, Oxford: Oxford University Press.

Colbert, Soyica Diggs (2011), *The African American Theatrical Body: Reception, Performance and the Stage*, Cambridge: Cambridge University Press.

Colbert, Soyica Diggs (2017), *Black Movements: Performance and Cultural Politics*, New Brunswick: Rutgers University Press.

Elam, Harry J. and Alice Rayner (2001), "Echoes from the Black (W)hole: An Examination of *The America Play* by Suzan-Lori Parks," in Jeffrey D. Mason and J. Ellen Gainor (eds.), *Performing America: Cultural*

Nationalism in American Theater, 178–92, Ann Arbor, MI: University of Michigan Press.

Geis, Deborah R. (2008), "Choral Explorations of Race and Politics," in *Suzan-Lori Parks*, 44–74, Ann Arbor, MI: University of Michigan Press.

Glick, Jeremy Matthew (2016), *The Black Radical Tragic: Performance, Aesthetics, and the Unfinished Haitian Revolution*, New York: New York University Press.

Hull, Gloria T. (1978), "Notes on a Marxist Interpretation of Black American Literature," *Black American Literature Forum* 12 (4): 148–53.

Hegel, Georg Wilhelm Friedrich ([1835] 1975), *Hegel's Aesthetics: Lectures on Fine Art*, vol. 2, translated by T. M. Knox, Oxford: Oxford University Press.

Miller, Arthur ([1949] 1996), "Tragedy and the Common Man," reprinted in *The Theater Essays of Arthur Miller*, revised and expanded edition, Robert A. Martin and Steven R. Centola (eds.), 3–7, New York: Da Capo Press. Available online: http://www.nytimes.com/books/00/11/12/specials/miller-common.html (accessed January 15, 2017).

Parks, Suzan-Lori (1995), *The America Play and Other Works*, New York: Theatre Communications Group.

Parks, Suzan-Lori (2001), *The Red Letter Plays*, New York: Theatre Communications Group.

Parks, Suzan-Lori (2002), *Topdog/Underdog*, New York: Theatre Communications Group.

Parks, Suzan-Lori (2015), *Father Comes Home from the Wars (Parts 1, 2 & 3)*, New York: Theatre Communications Group.

Poole, Adrian (2005), *Tragedy: A Very Short Introduction*, Oxford: Oxford University Press.

Schneider, Rebecca (2011), *Performing Remains: Art and War in Times of Theatrical Reenactment*, New York: Routledge.

Young, Harvey (2007), "Choral Compassion: *In the Blood* and *Venus*" in Kevin J. Wetmore Jr. and Alycia Smith-Howard (eds.), *Suzan-Lori Parks: A Casebook*, 29–47, New York: Routledge.

Williams, Raymond ([1966] 2006), *Modern Tragedy*, Pamela McCallum (ed.), Toronto: Broadview Encore Editions.

18

American Theatre since 1990

Toby Zinman
University of the Arts

"History is happening." That paradoxical line from *Hamilton*, the runaway hit musical by Lin-Manuel Miranda, is the governing thought of this chapter. The word "happening" is intended in both its literal and slang meanings: the obvious—the past influencing the present, suggesting the important and the lasting—as well as the trendy, the urgent, the reevaluated, the reassessed; history can be a place where the traditional and the experimental merge, in drama as in life. In creating parameters for this chapter—there had to be some for an essay about twenty-five years of plays or the essay would have become merely a long list—I have focused on plays about American history, and history, it turns out, is often about war, sociological as well as military. This focus eliminates the large and easy category of family drama (the dominant mode of American playwrights) and focuses on plays that emphasize ideas as well as emotion, philosophy as well as psychology. Tragedy demands more of us than tears.

In the last broadcast of *The Daily Show*, television satirist Jon Stewart said, "If comedy is tragedy plus time, I need more [bleep]ing time. But I would really settle for less [bleep]ing tragedy." This often-used definition of comedy, "humor is tragedy plus time," ascribed to at least a dozen comic writers but most frequently to Mark Twain, that most American of tragicomic voices, implies that with temporal distance and the resulting perspective, the tragic becomes a source of humor. This seems to echo Charlie Chaplin's filmic wisdom: "Life is a tragedy when seen in close-up, but a comedy in long shot." The painful and sometimes bizarre humor provided by the plays included in this chapter is their most contemporary signature.

I purposely have omitted from this chapter contemporary plays that are discussed in the chapters preceding this one, for example, Edward Albee's *The Goat, or Who Is Sylvia?* the subtitle of which is *Notes Toward a Definition of Tragedy*. The plays I have selected are those I admire both theatrically and intellectually, plays that thrilled me in performance and lingered in my mind long after reading. They are radical experiments in stagecraft, making them contemporary in ways far more important than mere chronology, and thus this final chapter of this volume brings, I hope, news as well as views.

The tragedy of history

Karl Marx told us that "History repeats itself, first as tragedy, second as farce." Perhaps it repeats for a third time as musical theatre. Consider *Assassins* by Stephen Sondheim and *Hamilton* by Lin-Manuel Miranda. Both of these shows are revolutionary theatre in subject matter and in style and in tone. Both suggest, in complex and very contemporary ways, the tragic arc of American history as it is shaped by guns, and both take real-life figures as their main characters and take past events as the basis of their narrative. Further, both musicals suggest how fundamental to American history immigrants are—one of the basic ways of defining American exceptionalism; another way of defining American exceptionalism is to call it hubris. Hubris is of course central to the definition of tragedy, but it is also sadly fundamental to human nature: nobody, from Laius onward, wants to yield to fate without a fight.

Sondheim, regarded as the greatest living genius of musical theatre, has shocked audiences over and over again, but in *Assassins*, he is at his most American and most heartbreaking. And, as is often true of the other plays considered here, *Assassins* is outrageously funny.

Assassins premiered in 1991. Its outlandish subject is presidential assassinations; its tone is darkly comic; its central characters are the villains of the piece: the assassins and would-be assassins, from John Wilkes Booth, who killed Abraham Lincoln, to Lee Harvey Oswald, who killed John F. Kennedy. The villains are surprisingly humanized and not easy targets of our collective rage and scorn. The richness and complexity of the show's effect is perfectly revealed in the Preface to the published script where André Bishop, then the artistic director of Playwrights Horizons, recounts this exchange between two audience members: "'I liked it, but who are you supposed to feel for?' His companion replied, her eyes filled with tears, 'Us. You're supposed to feel for us.'" Bishop sums up with this: "you went out into the night thinking how much you loved your country despite how troubled it had become, and you felt happy and sad to be an American" (Sondheim 1991: xi).

It is America, flawed but great, that becomes the tragic hero, a far larger, more thrilling and troubling focus than any one of the dead presidents, eliciting from us the Aristotelian responses to tragedy of terror and pity. And it is this idea of America as a tragic hero that informs this chapter, opening a wide vista on the ways drama can "hold a mirror up to Nature," revealing ourselves to ourselves. Many of the issues that turn tragic in the contemporary world are global and not, therefore, particularly American: racism, sexism, homophobia, classism, family dysfunction, terrorism, crime, drug addictions. But the position of the United States in the world, both as it is seen by other nations and as it self-identifies, lends itself to tragic heroism and a tragic fall. America onstage turns out to be material as rich and various and enormous as the country is in life: the arc of history happening creates the tragic narrative.

As in any good musical, the opening song/scene of *Assassins* establishes the main characters and the setting; the first line of the stage directions reads: "*A Shooting Gallery in a fairground.*" With its flashing red, white, and blue lights and calliope music, its sleazy Proprietor sings to each of the assassins, all disgruntled, down-on-their-luck folks, playing on the American audience's instinctive sympathy for the underdog, and then grotesquely inviting them to "C'mere and kill a President." He entices them with the bouncy refrain, "Everybody's / Got the right / To be happy," and it is this distortion of the *Declaration of Independence*—guaranteeing not happiness but the pursuit of happiness—that generates the action. The sense of entitlement, like the tawdry prizes in the Proprietor's booth, suggests the cheapening of the American Dream, the exchange of moral values for goods. This is underscored by how many of the assassins and would-be assassins are immigrants, members of the "tired, the poor, the huddled masses yearning to breathe free" acknowledged on the Statue of Liberty, a circumstance that now resounds with increased urgency and misery as the immigrant crisis and the consequent debate worsens both in the United States and throughout Europe. And even more relevant is the controversy over gun control in the United States, as the Proprietor sells each assassin a weapon in this carnival of horror. Brecht tried for this effect, but as Sondheim adds the element of history—events that are enshrined in both textbooks and living memory—the horror quotient rises as the theatrical and the factual collide.

In Scene 2 Sondheim creates the Balladeer, a twentieth-century folksinger *à la* Woody Guthrie or Pete Seeger, a musical chronicler of Americana: "Someone tell the story / Someone sing the song / Every now and then / The country goes a little wrong." Balladeer's first song is about John Wilkes Booth (the stage actor who killed President Lincoln) and asks, "Why did you do it, Johnny? / Nobody agrees. You who had everything, what made you bring a nation to its knees?" and sings all the motives ascribed to this national mystery. One of the clues is the Southern dandy's racism ("How the Union can never recover / From that vulgar, High and mighty / Niggerlover, Never–!"). Part of the tragedy of America is racism, the legacy of slavery, recurring in play after American play, as the mayhem of racially related murders has rapidly increased in recent years.

With the gleeful media egging them on, the parade of assassins rolls by—Zangara, Guiteau, Hinckley, Czolgosz, Fromme, Moore, Byck—and the show's style becomes more and more farcical, and thereby more and more appalling as well as more and more entertaining. Sam Byck planned to "drop a 747 on the White House" and thus assassinate Richard Nixon, a preposterous notion that is not at all funny after the fact of 9/11 and seems an eerie bit of clairvoyance. Finally, as time conflates and history happens, *Assassins* turns ice cold: Booth appears on stage out of the past to encourage Lee Harvey Oswald to shoot Kennedy.

Booth revels in the fact that his name is remembered, alluding to the famous line in Arthur Miller's *Death of a Salesman* when he declares, "Attention has been paid." Earlier in the show, Byck's long monologue of despair about the deterioration of the body politic ("Grandma Lives in Packing Crate!," "Sewage Closes Jersey Beaches," "Saudi Prince Buys Howard Johnson's") also quotes from Willy Loman: "The woods are burning." Booth offers Oswald, "The past you never had, the future you'd abandoned—it's called history, Lee." Willy Loman is the ur-underdog, fundamental to any discussion of American tragedy; Booth tells Oswald, "I've seen the future, Lee. And you are it." We, the audience, are cast as witnesses to this display of our tragic history; the stage directions read: "*Crowd noises, blending into a slow, wordless lamentation.*" And most shocking is the reprise of "Everybody's/ Got the right/ To be happy" when all the assassins reappear on stage, point their guns at the audience, and, as the last stage directions indicate, we hear "*the final chord as all the guns go off—BLAM—then blackout.*"

To quote André Bishop again, "you went out into the night thinking how much you loved your country despite how troubled it had become, and you felt happy and sad to be an American." Many plays in the next twenty-five years of American drama will send us out into similar nights.

Let me mention here briefly Suzan-Lori Parks's play *Topdog/ Underdog* (2002), which is taken up in greater detail in an earlier chapter in this volume. The two characters in *Topdog/Underdog*, both African American, are named Lincoln and Booth. Despite Parks's interpretive warning in the documentary film *Stage on Screen: The Topdog Diaries* that they do not act under the historical imperative of their names (their father's idea of a "joke," we are told), the relevance of Parks's play in light of *Assassins* seems pertinent. Like Sondheim, who sets *Assassins* in a carnival, Parks has Lincoln working in a similarly seedy amusement park where people pay for the chance to shoot him. When his brother Booth tries to coach him into a more dramatic death scene, Lincoln replies, "People are funny about they Lincoln shit. It's historical. People like they historical shit ... to unfold the way they folded it up. Neatly like a book. Not raggedy and bloody and screaming" (50). In that distinction is her indictment of our tidy and comforting ideas about American history and how they veil the violence and enduring injustice of racism. In her brilliant conceit of people lining up to play Lincoln's assassin, Parks unfolds the map of history.

Another play that messily unfolds the first chapter of America's enshrined history is James Ijames's *The Most Spectacularly Lamentable Trial of Miz Martha Washington* (2014). With fantasia-style theatricality, the play presents the Washington household, understandably tense now that George Washington is dead and his widow is dying; his will releases their slaves after her death. She is on trial for all the obvious crimes: kidnapping, unlawful imprisonment, physical and psychological abuse. Several of the Founding Fathers make cameo appearances in *Miz Martha*, and they are played by the same African American actors who play the slaves. The complex implications and indictments are brought home when at the play's end the slaves reach the verdict "Guilty," and she asks, "What do you want from me?!" (93). They reply in *Thunderous Unison*: "JESUS WOMAN! FREE US!" (94). In the brief dream state after her death, she tells a slave boy, "I ... I'm going to tell you a story" (95). That story is the fraudulent and tragic story of American history.

Hamilton, music, lyrics, and book by Lin-Manuel Miranda, the runaway hit of recent New York seasons, praised by Sondheim as "groundbreaking," is a work of revolutionary musical theatre about the American Revolution, the Founding Fathers, and the world-astonishing invention of the United States. Miranda refuses to dumb down American history or to yield to cheap cynicism, as the show reveals the grandeur of a vision of a new nation, a nation often stymied by political backbiting and infighting, and built by immigrants. History's relevance never has been more apparent.

The book follows the life of Alexander Hamilton—based on the celebrated biography by Ron Chernow—from orphaned teenager arriving in the colonies from his hurricane-destroyed Caribbean home to Founding Father and Secretary of the Treasury. He is dazzlingly articulate, an ambitious workaholic who is compelled by words: he wrote most of the *Federalist Papers* in only a few months. Those talents and inclinations make rap, with its endless rhymes and word play and driving electric energy, the perfect stylistic medium for this character and this story. But the score is a melting pot, a complex and witty compilation of many musical styles from lyrical ballads to jazzy tunes to pop, with flash references to everything from *South Pacific* to *The Pirates of Penzance* (George Washington refers to himself as "the very model of a modern major general"). Thus *Hamilton* is also about the history of musical theatre.

Alexander Hamilton's first friend in the New World will become his mortal enemy: Aaron Burr. The show gives the antihero equal time, both narratively and musically; like Sondheim in *Assassins*, Miranda is interested in finding the human in the villain. Burr is an opportunist, a man without honor, who smiles and waits. Hamilton is ambitious and vigorous; his musical refrain is, "I am not throwing away my shot." Ironically, the duel that ends his life (the only thing most people know about Alexander Hamilton is his fatal duel with Burr) happens when he, literally and honorably, throws away his shot by pointing his pistol to the sky.

All the Founding Fathers are played by actors of color, and they stand in contrast to the very white and hilariously weak King George who at first cannot believe the upstarts will succeed. Hamilton's love life is complicated by his marrying Eliza, whose sister Angelica— another pair of opposites played by actors of different races—also loves him. The family drama, though it contains humanizing plot events, is given far less time than the national events, indicating that Miranda is interested in something bigger than a family drama. The birth of Hamilton's son and Burr's daughter at the same time yields the lovely duet sung by both characters about paternal love and the future into which their children will grow. This is followed immediately by a letter from the father of John Laurens announcing the battlefield death of his son, who "dreamed of emancipating and recruiting 3000 men for the first all-black military regiment. His dream of freedom for these men dies with him." Laurens's death is, then, an enormous historical loss and not just his family's loss, a preamble to the last sad song at the show's conclusion: Eliza spends fifty years after her husband's death trying to do what Hamilton would have done in speaking out against slavery, leaving us to imagine that the tragic history of racism in America might have been different. Hamilton's anti-slavery stance is briefly glimpsed in his debate with Jefferson:

> A new line of credit, a financial diuretic
> How do you not get it? If we're aggressive and competitive
> The union gets a boost. You'd rather give it a sedative?
> A civics lesson from a slaver. Hey neighbor.
> Your debts are paid cuz you don't pay for labor

"We plant seeds in the South. We create." Yeah, keep ranting.
We know who's really doing the planting.
Don't lecture me about the war, you didn't fight in it. (161)

This last barb makes Jefferson's entrance into the play even funnier: he bounds into the group of politicians in 1789, having been in France as Ambassador for years, saying, "So, what'd I miss?" That he is seen as a Francophile and thus an elitist is wittily underscored by the same actor's playing Lafayette in Act 1.

The tragic cost of Hamilton's murder can be measured by his accomplishments and the loss of a great political and intellectual talent; dead before he was fifty years old, he already had created the *New York Post* newspaper, established the national banking system, founded the Coast Guard, created the US Mint, and served as the first Secretary of the Treasury. The show's final song has the company sing, "Every other founding father story gets told. / Every other founding father gets to grow old. / And when you're gone, who remembers your name?" (281). An additional if minor tragedy was averted when President Obama abandoned his plans to replace Hamilton's picture on the $10 bill—I suspect largely because of the power of this show.

The huge and talented chorus of multiracial singers/dancers all wear fascinating costumes that modulate through centuries of styles just as the show's linguistic and musical styles do; they bend genders and fill the edges of the stage with the new American population. The stirring song "They'll tell the story of tonight" echoes Henry V's Agincourt speech, reaching for and achieving glory, although not in the context of war as Shakespeare has it but in the context of political daring and revolutionary risk-taking as the young colonies declare their independence from England.

Hamilton is, like *Assassins*, both patriotic and optimistic—a new nation is created—as well as critical and pessimistic. And like the ancient Greek tragedies, like Shakespeare's history plays, *Hamilton* is about statecraft, the relationship between a great man and the state; it is not merely a single life that is at stake but something much larger and more enduring. Statesmanship is a crucial gauge of the historic tragic hero. As he is dying, Hamilton sings:

What is a legacy?
It's planting seeds in a garden you never get to see

I wrote some notes at the beginning of a song someone will sing
   for me
America, you great unfinished symphony,
You sent for me
You let me make a difference
A place where even orphan immigrants can leave their
   fingerprints and rise up. (273)

At the end of the show, the entire company sings, without Hamilton,
"Who lives, who dies, who tells your story?" and that telling, as all
the great playwrights knew, is the only way there can be tragedy:
somebody has to tell the story.

The tragedy of social legacy

Societal legacy is another form of history, and the clutch of new
plays discussed here is intended to stand for the many, many
scripts that take up similar issues, especially racism and the
deterioration of the communal fabric. Their central similarity is
thematic: the fabric of old-fashioned values of generosity and
loyalty continues to be shredded through narcissism and greed,
drugs and poverty.

An obvious example is Tracy Letts's 2008 Pulitzer Prize–
winning *August: Osage County* that often is read/performed as a
dysfunctional family drama with all the usual havoc around the
usual kitchen table: incest, drugs, alcoholism, suicide. But it is
crucial to remember Johnna, a seemingly minor character who is
a Cheyenne Indian with a gender-inclusive name; she is the Native
American stashed in the attic, the family's servant but also the
nation's shame. Notice the pivotal lines offhandedly delivered in the
middle of the second act in the middle of this very long play: "This
country, this experiment, America, this hubris: What a lament, if no
one saw it go. Here today, gone tomorrow" (192). History is still
happening.

Maybe all ambitious family dramas—"dysfunctional" almost
goes without saying, consider the *Oresteia* and *King Lear*—use the
drama of family as a way of talking about the drama of nation
("Something is rotten in the state of Denmark."). To extend the
geographic symbolism, we're in Oklahoma, on The Plains—"a state

of mind, right, some spiritual affliction, like the blues"—everybody in Osage County has got The Plains. Unlike classical tragedies, this one is laugh-out-loud funny, an emotional stew particular to contemporary American tragedy.

Stand-up tragedy is an actual category of performance art, like stand-up comedy turned inside out or standing on its head. But, unlike the usual solo rants of stand-up tragedy that are autobiographical and ultimately demand sympathy, Bill Cain's drama *Stand-Up Tragedy* (1991) explores the limits not of our sympathy but of our empathy, as true tragedy must and as self-pity cannot. This also illustrates the difference between agitprop and a theatre of societal awareness, revealing, according to the playwright's notes, a "tragedy so vast that it feels like ... our version of the Final Solution" (177). Despite this shocking overstatement, what Cain seems to be suggesting is that, like the plague in Thebes, like the rotten core of the state of Denmark, something in contemporary American society is deeply wrong. *Stand-Up Tragedy* reaches for these mighty predecessors, and Cain's prefatory "Note" concludes with, "There is always a sense of absurdity even at the most critical moments on the Lower East Side"—he is referring to a dangerous neighborhood in New York City, where young men regularly are killed by guns. But, as with *August: Osage County*, specific locales always stand for a larger world.

Stand-Up Tragedy takes place in a small Catholic school for Hispanic boys, as well as various apartments and mean streets, although the script specifically rejects all realistic sets and props, depending on light and sound for its effects. The central character is a fourteen-year-old boy named Lee, a gifted artist who creates an illustrated rap epic about a hero named Saga—thus the hero and the story become one—which is intermittently performed throughout the play by the students. This imaginary world is populated by evil creatures representing Senora, Lee's cruel, manipulative mother, and Tyro, his violent, thuggish brother—roles played by the actor playing Lee with lightning-fast shifts. There also is a mythological beast, a griffin:

> Cross a lion and eagle and in the books I've read ...
> You get a lion's body with an eagle's head ...
> But after all that trouble you got to wonder why ...
> 'Cause it looks great on paper but it's never gonna fly. (24)

The griffin is the avatar of the young, idealistic teacher Tom Griffin, who befriends Lee with the best of intentions that "look great on paper" but have dire consequences; this is a particularly American play about the desperate needs of tragic heroes. Worth noting here is F. Scott Fitzgerald's remark: "Show me a hero and I'll write you a tragedy," which seems to be a commentary not only on the unavailability of heroes but also on the unavailability of tragedy. Lee's saga is about his super-hero Saga who is trapped in his saga as Lee is trapped by his own story of poverty and family and social environment:

Lee   The story's the story.

Griffin   Change it.

Lee   Your family's your fate ... You can't change the story! (51)

Just as Oedipus's family is his fate, despite Laius and Jocasta's desperately trying to "change the story," the hero is ensnared in the narrative net. As Saga grows up, he discovers the family he thought was his is a lie. Griffin and his students rap the pivotal scene:

When Saga was a boy he thought the Baron was his father.
He didn't ask questions, I mean, why should he bother?
You find a man in your house—if he ain't too bad
And he stays for a while—you call the dude Dad.
But Saga's growing up, it's time for him to realize
That all the Baron's stories are lies, lies, lies.
Now the Baron's not your father, you've been living in disguise.
If you don't believe me, take a look at your eyes.
Saga's eyes were empty like two deep holes,
Like a night without stars, like tunnels to his soul.
Your father had eyes that did the same thing,
The Baron's not your father—your father's the king! (52)

In *Oedipus the King*, Oedipus discovers too late that he was, all along, the rightful heir to the throne ("your father's the king!"). Sophocles gives us the oldest and most powerful metaphor in theatre history: Oedipus's blindness; when he is sighted he cannot see the truth, and he can endure the truth only after he is literally blind. The truth turns out to be elusive in *Stand-up Tragedy* because despite the best efforts of several good men and several desperate boys, despite everyone's being able to see the truth of Lee's situation, there seems to be no possible solution to what Griffin calls the "ecology of evil" of the streets. Americans historically embrace the Christian idea of truth leading to freedom ("The truth will set you free") in ways that suggest that anybody can "change the story," that any child can grow up to be president, but the empty eyes are the tragic truth here.

Like Thornton Wilder in *Our Town*, Stephen Adly Guirgis creates a community of characters in *Our Lady of 121st Street* (2004) who have known each other all their lives, but unlike Wilder's folks, this is a group of out-of-control, self-deluded, self-loathing, heartbreaking crazies, where guilt and hurt and loyalty and love and rage compete for their souls every day. The outcome, unlike the consolatory wisdom of Wilder, is both messy and tragic. The play's opening line tells it all—or, rather, asks it all—with a question that the play itself will answer: "What kinda fuckin' world is this?!"

The characters have gathered from all over the country for their beloved Sister Rose's funeral, having been her pupils at a Catholic school in Harlem (thus the title's 121st Street in New York) when they were kids. A wild, alcoholic, child-rescuing nun, Sister Rose was found dead on the sidewalk. Contrary to easy expectations this is not a murder mystery; the immediate cause for outrage is that Sister Rose's corpse has been stolen, and everybody has to wait until the crime is solved. This old-fashioned locked-room dramatic premise gives Guirgis both the absurdist foundation and the set-up for the characters' conversations and backstories.

Balthazar, the investigating detective, sets the play's fiercely snarky tone when one guy asks, "What are you, a cop?" "No, Vic, I'm a farmer. I came here to sell some eggs" (8). We will learn later that Balthazar is tortured by guilt for not have found the man who raped and murdered his young son years ago.

We learn also about Rooftop, now a blingy radio personality in Los Angeles who wants absolution for unconfessed sins from Father Lux, who fears his parishioners and is confined to a wheelchair ("Where your legs at, Father?" "Korea."). Rooftop's bitter, beautiful ex-wife, Inez, still blames him for her "scorched-up heart." Rooftop finally explodes with despair and self-disgust: "I'm afraid that the person I'll like least wherever I go will always be me" (34).

Edwin is a guy trapped in the martyrdom of looking after his brain-damaged brother, Pinky, onto whose head he dropped a brick when they were boys. Flip, who imagines nobody knew he was gay, is now a lawyer in Wisconsin, and tries desperately to tone down his super-swishy partner, Gail. Norca is a woman who is still "venomous like some kind of no-ear pit-bull" (29), and Sister Rose's niece, Marcia, and her friend Sonia are suburban white girls caught in her cross fire.

This is a world of pain, and Guirgis's ear for street language creates dialogue that is jokey and heart-wrenching and appalling. *Our Lady* ends inconclusively, without either absolution or solution. They find only half of Sister Rose's body, and we never even hear which half. That, it seems, answers the play's opening question: that's what kind of a world this is.

Perhaps the most profoundly American and universal of these contemporary tragedies is Richard Greenberg's *Take Me Out* (2003), a play about that most American of sports, baseball. The title refers to a traditional song, a social legacy, that begins, "Take me out to the ball game" and continues with "Root, root, root for the home team/ If they don't win it's a shame/ For it's one, two, three strikes you're out at the old ball game." The title's phrase "take me out" also suggests the much more contemporary and murderous slang meaning: kill me. It also suggests going on a date. Further, "take me out" suggests the ecstatic pleasures of fandom. Mason, the narrating character, a gay man who initially knows nothing about baseball, is assigned to manage the money of the country's most idolized ball player, Darren, and he discovers the joy of having his spirit lifted:

> I don't know why I feel exalted when we win.
> I don't know why I feel diminished when we lose.
> I don't know why I'm saying "we" ...!
> Life is so ... tiny, so *daily*. This ... you ... take me out of it. (72)

And that joy, as well as a tribalistic sense of "we," may be the reasons, beneath all the other reasons, that sports fans worship their heroes, finding community in their worship. As Mason remarks, "Baseball is ... unrelentingly meaningful" (68). Early in the play, Mason explains how "baseball achieves the tragic vision democracy evades" because "baseball acknowledges loss ... Democracy is lovely, but baseball's more mature" (37). Like tragic drama, a home run provides the crowd with a catharsis, and it is no accident that in a game based on multiples of three, Greenberg has written that rare contemporary play with three acts. Furthermore, Darren Lemming, like all classical tragic heroes, has a flaw, and, as was true for many of his classical predecessors, that flaw is hubris. In this tangled plot of racism, homophobia, Christian self-righteousness, and back-country ignorance, Darren's best friend Davey Battle is killed by an intentionally lethal pitch thrown by Shane Mungitt.

The idea of a "home team," a community of a mutually supportive individuals relying on trust and affection—a metaphor for America's best image of itself—falls to pieces when Darren, apparently on impulse, reveals during a media interview that he is gay. Why does he do it? Because he's "goofin"? Because he wants to help gay kids? Because he wants to close the private/public gap in his life? Because he wants, hubristically, to test his immunity? Because he himself has no idea why?

Shane has been brought in as a pitcher, a "closer"—a term of art which becomes a term of literal truth—to rescue the team from its slump. He is so psychologically deformed and uneducated as to be nearly amoral and language-less. He has his own wretched history, having watched his parents' murder/suicide; he was fourteen months old and was not found for three days after the event, starving and covered in filth. No wonder he has a "cleanliness thing" that requires three ritualized showers before and after a game. When mixed-race Darren kisses Shane in the shower to bait him, he essentially arms this white racist homophobe as a deadly weapon against African American Davey Battle, Darren's best friend. When Shane relates the horror story of his childhood, he laughs. Darren asks why he's laughing, and Shane replies, in what may be the most chilling moment of a play filled with chilling moments, "What's not funny?"

In the play's last scene Darren invites Mason to be his date at the victory party after the Empires have once again won the World Series: "It'll be a goof." He gives him his World Series commemorative ring and tosses him the ball. Darren says, cavalierly, "What a fuck of a season, huh?" and Mason replies, "Yes, it was, it was a fuck of a season. It was … tragic." He then repeats to himself, "It *was*—tragic" (116). If, classically, tragedy moves from action through suffering, to perception, self-knowledge always comes too late, thus the tragic outcome. At the end of *Take Me Out*, Darren, the man who is the contemporary American equivalent of an ancient king, has fallen from a great height, but never fully comprehends his tragic drama. It is for Mason, the outsider who tells the story, to understand that. Like America, the Empires are a multinational, multiracial team: Japanese Kawabata lives in silence since he cannot speak English and does not wish to; Martinez and Rodriguez speak Spanish and thus exclude the others; Kippy is an over-articulate, intellectual Swede, while Mason, nicknamed "Mars," might as well be from Mars, the total outsider, since he not only is gay in this world of male athletes but thoroughly rejected by the gay community. That there are so many soliloquys in the play highlights the silence, a problem fundamental to both the pride and the loneliness of living in a country of immigrants.

The tragedy of war

War is, of course, deeply embedded in the history of most countries. The past two decades of American history, the decades with which I have been tasked in this chapter, are colored by the wars in Iraq and Afghanistan. The plays of recent years have examined the terrible cost of those wars by doing what media pundits and statistics cannot do: revealing the emotional truth of war. Significant contemporary American tragedies explore modern war by writing about ancient ones.

In *An Iliad* (2013), by Lisa Peterson and Denis O'Hare, a weary, barefoot man carrying an old suitcase, speaking ancient Greek enters a bare stage. He has been travelling 3,000 years to sing his song again, and this solo play revives the ancient, travelling rhapsode's oral tradition as this latter-day Homer recounts once again the story of the war between Greece and Troy. Peterson and O'Hare's script combines Robert Fagles's celebrated translation of Homer with a moving and persuasive contemporary play that uses the classic epic form to recount an updated heroic national narrative. But where Homer's epic sometimes is seen as a celebration of the glories and heroism of war, Petersen and O'Hare's rendering expresses distinctively antiwar sentiments. What does it say about contemporary Western civilization that everyone knows the name "Achilles," but hardly anyone knows the name "Hector"? History—and the recounting of history—belongs to the victors. The ancient poet embodies Sondheim's Balladeer's lines, "Someone tell the story / Someone sing the song" just as the finale in Miranda's *Hamilton* asks, "Who lives, who dies, who tells your story?"

If we have been taught to revere the ancient Greeks as heroes, the splendid creators of Western civilization, this play makes us rethink whose side we are on and takes us to the iconic ancient works through a revisionist lens. *An Iliad* is two hours of impassioned, uninterrupted speech, performed without props, requiring a virtuoso actor who can convincingly shift between characters, from the horrorstruck Hecuba to the desolate Andromache, the feckless Paris, the "shining" Hector, the proud Achilles, and a reflective Helen ("bitch that I am, vicious, scheming," 24), all while continuously holding the stage as the Poet. The Homeric devices of repetition and incantation ("The end closed in around him … and his soul went winging down to the House of Death") are part of the enthralling power of this play, but among its most effective devices is Homeric list-making:

Fighters from Coronea, Haleartus deep in meadows,
And the men who held Plataea and lived in Glisas,
Men who held the rough-hewn gates of Lower Thebes
On-kee-stus the holy, Poseidon's sun-filled grove,
Men from the town of Arne green with vineyards … (12)

And then he continues:

boys from every small town in Ohio, from farmlands, from fishing villages … the boys of Nebraska and South Dakota … from Springfield, Illinois; Evanston, Illinois; Chicago, Illinois; Buffalo, New York; Cooperstown, New York; Brooklyn, Queens … the Bronx.

This list goes on and on, ending finally with, "You get the point" (12–13).

This technique is most devastating as the Poet begins a list of wars, beginning with the Peloponnesian War, continuing through the Crusades, through Hiroshima, Vietnam, Sarajevo, and stopping—only for the moment—with Syria. The list is four pages long—single-spaced. As the Poet sadly tells us, "Every time I sing this song, I hope it's the last time" (10). And that's the point.

An Iliad also depends on the audience's being made to viscerally respond to the script—the intoxicating violence of "RAGE" as the Poet demonstrates "some trick of the blood" that makes us feel contemporary road rage along with these wild ancient warriors. What was Oedipus's slaying of his father but an episode of road rage?

Again and again, the Poet draws a breath and then says to us, "Do you see?" He explains that the gods "never die. They change ... they burrow inside us ... They *become* us, they become our impulses. Lust? Aphrodite. Mischief? Hermes. A good idea? Athena ..." (15). The Greeks' gods have become our psychology, a word of Greek origin which literally means "science of the soul." The play ends with a simple, powerful line: "You see?" followed by a blackout. Thus, ancient Greek tragedy is transformed into contemporary American tragedy, perhaps proving that the real source of tragedy is man's nature, a notion I will take up again later in discussing *Bengal Tiger in the Baghdad Zoo*.

Paula Vogel's 2014 play *Don Juan Comes Home from Iraq* dons a similar Homeric coat in a radical way: in a fierce antiwar play, she takes up the story of a young man called Juan both during and after his last tour of duty. Vogel's voice always has been courageous, daring to say what needs to be said, unafraid of moral ambiguity. Her plays (*Baltimore Waltz, How I Learned to Drive, Hot 'n' Throbbin'*, among many others) all are vastly different from one another, but none falls into the easy trap of linearity or its comfy cousin causality. Here Vogel is revisiting Odon van Horvath's *Don Juan Comes Back from the War*, where the satiric targets are both the womanizer and the horrors of war, although for van Horvath it is the First World War.

Don Juan Comes Home from Iraq is a memory play, spiraling back through time and event. It is also a woeful and shocking portrait of Americans' lack of knowledge about history.

The play's feminist point ("Don Juan" is shorthand for a womanizer) was made at a remarkably timely moment: just when various sex scandals were making headlines as male military officers exerted their power over the women under their command in order to take sexual advantage of them, a crime which is basic to Juan's *modus operandi*. Factor in the photographs of female soldiers humiliating male prisoners in Abu Ghraib, plus the triumphant video clips in August 2015 of the first two women to graduate from the legendarily tough Army Ranger training course, and the complexity of gender issues in today's military is revealed.

Vogel's Don Juan is up to his usual seductive, ruthless no-good when he finds himself on leave and a tourist in Philadelphia, where he meets a woman named Cressida. Later, as a Marine Captain, he is back in Philadelphia after four deployments in Iraq, suffering from unbearable pain both in his head and in his conscience and a numbness in his soul. He is searching for Cressida, his "girl back home." Her name evokes the Trojan War. As we know from Shakespeare's *Troilus and Cressida* if not from earlier sources (Boccaccio, Chaucer), she is an ambiguous character, both a faithless lover and betrayed woman.

Don Juan's search for her takes him through time as well as space: Philadelphia's seventeenth-century Tun Tavern, where the Marine Corps began; Osage Avenue during the MOVE bombings (one of the great blights on the city's twentieth-century history); the Mutter Museum, an archive of the gruesome and grotesque; Old City both then the section of Philadelphia where Ben Franklin lived and worked and now a neighborhood that is both elegant and arty. As Vogel's setting, Philadelphia is cast as hell and Don Juan is in it. After wandering the streets, he winds up homeless on a bitter cold night, waiting for his now ghostly Cressida to sit with him: "I've got your back."

Standing in contrast to the Marine Corps' motto, *Semper Fi* ("always faithful") is Vogel's litany repeated over and over: "Betrayed, abandoned, lied to." This describes the general condition: Cressida and numerous other women by Don Juan; Mother Theresa, here called "Colonel Mother," who has been betrayed by God and tells Juan, "We have much in common, Captain. Any charlatan can sell a cause she believes in. It takes the Gift of God to peddle the empty promise"; female soldiers who are betrayed, abandoned and lied to by their recruiters ("You will never deploy," they tell Cressida); Marines betrayed by their daredevil officer, Captain Juan, who orders them into "Suicide Alley." Ultimately, this indictment extends to the Iraqi citizens who have been betrayed, abandoned, and lied to by the US military.

Don Juan Comes Home from Iraq is about an America that has lost its way, its values, and its soul: this is tragedy on a massive scale. Near the end of the play we hear Cressida ask Don Juan the same question she asked him at the start, "Are you lost?" And now we know the answer. This echoing answer to a first-line question recalls the opening question in Guirgis's *Our Lady of 121st Street*: "What kinda fuckin' world is this?!'"

In *Dying City* ([2006] 2013), Christopher Shinn takes up the tragedy of another contemporary soldier in Iraq whose soul or psyche (these are the same word in ancient Greek) has become so polluted by the atrocities of war that he shoots himself. The play depends on disorienting shifts in tone that echo the disorienting shifts in time and perspective as we watch first Peter, a gay actor who has just walked offstage in the middle of a performance of O'Neill's *Long Day's Journey Into Night*, and then his identical twin, Craig, a soldier who died a year earlier in Iraq. They are, of course, played by the same actor, who has to delineate subtle distinctions between them. Craig was married to Kelly, a psychotherapist, and the play begins with Peter's unexpected, uninvited visit to his widowed sister-in-law's apartment. He is armed with a sheaf of printed-out emails sent by Craig to his brother from the battlefield. Later, when Craig emerges from the bedroom—a room Peter entered moments before—the time has shifted, unannounced, to a year prior. That was the night before Craig left for Iraq, the night he confessed to Kelly that he no longer loved her, although their lost marriage is the least of the play's sad concerns.

The dying city of the play's title is Baghdad: "The city is dying and we're the ones who are killing it" (400), Craig writes from Iraq. But Shinn also seems to mean New York, where the play takes place. He draws a straight, causal connecting line between the 9/11 attack on the Twin Towers and the war in Iraq, followed by the surge in Afghanistan and America's continued military presence there. The dying is both public and private, political and personal, American and Iraqi. Baghdad is where Craig shoots himself—a suicide called "an accident" by the US Army and by the family.

The backstory ("Oh, you know, everyone has a childhood") reveals that Peter and Craig's father was a Vietnam veteran whose repressed rage caused him once to smash the car's windshield with his fist during a battlefield flashback. This brief recollection is included in one of Craig's emails. The event becomes significant in retrospect: it took place when the family was in the car and the twins were six years old, but Peter has no recollection of it, whereas Craig's memory is vivid. Craig wrote this powerful account, which Peter reads aloud to Kelly:

I looked up and the windshield was like a spiderweb, and there was Dad's bleeding fist, gripping the steering wheel tight ... I looked over at Mom and I remember thinking that she was going to look a certain way, upset or scared ... but instead I saw her grinning. A little creeping grin on her face. I looked over at you. You were looking out the window like you hadn't noticed anything, so I punched you in the arm. You said "Ow," and Dad looked back for a second, then turned back to the road. That's all I remember. I think I've remembered this now, after so many years, because what I learned in that instant—that to be married to a man so powerful he could put his fist through glass was what made our mother smile—is exactly how I feel here: so powerful I can't stop smiling, while suffering a wound I do not feel. (398)

Like Vogel's Don Juan, Craig's and his father's numbness is one of the costs of war and is what permits soldiers to commit atrocious acts. What this exposes about the link between sexual allure and male violence is another issue of *Dying City*'s text and subtext. Woven into the dialogue are repeated mentions of one of Kelly's patients, referred to by his repeated brag that becomes his nickname: "Fucked-her-so-hard-she- ..." Both Craig and Peter find this nickname amusing, although Kelly does not; it becomes more shocking when Peter recounts a night in a bar when Craig returns from what is, presumably, a sexual encounter in the restroom, saying "I think the bitch bit me." Both Peter and Kelly discover in that moment that Craig always has been a violent person: "the horror I feel here is not just a consequence of the war, but is horror of the core of me, of who I have always been ... I haven't felt the overwhelming need to sexually demean women that has haunted me my entire life, and haven't fucked since leaving Ford Benning" (401), implying that war violence provides a release that substitutes for sex.

In *Dying City*, the TV, used by the characters as distraction and comfort after a harrowing series of discoveries, provides the shocking sounds of "laughter, applause," which conclude the play as Jon Stewart's *The Daily Show* begins. (Recall the quotation in my opening section of this chapter: "If comedy is tragedy plus time, I need more [bleep]ing time. But I would really settle for less [bleep]ing tragedy.") Earlier, Peter has recalled a man at a party saying,

"Bush is as bad as Hitler." *Then* he starts talking about how hilarious *The Daily Show* is. And I thought—if you were in Germany in the 1930s, would you watch a show where some smartass made fun of Hitler? Little mustache jokes while he's throwing Jews in the ovens? I mean if you really think George Bush is evil, then how can you laugh at "George Bush is dumb" jokes? (392)

Kelly's reply gets to the heart of the problem of contemporary tragedy: "It's the sensibility. The sensibility comes closer to conveying the truth than the real news does" (392). Shinn has refused to write a *Daily Show* sort of play.

Also revelatory of the American sense of tragedy is the full-throated literature Craig was studying: Melville, Hawthorne, Hemingway, and Faulkner—big books filled with big ideas about America, the kind of worthy stuff we feel is required for the grandeur of the tragic but also the kind of stuff where we tend to lose an authentic experience of tragedy as we are subsumed and thus protected in the worthiness of the works' fictional narratives. Craig's love of American literature may indicate his attempt to find comfort and release in the power of stories, a role that national narratives often perform when events challenge citizens' faith.

Significant, too, is Peter's starring as Edmund in *Long Day's Journey Into Night,* perhaps the premier American tragedy; it is a drama, as *Dying City* is, about two very different brothers and their abusive father. O'Neill, however, believed in an enlightening tragic despair that Shinn seems to reject: Peter is after all only an actor here, a pretender in a presentation. Perhaps this reveals Shinn's impulse to deny the power of the tragic that is at the heart of his dramatic vision. Kelly's two favorite TiVo solaces are Jon Stewart and *Law & Order.* The source of comfort in the latter is, "someone dies, and a whole team of specialists springs up to figure out how to solve the mystery of the person's death ... [whereby the mystery and thus the death itself are] therefore symbolically reversed" (380). In *Dying City* Shinn seems to suggest that we similarly live in a confusingly inconsistent world of our own images, never fully understanding or explaining our tragedies, no matter how great the loss and its emotional toll; we simply paper them over with stories that somehow enable us to go on, engaging in a quintessential American pragmatism that is both a self-protecting virtue and a self-deluding vice, until, as happened to Craig, we cannot go on. Tragedy does not lead to enlightenment for Shinn, merely finality.

Rajiv Joseph's electrifying play *Bengal Tiger at the Baghdad Zoo* (2010) takes place in Iraq in 2003. Based on an actual event when the Baghdad zoo was bombed inadvertently and many of the animals escaped into the city, Joseph's drama begins when the lions have all been hunted down and shot, but the Bengal tiger, played by an actor specified as wearing clothes and not a tiger costume, is still in his cage. Guarding his cage are two American Marines, Tom and Kev, both painfully young and dangerously stupid. When Tom decides the tiger looks hungry, he tries to feed it a Slim Jim, and the tiger bites his hand off ("... the hand that feeds it"—a teasing metaphor for the relationship between the Iraqis and the American military). Kev shoots and kills the tiger, who becomes a ghost and the play's central character. Undergoing an "existential quandary," he raises the play's big theological questions; for example, pointing to the logical conundrum of *Genesis*, he asks, "What kind of twisted bastard creates a predator and then punishes him for preying?"(214). Thus, by extension, he questions man's nature and wonders if violence, cruelty, and war are inevitable results for which human beings are programmed.

Kev's weapon is a solid gold gun that Tom had looted from the palace when they found and killed Saddam Hussein and his two insane sons, Uday and Qusay. The ghost of Uday denies being a Midas figure despite his love of gold. (Tom will return to Iraq with a bionic hand to find Uday's gold toilet seat that he buried in the desert). Uday roams through the play, carrying his brother's head, sometimes pretending the head is whispering in his ear, providing moments of grotesque hilarity.

For sheer shocking relevance, it is no accident that the central character—setting aside the tiger—is an Iraqi named Musa, who was a gardener in Uday's employ. The Hanging Gardens of Babylon, one of the Seven Wonders of the Ancient World, was less than fifty-five miles from modern day Baghdad, and biblical scholars locate the Garden of Eden on the site of the present-day city. Musa had created a wondrous garden, a zoo of topiary animals, and when he brought his little sister to see them, she was captured by Uday to be tortured, raped and gruesomely murdered. Tiger asks Musa, "Did you make this place? ... Are You who I think You are? ... At first it's pretty cool: the limitless fruit of knowledge hanging low in

your path. Then you realize it's the only thing to eat around here"
(213). Calling Baghdad "paradise lost" doesn't begin to capture the
irony. This is tragedy extending back to the foundational myth of
the Western world. As the tiger says, "It's like God's revenge, you
know? He's got us chasing our own tails here" (213).

Among much else, *Bengal Tiger at the Baghdad Zoo* is a play
about language; Joseph specifies in his stage directions that there
should be no subtitles for the Arabic dialogue (which is translated
on the page), giving the audience a taste of what it feels like to be
missing important information. Musa is a "terp" (military slang for
interpreter). Apparently, we all need terps; we are working in the
dark, in a language we don't understand, raising the question of the
profound connection between language and tragedy: the story must
be told, and there must be language to tell it in.

Conclusion

And to return to where I began: Alexander Hamilton wrote many of
the Federalist Papers in the eighteenth century, but his observations
about the US government seem startlingly apt today; consider this,
from Hamilton's *Federalist Paper #1*:

> It has been frequently remarked that it seems to have been
> reserved to the people of this country, by their conduct and
> example, to decide the important question, whether societies of
> men are really capable or not of establishing good government
> from reflection and choice, or whether they are forever destined
> to depend for their political constitutions on accident and force.

This last query is at the heart of contemporary tragedy, where "accident
and force" seem to run the show and shape the narrative, and thus
there are so many recent plays about recent wars, societal and military.

Finally, I return to Stephen Sondheim. Early in *Assassins,*
Balladeer sings:

> Someone tell the story,
> Someone sing the song.
> Every now and then
> The country

Goes a little wrong. [...]
Doesn't stop the story –
Story's pretty strong.
Doesn't change the song ...

This thrilling if naïve American optimism raises the hard question of this chapter: has America changed and with it American drama? American playwrights have found new ways to express our pity and our fear. Like the couple in my introduction, we go out into the night richer and sadder for having seen these plays.

References

Note: In the case of scripts not yet published at the time I was drafting this chapter in the spring of 2016, I have relied on generously provided rehearsal scripts.

Cain, Bill (1991), *Stand-Up Tragedy*, New York: Samuel French.
Greenberg, Richard (2003), *Take Me Out*, New York: Faber and Faber.
Guirgis, Stephen Adly (2004), *Our Lady of 121st Street*, New York: Dramatists Play Service.
Ijames, James (2014), *The Most Spectacularly Lamentable Trial of Miz Martha Washington*, rehearsal draft, June.
Joseph, Rajiv (2010), *Gruesome Playground Injuries; Animals Out of Paper; Bengal Tiger at the Baghdad Zoo: Three Plays*, Berkeley, CA: Soft Skull Press.
Letts, Tracy (2008), *August: Osage County*, New York: Theatre Communications Group.
Miranda, Lin-Manuel and Jeremy McCarter (2016), *Hamilton: The Revolution*, New York: Grand Central Publishing.
Parks, Suzan-Lori (2002), *Topdog/Underdog*, New York: Theatre Communications Group.
Peterson, Lisa and Denis O'Hare (2013), *An Iliad*, New York: Dramatists Play Service.
Shinn, Christopher ([2006] 2013), *Dying City*, reprinted in Sarah Benson (ed.), *The Methuen Drama Book of New American Plays*, London: Bloomsbury.
Sondheim, Stephen and John Weidman (1991), *Assassins*, New York: Theatre Communications Group.
Stage on Screen: The Topdog Diaries (2002) [Film], Dir. Oren Jacoby, United States: Independent Television Service (ITVS), Storyville Films, PBS.
Vogel, Paula (2014), *Don Juan Comes Home from Iraq*, rehearsal draft, March.

PERMISSIONS

I am grateful to the South Coast Repertory Company in Costa Mesa, California, for permission to use the image of Curtis McClarin in their 2012 production of Suzan-Lori Parks's *Topdog/Underdog* as the cover image for this volume. Photograph by Henry DiRocco. Web link: www.scr.org.

I am grateful to Grove/Atlantic for permission for Harvey Young to reprint the first stanza of Amiri Baraka's poem "An Agony. As Now" in his essay on Baraka here.

I am grateful to the University of Minnesota Press for permission for Werner Sollors to adapt and expand his essay here from his introduction to *The Adrienne Kennedy Reader* (2001).

The idea for this anthology emerged from a plenary round-table discussion I organized at the Comparative Drama Conference at Stevenson University in Baltimore in April 2015. Eight of the contributors here also participated in that discussion: Jeffery Kennedy on Eugene O'Neill, Sharon Friedman on Susan Glaspell, Jackson R. Bryer on Thornton Wilder, Susan C. W. Abbotson on Tennessee Williams, Stephen Marino on Arthur Miller, Natka Bianchini on Edward Albee, Brenda Murphy on David Mamet, and Sandra G. Shannon on August Wilson. The moderator was J. Chris Westgate. Remarks from that discussion were published in the Comparative Drama Conference's annual *Text & Presentation, 2015* (Jefferson, NC: McFarland, 2016). I thank Laura Snyder, her assistant Chelsea Dove, and their staff for their excellent work in organizing this conference, and Graley Herren, the editor of *Text & Presentation*, for his help in securing permissions from McFarland.

INDEX